Russian Experimental Fiction

*

Russian Experimental Fiction

RESISTING IDEOLOGY
AFTER UTOPIA

*

EDITH W. CLOWES

PRINCETON UNIVERSITY PRESS

PRINCETON, NEW JERSEY

Copyright © 1993 by Princeton University Press
Published by Princeton University Press, 41 William Street,
Princeton, New Jersey 08540
In the United Kingdom: Princeton University Press,
Chichester, West Sussex
All Rights Reserved

Library of Congress Cataloging-in-Publication Data
Clowes, Edith W.
Russian experimental fiction : resisting ideology
after Utopia /Edith W. Clowes.
p. cm.
Includes bibliographical references and index.
ISBN 0-691-03222-X
1. Russian fiction—20th century—History and criticism.
2. Utopias in literature. 3. Experimental fiction—
Russia (Federation)—History and criticism. I. Title.
PG3096.U94C56 1993
891.73′409372—dc20 92-46315

This book has been composed in Adobe Utopia

Princeton University Press books are printed
on acid-free paper and meet the guidelines
for permanence and durability of the Committee
on Production Guidelines for Book Longevity
of the Council on Library Resources

Some information in this book is based on
research that was first published in *The Russian
Review* 51, no. 3 (July 1992).
Copyright 1992 The Ohio State University Press.
All rights reserved.

Printed in the United States of America

1 3 5 7 9 10 8 6 4 2

TO CRAIG, SAM, AND NED

*

Contents

Preface and Acknowledgments	ix
Note on Transliteration and Translation	xiii
List of Abbreviations	xv

PART ONE:
EXPERIMENTAL FICTION AGAINST IDEOLOGICAL FIXATION

CHAPTER ONE
Meta-utopian Writing: The Problem of Utopia as Ideology 3

CHAPTER TWO
Publishing the Dystopian Heritage: The Glasnost Debate about Literary Experiment and Utopian Ideology 25

PART TWO:
THE META-UTOPIAN EXPERIMENT IN FICTION: ELEMENTS OF LITERARY AND IDEOLOGICAL REANIMATION

CHAPTER THREE
Charting Meta-utopia: Chronotopes of Disorientation 41

CHAPTER FOUR
Science, Ideology, and the Structure of Meta-utopian Narrative 70

CHAPTER FIVE
The Meta-utopian Language Problem, or Utopia as a Bump on a -log- 94

CHAPTER SIX
Meta-utopian Consciousness 122

PART THREE:
THE READER IN THE TEXT: POPULARIZING THE META-UTOPIAN MENTALITY

CHAPTER SEVEN
Making Meta-utopia Accessible: Zinoviev's *The Radiant Future* 145

CONTENTS

CHAPTER EIGHT
Utopia, Imagination, and Memory: The Strugatsky Brothers'
The Ugly Swans, Tendriakov's *A Potshot at Mirages*, and
Aksënov's *The Island of Crimea* — 162

CHAPTER NINE
Parody of Popular Forms in Iskander's *Rabbits and Boa
Constrictors* and Voinovich's *Moscow 2042* — 183

CHAPTER TEN
Play with Closure in Petrushevskaia's "The New Robinsons"
and Kabakov's "The Deserter" — 198

CONCLUSION
The Utopian Impulse after 1968: Russian Meta-utopian
Fiction in a European Context — 208

Bibliography — 223

Index — 233

* *Preface and Acknowledgments* *

THIS BOOK explores the challenge that literary play poses to ideological fixation. Since the death of Stalin experimental fiction has been more openly contested and its authors more severely punished than so-called realist fiction and its authors. Beginning with the experiments of Abram Terts (Andrei Siniavsky) and Nikolai Arzhak (Iuly Daniel) in the late 1950s, Soviet courts, censors, and editorial boards put ludic art on trial and then consistently kept it off the printed page. Clearly this kind of art offers more than the vacuous aestheticism that its critics have seen in it.

The focal point of this study is a considerable body of fiction that responds to the heritage of utopian thought and conceives of contemporary Soviet reality ironically, in terms of a realized utopia. It spans the post-Stalinist period, starting with Terts's "What Is Socialist Realism?" in 1959 and concluding with stories by Liudmila Petrushevskaia and Aleksandr Kabakov of the late 1980s. Included in this discussion are, among others, Terts's *Liubimov*, Venedikt Erofeev's *Moscow-Petushki*, Aleksandr Zinoviev's *Yawning Heights*, Vladimir Voinovich's *Moscow 2042*, *The Ugly Swans* by the Strugatsky brothers, and Vasily Aksënov's *The Island of Crimea*. All of these works deal centrally with the question of social imagination: how alternative worlds are framed and what impact they have on our perception of social "reality" and our behavior in society. I have used the term *meta-utopian* to describe this fiction. My definition includes that of Saul Morson in *The Boundaries of Genre*, that is, a form of literary play involving parody of parody, but it probes beyond this purely formal aspect to questions of social mentality. The term *meta-utopian* is meant to signal an ideological and imaginative scope quite different from that of traditional utopian, dystopian, anti-utopian, and counterutopian fiction. If metaphysics traditionally takes as its problem the prime causes of the physical, material world, so the meta-utopian imagination searches out the linguistic, psychological, and political structures that inform the process of generating and realizing social dreams. Skeptical toward all distinct valences of utopian writing, it entertains a variety of utopian scenarios and seeks to expose their common, underlying motivations and assumptions.

Among the key elements of dogmatic thinking that meta-utopian writing probes is a simple binary system of values, an "either/or," "we/they" mentality that informs much Russian utopian thinking and certainly Marxism-Leninism. Revealing the essentially similar mindset behind the two aesthetic opponents, Socialist Realism and post-Stalinist critical realism—with their competing ideologies of Marxism-Leninism and conservative, Russian nationalism—meta-utopias show the even stronger hostility of both to aesthetic play and social critique. By pointing out the poverty of existing social scripts available in contemporary Russian culture, these works at least implicitly open a middle ground for greater ideological complexity.

My study is divided into three parts. The first part provides a theoretical and historical framework for understanding meta-utopian experiments and their importance for Russian culture. The second is a structural analysis of meta-utopian fictions, how they interrogate narrative forms, language use, and concepts of space and time to uncover the valuative structures inherent in them. The third part provides an examination of the "implied reader," the reader projected in the text, and how experimental writers carry out an implicit claim to refine their readers' aesthetic, social, and political sensibilities.

The subject of this book bears an important, if not immediately obvious, relationship to the rethinking of utopia in Western culture that has accompanied the quincentenary of Columbus's discovery/invention of the New World. It is obvious to everyone that the communist world has collapsed, and it is becoming increasingly clear that the Western world also faces a crisis of social and political imagination. If the celebration of Columbus makes us wonder about the reality of the imagined and constructed *geography* of the New World, this same year of 1992 highlights a key juncture in Russian Orthodox *eschatology*. The year 1992, strange as it may sound, is the quincentenary of the apocalypse, the end of the world according to the Eastern Orthodox tradition. Around the year 1492 social-political images took hold, in both East and West, that were to resonate throughout the modern era. Just as the idea of the New World gave a rationale for westward voyages and legitimacy to the often brutal conquest, colonization, and enslavement of native populations to the south and west, so the ancient "Legend of the White Cowl" and the image of Moscow as the Third Rome fed a Russian, messianic idea of nationhood that, in turn, justified imperial expansion to the south and east. Russia was to be the salvation of the world.

PREFACE AND ACKNOWLEDGMENTS

Perhaps it is not surprising that both Russian and Western utopian ideas have been severely challenged, if not discredited, five hundred years, almost to the year, after their symbolic inception. The most recent expression of Russian messianism, the Soviet state, caved in at much the same time that the "New World," and particularly the United States, is wondering exactly *who* Columbus was and *what* "world" he "discovered." Eastern and Western utopian visions have sparred against one another for as long as they have existed, each serving more or less intensely as the binary opposite against which the other defined itself. Now, in the ashes of the cold war, both "Russia" and the "New World" are confronted with ideological emptiness, the question of what they really are and to what purpose they exist.

Meta-utopian fiction, along with the Russian apartment art movement, conceptualist art, and much experimental poetry and theater of the 1970s and 1980s, is part of a broad cultural groundswell that focuses on ideological petrification and challenges Soviet orthodoxy at every point. Obviously there are many examples of cultural texts that combine aesthetic experiment and ideological critique that do not receive attention here. For example, some readers may miss discussion of other experimental narratives, such as Sokolov's *Palisandriia* or Bitov's *Pushkin House*, that parody dogma. These and many other fictions are not included because they do not engage in utopian discourse. But while this book does not offer a comprehensive historical treatment of the Soviet underground, it is hoped that its interpretive framework deals fully enough with the relationship between aesthetic experiment and ideological critique to offer an approach to other kinds of texts.

I wish to thank the people who encouraged this project along the way. Ellen Chances spent hours discussing utopian ideas and recent Soviet literature with me and provided valuable information about the contemporary scene. Jay West and Bernice Rosenthal commented on various versions of the manuscript. Deming Brown, Natalia Ivanova, Thomas Lahusen, Nadia Peterson, Laura Beraha, David Bethea, Svetlana Boym, and Boris Gasparov variously lent materials and critical sense. Colleagues at Purdue University, Jay Rosellini, Zina Breschinsky, Djelal Kadir, Floyd Merrill, Cal Schrag, Larry May, Marilyn Friedman, and Leonard Harris were generous with discussion, comments, and questions. I particularly want to thank my students from the seminar "Utopia and Modernity" who gave me an education in non-Russian utopian discourse, from Che Guevara to Ronald Reagan.

The Purdue Research Foundation granted me summer and sabbatical support to work on this project. The Summer Slavic Research Laboratory at the University of Illinois provided, as always, a very congenial setting in which to do research. The staff at the Interlibrary Loan Office at Purdue were very friendly and efficient in processing a large number of requests. My research assistant, Karen Knight, did a great deal of legwork and helped to track down several invaluable sources. Special thanks are due to Robert Brown at Princeton University Press for his enthusiasm and support for this project and to Annette Theuring, also of the Press, for her careful editing work.

I am grateful to the editors and publisher of *The Russian Review* for permission to use material that first appeared in that publication.

Note on Transliteration and Translation

THE SYSTEM of transliteration used throughout this book is Thomas Shaw's System II. To make the text easier to read, however, I have made a few modifications. Although Russian titles of written works are transliterated according to System II, names of people are altered. All diacritical marks are omitted. Names ending in *-ii* have been shortened to end in *-y*, as in Gorky or Siniavsky. For the sake of correct pronunciation I have chosen to write the last name Zinov'ev as Zinoviev. To convey the sound *yo*, I have used *ë*, as in Lënia Tikhomirov.

Unless otherwise specified, all translations are my own.

List of Abbreviations

PRIMARY WORKS analyzed will be cited in the text by the relevant abbreviation and page number. In the text, the first date given in parentheses after the title of a work is the date of writing or of first publication. If a second date is given, it is the date of first publication in the Soviet Union.

CC   Arkadii Strugatskii and Boris Strugatskii, "Grad obrechennyi," *Neva*, no. 9 (1988): 64–117; no. 10 (1988): 86–128. No translation is available.

D   Aleksandr Kabakov, "Nevozvrashchenets," *Iskusstvo kino*, no. 6 (1989): 150–75. Translated as *No Return*, ed. D. Stumpf, trans. T. Whitney (New York: Morrow, 1990). Citations are from the original. In the text, I have translated the title as "The Deserter."

IC   Vasilii Aksënov, *Ostrov Krym* (Ann Arbor: Ardis, 1981). Citations are from *The Island of Crimea*, trans. M. H. Heim (New York: Vintage, 1984).

L   Abram Terts (Andrei Siniavskii), *Liubimov*, in *Tsena metafory ili prestuplenie i nakazanie Siniavskogo i Danielia*, ed. L. S. Eremina (Moscow: Kniga, 1989), 336–424. Translated as *The Makepeace Experiment*, trans. M. Harari (Evanston, Ill.: Northwestern University Press, 1989). Citations are from the original. In the text, I have used the title *Liubimov*.

M   Vladimir Voinovich, *Moskva 2042* (Ann Arbor: Ardis, 1987). Translated as *Moscow 2042*, trans. R. Lourie (New York: Harcourt Brace, 1990). Citations are from the original.

MP   Venedikt Erofeev, *Moskva-Petushki* (Paris: YMCA-Press, 1977). Translated as *Moscow to the End of the Line*, trans. H. W. Tjalsma (New York: Taplinger, 1980). Citations are from the original. In the text, I have translated the title as *Moscow-Petushki*.

MS   Nikolai Arzhak (Iulii Daniel'), *Govorit Moskva* (New York: Inter-Language Literary Associates, 1966). Translated as "This Is Moscow Speaking," in *This Is Moscow Speaking, and Other Stories*, trans. S. Hood, H. Shukman, and J. Richardson

ABBREVIATIONS

(London: Collins, 1968). Citations are from the original. In the text, I have translated the title as *Moscow Speaking*.

NR   Liudmila Petrushevskaia, "Novye Robinzony," *Novyi mir*, no. 8 (1989): 166–72. No translation is available.

PM   Vladimir Tendriakov, "Pokushenie na mirazhi," *Novyi mir*, no. 4 (1987): 59–116; no. 5 (1987): 89–164. No translation is available.

RB   Fazil' Iskander, *Kroliki i udavy* (Moscow: Knizhnaia palata, 1988). Translated as *Rabbits and Boa Constrictors*, trans. R. E. Peterson (Ann Arbor: Ardis, 1989). Citations are from the original.

RF   Aleksandr Zinov'ev, *Svetloe budushchee* (Lausanne: L'age d'homme, 1978). Citations, except where noted, are taken from *The Radiant Future*, trans. G. Clough (London: The Bodley Head, 1981).

SR   Abram Terts (Andrei Siniavskii), "Chto takoe sotsialisticheskii realizm?"in *Tsena metafory ili prestuplenie i nakazanie Siniavskogo i Danielia*, ed. L. S. Eremina (Moscow: Kniga, 1989), 425–59. Citations are from "On Socialist Realism," in *"The Trial Begins" and "On Socialist Realism"*, trans. G. Dennis (New York: Vintage, 1960), 147–219.

US   Arkadii Strugatskii and Boris Strugatskii, *Gadkie lebedi* (Frankfurt: Posev, 1972). Citations are from *The Ugly Swans*, trans. A. Nakhimovsky and A. S. Nakhimovsky (New York: Macmillan, 1979).

YH   Aleksandr Zinov'ev, *Ziiaiushchie vysoty* (Lausanne: L'age d'homme, 1976). Translated as *The Yawning Heights*, trans. G. Clough (New York: Random House, 1979). Citations are from the original.

PART ONE

EXPERIMENTAL FICTION AGAINST IDEOLOGICAL FIXATION

*

* CHAPTER ONE *

Meta-utopian Writing

THE PROBLEM OF UTOPIA

AS IDEOLOGY

IN THE SHORT period since 1987 when Gorbachev made his speech about filling in the "blank passages" of Soviet Russian history, Russian intellectuals have confronted a serious crisis of social imagination. While it is clear that the old monopolistic, authoritarian communist ideology is in retreat, many people, and not just the old hardliners, fear that the absence of an authoritarian hierarchy portends an apocalypse, the onslaught of complete political and economic disorder. On the other hand, particularly since the failed coup of August 1991, a significant number of citizens have proved that they are probing some wholly different notion of social-cultural discourse, rejecting the mental sphere that limited them to the two extremes of authority and anarchy. Instead, they are proceeding from the assumption that some negotiated middle ground of compromise and common interest is preferable to either extreme, that one can achieve a better society through communication between radically differing interests—in short, through a notion of consensus.

Literary life, as manifested in both the literary press and fiction currently being published and discussed, has played a crucial role in articulating a new mentality. Early on, experimental fiction and ideological critique burst onto the center stage of literary-intellectual discussion to tear down what credibility party centralism still enjoyed. We have only to consider the publication and broad discussions of Tolstaia's, Narbikova's, and Popov's "anti-ideologizing" fiction, the first Soviet publication of ideologically heretical, modernist "classics," such as Zamiatin's *We*, Nabokov's oeuvre, Kafka's *The Castle*, the current interest in Western antiauthoritarian modes of thinking, such as that illustrated by the concept of "deconstructionism."[1]

[1] Galina Belaia, *Zatonuvshaia Atlantida*, Biblioteka "Ogonek," vol. 14 (Moscow: Ogonek, 1991), 42. Belaia maintains that what has been called the "other prose" rejects "any violent ideologization of content." On deconstructionist theories, see, for

During the first two or three years of glasnost these literary events bolstered the debate about the merits of Marxism-Leninism and the historical exposés of the Civil War era implicating Lenin in the later formation of Stalinist totalitarianism.

One of the central issues in the literary debate has been the question of utopia and the relationship between the different uses of utopia: as fictional experiment, as ideological construct, and as social practice. The appearance of the modernist "dystopian" novels of Zamiatin, Platonov, and Orwell has aroused heated discussion about the importance of "alternative," experimental fiction as a needed challenge to established ideology, a kind of "warning" about dogmatism.[2] The present study is about a more recent body of fiction, written in the underground since Stalin's death, that is of possibly even greater importance to the process of imagining and articulating kinds of social consciousness other than the authoritarian ones traditional in Russian life. This fiction can be called "meta-utopian" since it is positioned on the borders of the utopian tradition and yet mediates between a variety of utopian modes.[3] Spawned as it was in the underground of the post-Stalinist years, meta-utopian fiction represents a much greater immediate challenge to current leaders, whether of communist or any other political stripe, than dystopian novels do. It is clearly not by chance that some of its most radical exemplars, for example, Zinoviev's *The Yawning Heights*, Siniavsky-Terts's *Liubimov*, and Voinovich's *Moscow 2042*, are only just becoming available now in the early 1990s. They are important, if hidden and unacknowledged, pathbreakers to the seeming transformation of mentality that we now witness.[4] Unlike their dystopian predecessors, they fit as part of this postcommunist time and its ideologically fragmented cul-

---

example, A. A. Griakalov and Iu. Iu. Dorokhov, "Ot strukturalizma k dekonstruktsii (zapadnye esteticheskie teorii 70-80-kh godov XX veka)," *Russkaia literatura*, no. 1 (1990), 236–49.

[2] See, for example, V. Lakshin's introduction to the first Soviet Russian printing of *We*. "'Antiutopiia' Evgeniia Zamiatina," *Znamia*, no. 4 (1988): 128.

[3] I take the term *meta-utopia* from Gary Saul Morson, *The Boundaries of Genre: Dostoevsky's Diary of a Writer and the Traditions of Literary Utopia* (1981; Evanston, Ill.: Northwestern University Press, n.d.), 146. While Morson uses the term as a generic category, I have used it here to refer to a social consciousness involving social and cultural pluralism.

[4] For some recent discussions of their importance see N. Azhgikhina, "Vozvrashchenie Siniavskogo i Danielia," *Oktiabr'*, no. 8 (1990): 203–5; Karl Kantor, "Siiaiushchaia vysota slovesnosti," *Oktiabr'*, no. 1 (1991): 30–35.

ture: through them the cultural soil that produced a phenomenon like glasnost becomes more palpable.

This writing "about utopia," with its penetrating insight into utopian modes of thinking, is a powerful stimulus to those seeking social and political alternatives to a long-standing authoritarian culture. Mikhail Suslov, the Soviet Union's chief ideologue of the post-Stalinist era, thought Zinoviev an enemy of Soviet power more terrible even than that longtime moral counterweight to the Soviet regime Aleksandr Solzhenitsyn. According to an old friend of Zinoviev, Karl Kantor, Suslov reasoned thus: "While Solzhenitsyn revealed the secret of the horrors of the GULAG [the concentration camps], Zinoviev pictured normal, everyday life outside the GULAG as the kind of life in which the GULAG would fit naturally, at least at the stage of the birth and development of 'real communism.'"[5] By contrast, those meta-utopian works that have become available enjoy tremendous popularity. The most recent meta-utopian narratives, Petrushevskaia's "The New Robinsons" and Kabakov's "The Deserter," have been hailed as best-sellers and are counted among the most important fiction of the glasnost period. Here, too, some critics have compared these works to those of Solzhenitsyn as a measure of their overwhelming significance for their time.[6]

In the following discussion my chief concern is to examine how experiment with literary style and narrative form relates to the deeper cultural-ideological problem of the reinvigoration and reframing of social imagination. The major question here concerns the function of such fiction vis-à-vis existing ideological frameworks. Does it, like traditional utopian narratives, offer a single, "progressive" alternative to the existing social and political system? Like counterutopian visions, does it provide a nostalgic revision of some past age? Or instead, like anti-utopian or dystopian writing, does meta-utopian fiction deconstruct utopian schemes, only then to abandon the notion of a beneficial social imagination? Or, and I believe this to be the closest to the truth, does meta-utopian fiction take note of the proliferation of these different social attitudes, standing on the interface of dominant utopian ideologies, juxtaposing them, revealing the hidden similarities behind their more obvious, mutually adversarial

---

[5] Kantor, "Siiaiushchaia vysota," 34.

[6] Andrei Vasil'evskii, "Opyty zanimatel'noi futuro(eskhato)logii, II," *Novyi mir*, no. 5 (1990): 258–62. Belaia sees Solzhenitsyn's epic novels as the inheritors of a tradition of "authoritarian art" that the new avant-garde rejects. See *Zatonuvshaia Atlantida*, 42.

programs, thus opening a neutral space that permits the emergence of other possible patterns of social practice? The term *meta-utopian* best emphasizes this challenge not just to one kind of utopia but to a whole array of social constructs available in the Russian heritage.

My conceptualization of meta-utopian art builds on a project undertaken in the 1970s by the French literary scholar Paul Ricoeur to make more of "utopia" than merely a bastard literary-rhetorical genre, an artistically uninteresting form of social fantasy.[7] To achieve his goal Ricoeur recalled the efforts of Karl Mannheim in his book *Ideology and Utopia* (1929) to put the two notions of ideology and utopia into some conceptual relationship and thereby to salvage each from the flatness of a single, unchallenged social consciousness. Ideology and utopia, according to Mannheim, are the two major vehicles by which we model reality (which we can never know or evaluate in and of itself). As kinds of divergence from social reality, ideology and utopia offer competing formulations and evaluations of a perception broadly accepted as "reality." Each becomes more than opaque false consciousness in its resistance to the other. Ricoeur adds to this scenario his own concerns with the two terms as kinds of imagination that can interact with each other and with social reality in productive (or what he calls "constitutive") as well as reactive, nonproductive (or "pathological") ways. Each taken by itself, Ricoeur argues, can only provide a destructive model of reality: ideology tends to "fix" reality in a symbolic prison, some immutable form, while utopia tends to "escape" from reality into imaginative anarchy. In Ricoeur's view, the two function best if they partake in dialogue, in which ideology productively legitimizes a certain view of reality and utopia modifies and reanimates that view by challenging and subverting it. Utopia, as a form of irony or satire, points out the credibility gap normally filled by ideology between the rulers' claim to power and the willingness of the citizenry to accept that claim.[8]

While Ricoeur's project is plausible and useful in its effort to give greater conceptual weight to utopia and to put it into a functional context, I see several problems with it. One is his opinion that ideology and utopia are qualitatively different. Both are sociopolitical constructs that legitimize some collective configuration, allocate power, define notions of justice, freedom, happiness, and so forth. The dif-

---

[7] Paul Ricoeur, *Lectures on Ideology and Utopia*, ed. G. H. Taylor (New York: Columbia University Press, 1986).

[8] Ibid. See especially pp. 298–303.

ference, it seems to me, has more to do with the relationship of the theoretical construct to an existing power base.

Another problem has to do with Ricoeur's positive valuation of what he calls "constitutive" thinking and almost wholly negative valuation of "pathologies." The one cannot exist without the other. As should be clear from the Soviet case study offered here, the constitutive element cannot become active until a pathology has been "diagnosed." New social options do not become thinkable until the familiar stagnation of Stalinist society and the knee-jerk reaction, the urge to escape, have both been acknowledged, contemplated, and evaluated.

Ricoeur has an overly optimistic view of utopia as a qualitatively new form of consciousness. He ignores an important element of the pathological side of utopia, that is, its hidden and sometimes destructive rehearsal of existing structures and archetypes of oppression. For example, in many nineteenth- and early-twentieth-century utopias, from Saint-Simon to the Russian Godbuilders, church dogma, hierarchy, and ritual are reanimated under the avowedly antireligious guise of rational, political faith or revolutionary passion.

A final problem is related to the supposed innovativeness of utopian thinking. It concerns the problem of language and consciousness in utopian schemes and the status of utopian writing as literature. Almost without exception, from Fourier to Chernyshevsky to Gorky (to Hitler and Stalin), utopians seem linguistically creative, coining new words and concepts, but their style in general tends to be, at best, sterile and derivative and, at worst, hackneyed and full of kitsch. Gorky's coinage of "Godbuilding" (*bogostroitel'stvo*), for example, is rooted in Dostoevsky's "Godman" (*bogochelovek*), Solovyov's idea of "Godmanhood" (*bogochelovechestvo*), and, later, the symbolists' concept of "Godseeking" (*bogoiskatel'stvo*).[9] Moreover, Gorky's most fervent utopian statements are couched in a cloying, kitschy style and form that certainly sabotage whatever ideas and plans for social renewal that he may have had.[10] Utopians' ability to call forth a plausible, truly new social order is circumscribed in part by their typically inadequate use of language.

[9] Jutta Scherrer, *Die Petersbürger Religiös-Philosophischen Vereinigungen* (Berlin-Wiesbaden: O. Harrasowitz, 1973), 310–12; Raimund Sesterhenn, *Das Bogostroitel'stvo bei Gor'kij und Lunačarskij bis 1909* (Munich: Otto Sagner, 1982), 21–23.

[10] See, for example, Gor'kii's "Chelovek" from 1904.

Despite the reservations we have mentioned, Ricoeur's idea of relating ideology and utopia as imaginative, ideational adversaries suggests a context for understanding the role of meta-utopian writing as a challenge to the Soviet social imagination. In the nineteenth century the two kinds of construct, ideology and utopia, were clearly divided: "ideology" represented the values of that social group presently in a position of power and privilege, and "utopia" provided an imaginative design for a better future society. When utopia was put into practice at all, for example, in France or in New England, it was only on the level of a very small, voluntary community of like-minded people in the role of alternative or adversary to legitimized power on the broader social scale.[11]

In twentieth-century totalitarianism, and particularly in Nazi Germany and Stalinist Russia, ideology and utopia lost their fruitful, adversarial relationship and became one and the same in a fusion of the traditional characteristics of each. Like traditional "ideology," this new construct legitimized an existing power structure. And like ideology, this ruling vision disclaimed labels such as *ideology* or *utopia* that implied false consciousness and, preferring the epithet *scientific*, insisted on its ability to represent reality accurately. Like *utopia*, on the other hand, it put before the citizenry a bright picture of an ideal society, promising to make that society come true in the near future. Like utopia, this new "utopian ideology" assumed an adversarial position vis-à-vis an actually existing ideology, for example, bourgeois capitalism, and promised to realize its program through waging war on this enemy. This conjoining of ideology and utopia closed the circle off from critical challenge, from open discreditation, by curtailing the forms available to memory and imagination in historiography and art. Really what was achieved in both systems was a new catholic faith, only now not in a deity but in a substitute, the state.

The question arises: Has any form of imaginative play arisen to answer this dilemma, this disastrous flattening of the horizon of social imagination? If dystopian fiction pointed out the failure of social imagination, are there other forms of utopian thinking that somehow go beyond this impasse? Does the current cultural debate in general divulge only "pathology," that is, a dead-end–apocalyptic mentality, or is there "health," in the sense of promising social scenarios to be

---

[11] Frank E. Manuel and Fritzie Manuel, *Utopian Thought in the Western World* (Cambridge, Mass.: Harvard University Press, 1979), 581–89.

realized in appropriately fresh language and form? In other words, has the post-Stalinist underground offered merely a dark mirror for the Stalinist "utopia" or has it offered to the imagination new alternatives?

If there is any fresh valuative framework, it is offered by the skeptical, "meta-utopian" thinking, of which Ricoeur's essay is an example, that has emerged in both West and East in the late twentieth century. If anti-utopian thinking and dystopian fiction have a significant pathological side, denying not only actual "realized" utopian schemes but also the very notion of a beneficial social imagination, meta-utopian thinking takes a critical stance on the borders *among* existing systems of social values. Its object is not to discard "old" valuative systems, but to juxtapose them, to expose, through debate, the pathologies inherent in them, and thus to make possible the emergence of other, more adequate forms of social imagination. Meta-utopian thinking certainly has its own pathologies: it is capable of degeneration into an anarchistic kind of relativism, reducing all valuative constructs to expressions of underlying power relationships. Another pathological scenario, and one familiar currently in the former Soviet Union and Eastern Europe, is the crumbling of a single totalitarian ideology into a large number of mini-totalitarianisms, each insisting on its own legitimacy. The result inevitably is war. Nonetheless, the strong penchant of meta-utopian thinking for pluralist discourse, its inherent effort to bring about a confrontation of opposing ideologies, promises a broadening of the social horizon.

It is true, as Galina Belaia has pointed out recently in *The Sunken Atlantis*, that much "alternative" art implicitly or explicitly challenges official ideological positions.[12] Like most underground literature, meta-utopian fiction belongs to what Donald Fanger has called the "other" tradition in Russian literary history, the tradition, starting with Pushkin and Gogol, that uses aesthetic play to call into question the "social imperative," the truth-seeking to which Russian writers have classically dedicated themselves.[13] Because of its rich allusions to Western and pre-twentieth-century Russian traditions of utopia, which themselves have been vital to articulating the domains of and relationships between social-moral and aesthetic impulses, meta-

[12] Belaia, *Zatonuvshaia Atlantida*, 40–43.

[13] Donald Fanger, "Conflicting Imperatives in the Model of the Russian Writer," in *Literature and History: Theoretical Problems and Russian Case Studies*, ed. G. S. Morson (Stanford: Stanford University Press, 1986), 117.

utopian writing is particularly well poised to provide insight into the very mental foundations, the ideological templates, on which systems of value have been cast.

What distinguishes meta-utopias from other alternative writing is their dual character as both "didactic" and "ludic" art. More than other kinds of underground writing, meta-utopias focus on the tension between social and aesthetic impulses: as has so often been the case, literary play here presents a threat to ideological system, promising to discredit its claims to absolute truth and to reduce it to a form of play. And yet instead of turning away from social forms of consciousness as being too confining for the aesthetic impulse, meta-utopian fictions tend to insist on the validity of "play" as a way of functioning in society, as a way of negotiating between otherwise intransigent social dogmas.

Meta-utopian writing departs from anti-utopian or dystopian precursors in a number of crucial ways. (In passing, we should mention that the term *anti-utopian* refers to a philosophy or worldview critical of positive utopian schemes. The term *dystopian* refers to a novelistic form of narrative that *depicts* a bad place or "dys-topia.") If a dystopian novel, such as *We*, envisions "utopia" as a single, exclusivist ideological system, which one either accepts or rejects, meta-utopian fiction entertains a number of possibilities that could be called "utopian thinking." That is, it envisions utopia in the plural as "utopias." Moreover, in contrast to the dystopian "either/or,"that is, either tyranny or anarchy, it countenances and challenges all kinds of authoritarian ideologies, each with its own vision of the ideal society, that insist on their own versions of rightness, justice, and truthfulness to the exclusion of all others. Meta-utopian works as different as Terts's very playful *Liubimov* and Tendriakov's rather conventional novel *A Potshot at Mirages* share a skepticism about all rigid, unitary ideological systems and a love of linguistic and narrative play as a vehicle for increased consciousness of the effects of ideological fixation. In contrast to anti-utopian thought, which turns away from social imagination altogether and reverts to "nature," to images of pre-civilized human existence or to inner, spiritual life, meta-utopias show a concern for a just *and* workable social order. In short, meta-utopian writing has a much more complex and ambiguous view of utopia than its dystopian counterparts.

It is interesting to note that, insofar as these authors (for example, Daniel, Zinoviev, and Voinovich) are aware of great dystopian antecedents, such as *We* or *1984*, they tend to oppose the primitivist visions offered in these novels. They do embrace separate aspects of the civilization achieved through the twentieth-century utopian experiment, although the utopian social experience as a whole is certainly judged to have failed. Both Zinoviev and Voinovich have gone so far as to insist that their works, *The Yawning Heights* and *Moscow 2042*, should *not* be read as "anti-utopias."[14]

What of the nature of aesthetic play in meta-utopian fiction? My discussion in Chapters 3 through 6 gives a great deal of attention to the use of three techniques in the interlocking processes of the renewal of literary language and social fantasy: parody, parable, and paradoxical thinking. Of particular importance is the functioning of what Iury Tynianov called serious parody, the exposure of automatized—indeed, hackneyed—literary styles and forms with the goal of opening a space for one's own innovations. Insofar as all literary forms have ideological assumptions embedded in them, this technique has implications for the reanimation of social fantasy.

Parabolic or allegorical language has long functioned in the Russian underground to foil censorship and to create space for criticism and dissent in a monological cultural context. In meta-utopian writing the language of secret political protest known as "Aesopian language" is exposed as a secret sharer in totalitarian culture. It will be reevaluated as part of a whole language practice that must be overcome if the process of liberating oneself from the totalitarian heritage is to succeed.

Another crucial technique for the exposure of systemic weakness in any exclusivist ideological construct is paradoxical thinking, most famously used by Dostoevsky in his anti-utopian *Notes from the Underground*. The use of contradictory statements that on closer inspection end up being true is essential to the effort to unmask the incongruities behind the façade not only of Marxist-Leninist thinking but also of the other social-ideological systems in the Russian tradition, such as Russian Orthodox nationalism, that appear to pose real alternatives to Marxism-Leninism.

[14] See the jacket flap for *Ziiaiushchie vysoty* (Lausanne: L'age d'homme, 1976): "It would be an oversimplification to see in this book just one more anti-utopia in the image of Zamiatin. Or, better put, it would be an inadmissible limitation." In an interview with *Literaturnaia gazeta*, Voinovich clearly stated the differences between *Moscow 2042* and Orwell's *1984*, calling his novel an "anti-anti-utopia." See Irina Rishina, "Ia vernulsia by," *Literaturnaia gazeta*, no. 25 (June 20, 1990): 8.

In their experiment with narrative form, meta-utopias again move well beyond their nearest precursor, the dystopian novel. While dystopias use "dialogical" techniques familiar in the novel form to uncover the spiritual oppression and physical coercion inherent in various kinds of socialist, utopian practice, meta-utopias parody a broad variety of narrative forms in order to expose ideological fixation of all kinds embedded in them. As the critic Vladimir Novikov has commented, the dystopian novel as a pure genre has been fully developed. He notes further: "The dystopia [he uses the Russian word *antiutopiia*] is already tending toward interaction with other genres and possibly toward dissolution in them."[15] As such, he feels, it can be very productive. In response, I would reiterate that these works, with their mixed genres, are no longer "dystopian," with the stress solely on revealing the isolated utopian society as a "bad place," but are "meta-utopian." That is, they meditate on the nature of all utopias—and, indeed, a larger set of ideologies—as the constructs that they are: fictional but vital to the formulation of social identity. Certainly Novikov is correct in pointing out the wide diversity of narrative forms in contemporary writing about utopia.

The works examined here include quite radical experiments that expose the tenuousness of the border between fact and fiction, such as near-fictionalized literary criticism in Terts's "What Is Socialist Realism?" (1959) and fictionalized sociological analysis in Aleksandr Zinoviev's *The Yawning Heights* (*Ziiaiushchie vysoty*, 1976). Several meta-utopias parody ideologically rigid popular forms. Among these are Terts's chronicle of a town *Liubimov* (1963), Fazil Iskander's fable *Rabbits and Boa Constrictors* (*Kroliki i udavy*, 1982, 1988), Vladimir Voinovich's science-fiction parody *Moscow 2042* (*Moskva 2042*, 1987), and Vasily Aksënov's international thriller *The Island of Crimea* (*Ostrov Krym*, 1981). Still other meta-utopian fictions play with middlebrow didactic genres. Here we find Iuly Daniel's absurdist confession *Moscow Speaking* (*Govorit Moskva*, 1961) and, among the finest and most pathological meta-utopias, Venedikt Erofeev's mock journey *Moscow-Petushki* (*Moskva-Petushki*, 1969). On the other hand, the meta-utopian corpus also has room for seemingly conventional, less obviously self-reflective works, such as the Strugatsky brothers' science-fiction novel *The Ugly Swans* (*Gadkie lebedi*, 1968,

---

[15] Vladimir Novikov, "Vozvrashchenie k zdravomu smyslu: Sub'ektivnye zametki chitatelia antiutopii," *Znamia*, no. 7 (1989): 214.

1989), Zinoviev's realist satire *The Radiant Future* (*Svetloe budushchee*, 1978), or Vladimir Tendriakov's novel about writing history *A Potshot at Mirages* (*Pokushenie na mirazhi*, 1979, 1987).

As to the issue of the reanimation of literary language, meta-utopian writers would agree with a Russian dystopian forebear Zamiatin that language play is essential to opening up perceptual and imaginative space and to realizing modes of consciousness. Zamiatin saw the relationship between ideology, utopia, and "reality" as a problem of language, and here post-Stalinist meta-utopians share a great deal with him. Zamiatin's verbal experiments were very much in keeping with general trends of the literary avant-garde of the 1920s, who, to borrow Viktor Shklovsky's phrase, believed that "form creates for itself content," that language and style were important determinants of consciousness.[16] As Zamiatin put it in his article "On Literature," literary play was important in resisting "entropy of thought," the tendency to slip inadvertently into ready-made ways of thinking.[17] Stylistic innovation, Zamiatin wrote, was essential to adequate perception of the new reality and to the creation of new consciousness. He sought to go beyond the schism of his day between realism and symbolism and the vying ideologies embedded in these styles: the utopian Godbuilding of radical Bolsheviks, such as Aleksandr Bogdanov, Maksim Gorky, and Anatoly Lunacharsky, and the mystical God-seeking of such symbolists as Aleksandr Blok, Viacheslav Ivanov, and Andrei Belyi. The old "realism," Zamiatin claimed, was too attached to the world of the senses. Although symbolism had made enormous linguistic strides in opening the transcendent world of the spirit, it too was inappropriate to the lived apocalypse of postrevolutionary Russia. Zamiatin suggested that a provisional style for the near future might be found in some fusion of classical realism and symbolist mysticism. The new art, he wrote, must synthesize an "ironic" outlook with a heightened, ecstatic acceptance of the moment, with its passions, colors, lines, and forms.[18] With the new style Zamiatin

---

[16] Viktor Shklovskii, "Sviaz' priemov siuzhetoslozheniia s obshchimi priemami stilia," in *O teorii prozy* (1929; Ann Arbor: Ardis, 1985), 35.

[17] Evgenii Zamiatin, "O literature, revoliutsii i entropii" (1923), in *Litsa* (New York: Inter-Language Literary Associates, 1967), 252.

[18] Ibid. For more on Zamiatin's critique of Godbuilding, see my "Beyond the Abyss: Nietzschean Myth in Zamiatin's *We* and Pasternak's *Doctor Zhivago*," in *Nietzsche and Soviet Culture*, ed. B. G. Rosenthal (Cambridge: Cambridge University Press, forthcoming).

particularly hoped to challenge the wooden "realism" practiced by Gorky and other "revolutionary" writers, and the petrification of consciousness that these styles and aesthetic attitudes seemed to promise. Zamiatin's dystopian novel *We*, which has finally won broad acclaim in the Soviet Union in the last few years, is a vital precedent for the current meta-utopian discussion about language and consciousness.

If Zamiatin optimistically embraced the living bond between consciousness, idea, and language and believed that verbal art, to be vital, must develop in correspondence to a changing reality, post-Stalinist meta-utopians are more pessimistic, perhaps more like that meta-utopian *avant la lettre* Andrei Platonov.[19] What the poet Joseph Brodsky has written about Platonov, utopian thinking, and language might be applied to the meta-utopian writers. Language is driven into a dead end when it must be made consistently to refer to a "reality" that does not exist:

> Being in the dead-end is not limited by anything, and if one can conceive that even there being defines consciousness and engenders its own psychology, then it is above all in language that this psychology is expressed. In general it should be noted that the first victim of talk about Utopia—desired or already attained—is grammar; for language, unable to keep up with thought, begins to gasp in the subjunctive mood and starts to gravitate toward timeless categories and constructions; as a consequence of which the ground starts to slip out from under even simple nouns, and an aura of arbitrariness arises around them.[20]

While it does not reject notions of an ideal society, most meta-utopian writing does uncover the emptiness at the heart of various actual utopian attempts to attain new consciousness through neologism. These writers suspect that language is more like a prison house, capable of expressing only a limited number of ideas, all of which have a doubtful relationship to anything one could call "reality."

In his diary-confession "Notes from Around the Corner," Andrei Bitov expresses a view of language that is quite close to that prevalent

---

[19] David M. Bethea, "Chevengur: On the Road with the Bolshevik Utopia," in *The Shape of Apocalypse in Modern Russian Fiction* (Princeton: Princeton University Press, 1989), 145–85.

[20] Joseph Brodsky, Preface to Andrei Platonov, *The Foundation Pit* (Ann Arbor: Ardis, 1973), ix.

in meta-utopian fiction. He speaks of a problem that he calls "bumping against the same old words."[21] The writer is in the predicament of using and reusing a limited number of words that are inherently "ideological" in the broadest sense; that is, they express ideas that have all been expressed before and are all, in any case, deceptive. The choice open to any writer is the one confronted by Fëdor Tiutchev: to remain silent and "wise," and thus stop being a writer, or to swing between the expression of illusion and the expression of disillusionment.

The chief illusion that Bitov accuses abstract, ideologically laden language of perpetrating is one of linguistic centralism, or, in a way, logocentrism: the impression that the world has one incontrovertible unitary meaning and purpose that has been bestowed upon it by a single idea. His thought is worth quoting at length, because it captures a resistance to abstract, unitary systems of value that we will also find in meta-utopias:

> One of the lies that condemns people to incongruity and torment is the notion that an idea is capable of changing the world. The world does change, but not the idea. Ideas are always around. People who don't know words consume [ideas], and then it seems to them that their actions are meaningful and directed. There has always existed one legendary personality that gave birth to an idea by which we, comrades, now live and breathe and find our happiness ... thus everything takes shape, and it appears as if all humanity were [already] developing in a directed and meaningful way, [and] as the fruit of that process, the idea of that remarkable personality emerged, and from that idea arose that splendid and ultimately meaningful and just world in which we live, grateful to the idea. It has always been that way in all epochs and among all peoples. And even honest people who grew up in this atmosphere of cardsharping and cheating nature have learned freely to reorder the pattern of events and their own thinking about them, so that [they believe that] the thought came first and only then action and never the other way around—and in this deception they perceive themselves to be rational beings, and in this deception it seems as if one's domination over the world

---

[21] Andrei Bitov, "Zapiski iz-za ugla," *Novyi mir*, no. 2 (1990): 144. Here Bitov follows Gershenzon's position in the similarly titled "Notes from Opposite Corners," his 1921 debate with the great symbolist theorist Viacheslav Ivanov about language, culture, and metaphysics.

means its subordination to one, and you are the king of nature, its summit, its crown, its halo.²²

Especially when one is not aware of the tricks that language in the service of abstract thought plays with reality, the chief illusion of an egocentric, anthropocentric universe takes hold and itself becomes "reality." The ultimate image of linguistic egocentrism, the idea of a greater-than-human personality who creates purpose and direction, and therefore meaning, in people's lives, is one that belongs in the utopian tradition (as well as, significantly, in religious mythology pertaining to the notion of paradise, the promised land, the Kingdom of Heaven, and the like). We find it in Plato's image of the philosopher-king, who brings fellow citizens beyond the cave; in More's King Utopus; in Hegel's "world-historical individual"; in Saint-Simon's characterization of himself at once as the new Socrates and the new Charlemagne; and even in the early-twentieth-century Russian Godbuilders' archetype of the artist-leader.²³ It is the function of ludic art, with its strong linguistic self-reflectiveness, to undermine such delusions and set them in a broader perspective.

This adversity of language in its aesthetic, ludic function to the fixedness of dogmatic uses of language is reinforced in more specific terms in Zinoviev's *The Yawning Heights* as a standoff between artistic institutions and political power: "Whatever the alliance of art and politics, sooner or later it will reveal itself as a misalliance" (YH, 220). Here Zinoviev implies conflicting drives within the creative process: to legitimize existing ideological structures or to challenge them. He argues that in all truly great art the need to subvert and unmask the reigning ideology outweighs the opposing desire for immediate recognition, privilege, and influence.

Another issue at the heart of our discussion is the place of meta-utopian fiction in Russian literary history. Spawned in the "basement" of the Soviet utopian skyscraper, it has existed for three decades in a timeless limbo. And, as is often the case with literature written in exile (whether internal or external), meta-utopian fiction

---

²² Ibid.

²³ On Saint-Simon, see Manuel and Manuel, *Utopian Thought in the Western World*, 583. For more information about this aspect of Godbuilding, see Scherrer, *Die Petersburger Religiös-Philosophischen Vereinigungen*; Sesterhenn, *Das Bogostroitel'stvo bei Gor'kij*; Edith W. Clowes, *The Revolution of Moral Consciousness: Nietzsche in Russian Literature, 1890–1914* (DeKalb: Northern Illinois University Press, 1988), 190–97.

from the late 1950s to the 1980s presents rather odd and unusual challenges to national literary history. Its access to immediate precursors and its possibilities for the kind of intertextual polemic necessary for aesthetic innovation were quite limited. What is more, its outlets to its intended audience were sharply curtailed. And now, during the glasnost years, Russian readers have developed a strange historical-cultural consciousness. Overwhelmed by the "classics" of modernism—works by Zamiatin, Joyce, Platonov, Kafka—that became accessible to most people for the first time, readers have remained relatively unaware of the rich store of underground writing in their own lifetime, during the Thaw and post-Thaw periods. As Nadezhda Azhgikhina remarks in her temptingly titled article "Destroyers in Search of Belief," the young writers of the 1980s, Viktoria Narbikova and others, undoubtedly have roots in the modernism of Belyi and Nabokov. What they need to realize is that for them "the experience of recent precursors—V. Aksënov, A. Zinoviev, V. Voinovich, Abram Terts and, of course, Ven[edikt] Erofeev—is closest of all."[24]

In the case of utopian fiction in general, modernist dystopian writing has suddenly become artificially more prominent than meta-utopian fiction of the postwar era. Although all, with the exception of Zinoviev's and Erofeev's works, have now become available as of late 1991, they have not received the broad attention that they deserve and will eventually receive.[25] In addition, Russian citizens are much too concerned now with social and political action, with rewriting the charter between society and state, and with actual physical survival to have time to read.[26] As Zinoviev lamented in a recent interview in the emigré newspaper *Novoe russkoe slovo*, it is good finally to be published in one's own homeland, but the time when such works would have exploded their intended readers' orthodox values was

[24] N. Azhgikhina, "Razrushiteli v poiskakh very (Novye cherty sovremennoi molodoi prozy," *Znamia*, no. 9 (1990), 225.

[25] See Vitalii Amurskii, "Ia—odinochka vo vsem," *Novoe russkoe slovo* (July 12, 1991), 14. In this interview, Zinoviev notes that fragments of *The Yawning Heights* have appeared in *Oktiabr'* (no. 1 [1991]: 36–97; no. 2 [1991]: 23–82; no. 3 [1991]: 59–81) and of *The Road to Golgotha* (*Idi na Golgofu*) in *Smena*. The only fragment of *Moscow-Petushki* that I have found so far is in *Trezvost' i kul'tura*, no. 12 (1988): 26–38; no. 1 (1989): 27–37.

[26] Karen Stepanian, "Nuzhna li nam literatura? (Zametki o proze ukhodiashchego goda)," *Znamia*, no. 12 (1990): 230.

two or three decades ago.²⁷ Despite these regrets, meta-utopian works were read at the very least in the big cities in an active underground network, and are of unequivocal importance now as voices in a complex cultural mix experimenting with pluralism.

Meta-utopian writing presents yet another problem to traditional literary history. While seeming at first glance to belong to a general tradition of utopian writing, these fictions respond creatively to no particular precursor or contemporary. One or two reveal at most a tangential relationship to Russian modernist dystopias that could not have been known until the last two decades to anyone but the closest friends and relatives of the authors. Nonetheless, post-Stalinist meta-utopian fiction does belong to a generally "modern" tradition in that it answers a deep-seated cultural need to challenge fixed aesthetic and social dogma. More specifically, it partakes of a tendency in Russian experimental prose at least since the appearance of Dostoevsky's *Notes from the Underground* to subvert a special kind of ideological construct predominant in Russian intellectual life of the last two centuries. This is the "scientific" or tractarian utopia, which its adherents believed to be "real"—that is, to be realizable in social practice.

It is ironic that modernist Russian dystopias that are the closest ideologically, as well as chronologically, to meta-utopian writing entered the general, literary-cultural dialogue that gave rise to the meta-utopian corpus well *after* a meta-utopian sensibility had been articulated. Thus, although separate meta-utopian works respond to a very diverse range of subtraditions within the utopian tradition, there are almost no allusions to the modernist heritage. Primarily we find reference to premodern sketches of the ideal state, such as Plato's *Republic*, that have always been freely available in the Soviet Union, as well as early modern works, for example, Campanella's *City of the Sun*, More's *Utopia*, Rabelais's *Gargantua and Pantagruel*, and Defoe's *Robinson Crusoe*.²⁸ None of the early-twentieth-century heritage of Russian utopian writing—the writings of the religious philosopher Nikolai Fedorov and the radical, Godbuilding founder of

---

²⁷ Amurskii, "Ia—odinochka vo vsem," 14.
²⁸ Soviets' admiration for Campanella is described by the Manuels in *Utopian Thought in the Western World*, 268, 272. For information about frequency of editions of utopian works in the decade following the Bolshevik Revolution, see Richard Stites, *Revolutionary Dreams: Utopian Vision and Experimental Life in the Russian Revolution* (New York: Oxford University Press, 1989), 168.

Proletcult, Bogdanov, the postrevolutionary anti-utopian experiments of Zamiatin and Bulgakov, and the meta-utopian novels of Platonov—were available until the late 1980s. It is not surprising, thus, that we do not find a creative response to them in any but the most recent meta-utopian fiction. The traces of a Platonovian-Fedorovian reception, for example, can be felt in Petrushevskaia's "The New Robinsons," published in 1989. A possible but unlikely allusion to *We* can be found in the Strugatskys' novel *The Condemned City*, written in the early 1970s, in their use of the image of a wall that separates the settlers of something known as "The Experiment" from whatever else may be in the cosmos.[29] Zamiatin's novel is first mentioned by name only in 1978 in Zinoviev's *The Radiant Future*.

Such Western dystopias as Orwell's *1984* (which was, in turn, strongly influenced by *We*) and *Animal Farm*, which circulated in samizdat, function much more actively as literary precursors in Russian meta-utopian writing.[30] For example, *1984*, with its two-minute hate sessions and festival of hate week, stands out as an important model for Iuly Daniel in his absurdist short novel *Moscow Speaking*, with its Open Murder Day, when anyone, with a few exceptions, is allowed to do away with anyone else. We can see an allusion to *Animal Farm* in Zinoviev's *The Yawning Heights*, in which the satirical double for Khrushchev is known as The Hog (Khriak), much as the Stalinist leaders of the coup at the animal farm are two pigs. Likewise, *Animal Farm* functions as an important subtext in Iskander's *Rabbits and Boa Constrictors*, an animal fable in part about the failure of realized utopia.[31] Parallel to the ten principles that hang on the wall of the barn in *Animal Farm*, over the throne of the Rabbit King in Iskander's fable hangs a large banner of the Cauliflower, a symbol of future welfare and happiness. Just as the wording of the ten principles changes to support the pigs' growing power, so the banner regularly changes colors, the more boldly exciting rabbits' hopes as their actual social condition worsens.

[29] The wall in *The Condemned City* is an opaque yellow one that may also have its origins in Leonid Andreev's story "The Wall" (1901).

[30] See Nikolai Loktev, "Allegorii Dzhordzha Oruella," *Literaturnyi Kirgizstan*, no. 1 (1989): 151. Loktev remarks that people read Orwell despite the censorship: his works "walked the country in editions of Xerox copies and pale offprints from ancient typewriters."

[31] Richard Chapple, "Fazil Iskander's *Rabbits and Boa Constrictors*: A Soviet Version of Orwell's *Animal Farm*," *Germano-Slavica*, nos. 1–2 (1985): 33–47.

Something should be said about how meta-utopian works differ from the brand of utopian literature that found acceptance in the pre-glasnost era within the borders of officially proscribed art. Works such as Anatoly Kim's *Gurin's Utopia* and the Strugatsky brothers' *The Snail on the Slope* stand out as narrative experiments using, for example, a limited or otherwise unreliable narrative perspective, mixing dream and reality, and disrupting chronological and spatial unity.[32] The key difference here is that they in no essential way attempt to challenge ideological fixation and the limits it puts on language and consciousness. While they criticize the Soviet utopian experiment, they do so wholly from within the system. Their themes are circumscribed and topical, pertaining more directly to current events and issues—for example, environmental policy or bureaucratic waste. We find here no metafictional inquiry into how we construct our fictions and what ideological predicates are embedded in the language and forms with which we express ourselves.

Chapters 7 through 10 address the other major issue at hand in Russian meta-utopian writing: its effort to reach a large audience and to educate that audience to a more nuanced and critical way of reading. In this concern meta-utopian experiments share more with classical utopian fiction and with recent Western "postmodernism" than with their most immediate historical antecedent, the modernist dystopian novel. In his classic essay "The Culture of Modernism" Irving Howe predicted that modernism would fade when avant-garde art was adopted in mainstream society, when the "rage against the official order" became a popular attitude, when parody and irony were everywhere predominant.[33] And, indeed, that is very much what has occurred in Russian meta-utopian fiction: the "rage against the official order"—radical, "difficult" experimentation in verbal art—is being "brought to the people." As Linda Hutcheon shows in *A Poetics of Postmodernism*, Western postmodernist fiction—for example, Maxine Hong Kingston's *Woman Warrior* or E. L. Doctorow's *Ragtime*—bridges the gap between elite and popular art, parodying popular forms, such as the detective novel, the western, and the historical

---

[32] Nadezhda L. Peterson, "Fantasy and Utopia in the Contemporary Soviet Novel, 1976–1981" (Ph.D. diss., Indiana University, 1986).

[33] Irving Howe, "The Culture of Modernism," in *The Decline of the New* (New York: Harcourt, Brace and World, 1970), 3.

romance.³⁴ In addition, it is, in her view, a "didactic" art, concerned with "teaching" the willing reader about the restrictions of the reigning ideology.³⁵ In much the same manner, Russian meta-utopias play with popular forms in a very sophisticated, almost "esoteric" way, but to ultimately didactic purpose.

Contemporary Russian critics voice a strong concern about the educative uses of literary experiment. The critic V. O. Ksepma notes with obvious regret: "That variety of forms that appeared in our culture at the beginning of the twentieth century did not have the chance to enter mass culture, literary imitations could not develop in the numbers needed to popularize the devices that had just been discovered. The invention of new forms was summarily cut short, and realism, rehabilitated, ... started to give birth to such chimeras of implausibility that no kind of modernism could ever invent."³⁶

In meta-utopian fiction popular taste arises as a major issue, precisely in connection with experimental art, both explicitly in dialogue between characters and implicitly in forms chosen and techniques used to educate the reader to a new style of interpretation. For example, the narrator of Zinoviev's novel *The Radiant Future* remarks on the popularity of modernist, avant-garde painting and the use of experimental techniques in recent widely acclaimed fiction, and he criticizes the stupidity of official policy that persists in condemning it. And as one of Zinoviev's characters argues in *The Yawning Heights*, great art must be mass-oriented, though emphatically not a naturalistic mirror pretending to reflect reality (YH, 276). The greatest art must rather be deformative and transformative; as examples he mentions Dante and Bosch (YH, 241). Thus, stylistic experimentation and the fantastic are far from being equated with an esoteric or elitist art. Their ability to have an impact on entrenched ideologies depends very much on their ability to reach the average educated reader.

It is enlightening to compare and contrast the Russian experience of meta-utopian thinking with contemporary Western phenomena of neo-Marxist and postmodernist thinking. Certainly, from one point

---

[34] Linda Hutcheon, *A Poetics of Postmodernism: History, Theory, Fiction* (New York: Routledge, 1988), 20.

[35] Ibid., 41.

[36] V. O. Ksepma, "'Po tu storonu lobnoi stenki': Konspekt neproiznesennogo dialoga po povodu nekotorykh sochinenii pisatelia A. G. Bitova," *Literaturnoe obozrenie*, no. 3 (1989): 26.

of view, this might seem to be comparing apples and oranges, since recent Russian and Western writing arise in wholly different socioeconomic and cultural contexts. The Russian experimentalist's attitude to utopia, for example, would seem to be typically quite different from that of a Westerner, since he or she has been born into and had to come to terms firsthand with an actual "realized" utopian society. But, as many contemporary social thinkers point out, Westerners have been born into another form of "realized" socialism that has some utopian characteristics, the liberal welfare state. The Soviet experiment, the "American Dream," and the notion of the welfare state have coexisted in the twentieth-century mind, embodying what the French social thinker Jean-François Lyotard calls the great Enlightenment "metanarrative" of emancipation.[37] All have failed to one degree or another in the late twentieth century, helping to kindle a reevaluation of ideological assumptions.

Thus, despite the obvious differences between developments in Eastern and Western thinking of the second half of the twentieth century, one finds in both a clear impulse to disengage language, memory, and imagination from ideological absolutes. Hence, from time to time throughout this study I have drawn on these Western sources in order better to illuminate aspects of the Russian meta-utopian mentality. The concluding chapter uses this contrastive technique to put into a broader context the issues around which our searching and very provisional late-twentieth-century mentality has formed.

The greatest challenge that meta-utopian fiction presents is to any kind of ideological maximalism, any either/ormentality in which two alternatives are inherently closely related to each other as in a vicious circle, both denying the validity of a moderating middle space. This tendency characterizes the Russian intellectual tradition especially strongly. It is not surprising that this valuative model has received special attention since the 1960s in Russian semiotics. In their classic article "The Role of Dual Models in the Dynamics of Russian Culture" Iury Lotman and Boris Uspensky argue that premodern and early modern Russian culture was built on polarized value systems, binary in their inherent structures and emerging in diametrically opposed

---

[37] Jean-François Lyotard, *The Postmodern Condition: A Report on Knowledge*, trans. G. Bennington and B. Massumi (Minneapolis: University of Minnesota Press, 1984), xxiv.

pairs.[38] In essential concepts of good/bad, true/false, virtuous/sinful, just/unjust, one system functioned as the mirror image, as it were, of its diametrical opposite. The effect was to create a valuative circle that was incapable of deep change of mentality but that did "revolve" occasionally in violent reversals of value. Lotman and Uspensky use this model to characterize major cultural revolutions in pre-nineteenth-century Russian history—among them, the medieval Russian Orthodox polemic on paganism, and later on Roman Catholicism, as well as the modernization and secularization of Russia under Peter the Great. They juxtapose this bipolar pattern to a tripartite model of cultural development that emerged in Western Europe in the early Renaissance. This model posited a neutral middle ground between the two poles, which in turn became the space in which truly new mentalities emerged.

It can certainly be argued that Stalinist and post-Stalinist culture has been strongly shaped by an either/or mentality, this time with the egalitarian, liberationist utopian project of Marxism-Leninism opposed by the conservative, patriarchal vision of Russian Orthodox nationalism.[39] Ironically, both are ultimately allies against any concept of moderation, any attempt to discredit ideological maximalism and defend some common middle ground. Meta-utopian fiction may be seen as a "playground" in which a tripartite "game" can be imagined and acted out. What these works as a whole strive for—and in this they represent a significant literary precedent for the "real-life" experiment in pluralist discourse in contemporary Russian society—is a recognition of the forms of the maximalist either/or mentality in post-Stalinist discourse and the positing of a genuine middle ground where dominant ideological polarities may be contemplated in terms of their common underlying mentality. Once this apocalyptic, maximalist mentality is defined for what it is and polarities reduced to one single ideological model, the question becomes whether meta-utopian fiction actually bears the seeds of a different new mentality or just expresses a tired skepticism toward the bipolarity underlying all ideological constructs. While ideological skepticism is certainly

---

[38] Jurij Lotman and Boris Uspenskij, "The Role of Dual Models in the Dynamics of Russian Culture," in *The Semiotics of Russian Culture*, ed. A. Shukman (Ann Arbor: Ardis, 1984), 3–35.

[39] Belaia makes this point most forcefully in her discussion of village prose. See *Zatonuvshaia Atlantida*, 37–38.

potent in this art, I will claim here that meta-utopian fiction goes beyond the dark, apocalyptic warnings of dystopia and beyond an apathetic, "what's-the-difference" attitude to sketch out a personal sphere that resists the claims of all ideologies on one's loyalty and defends *as a broad social strategy* the right of personal moral integrity and choice.

* CHAPTER TWO *

Publishing the Dystopian Heritage

THE GLASNOST DEBATE ABOUT

LITERARY EXPERIMENT AND

UTOPIAN IDEOLOGY

During glasnost among the strongest forms that the rethinking of social and cultural values has taken is a backlash against the utopian premises informing Soviet ideology. Such formulations are, in part, a response to the sudden appearance in Soviet journals of a large number of early- and mid-twentieth-century dystopian novels. The list is astounding. The year 1986 saw the publication of Platonov's "Juvenalian Sea" ("Iuvenil'noe more") in *Znamia*. In 1987 his *Foundation Pit* (*Kotlovan*) appeared in *Novyi mir*. In 1988 three more novels were published: Platonov's rather meta-utopian *Chevengur* in *Druzhba narodov*, Orwell's *Animal Farm* (*Skotnyi dvor*) in *Rodnik* in Latvia, and perhaps the most famous of Russian dystopias, Zamiatin's *We* (*My*), in *Znamia*. In the same year two works that in the West are not usually seen as dystopias were published and hailed for their anti-utopian qualities: Kafka's *The Castle* (*Zamok*) in two separate translations, in *Inostrannaia literatura* and *Neva*, and Arthur Koestler's *Darkness at Noon* (*Slepiashchaia t'ma*) in *Neva*. In 1989, Orwell's *1984* appeared in *Novyi mir*, and *Animal Farm* appeared in a second translation as *Ferma zhivotnykh* in *Literaturnyi Kirgizstan*. Many of these works have appeared since then as books in large editions.

This series of publications has triggered a much-belated shock of national self-recognition and has become an important focal point for ideological reevaluation. Perhaps it is appropriate to describe this anachronistic situation as an introduction to our study about a kind of fiction that both treats history as a problem and itself has so far been kept out of the flow of cultural-historical interaction. So we start not with the meta-utopian texts themselves but with their intended readers, and not with the reception of these works, which has barely begun, but with the reception of modernist dystopias, the chronological precursors that meta-utopian writers hardly knew. The point of this chapter is to set a historical anchor—to profile real Russian readers, their mentality, and how they perceive the relationship between experimental (dystopian) fiction and the entrenched (utopian) ideology during the one time in Soviet history when the two were allowed to engage in open dispute. We examine both the "constitutive" and "pathological" aspects of this intense reception process—that is, on the one hand, how it opens the future to new aesthetic and social possibilities and, on the other, how it dwells on lost chances and past and present horrors, closing the future off to a productive form of social imagination.[1] What we can see, I believe, is a readership overready for the kind of game that meta-utopian fiction proposes to play.

One of the healthy, constitutive functions of the current reception of dystopian fiction is the accessibility of the published texts to the general reader. Although one critic predicted that they would not become popular reading because of their emphasis on the antihero, on the protagonist victimized by state control, they and the discussion around them have appeared in journals of national scope, often with subscriptions running well over a million, as well as in smaller provincial journals.[2] In addition, critical responses have been published in journals and magazines of all political stripes, from the archconservative *Nash sovremennik* to the reformist journals *Novyi mir*, *Oktiabr'*, and *Znamia*, from the provincial *Sever* and *Don* to the national glossy magazines, like *Novoe vremia*, to such popular magazines as *Znanie—sila*. It is interesting that, according to a poll of readers published in *Izvestiia* early in 1989, the vast majority of readers had either heard of (36.1 percent) or read (34 percent) *The Foundation Pit*, which had appeared over a year before. A much smaller but still sizable number had either heard of (29.3 percent) or read (14.5 percent) *We*, which had been available for only a little over six months. This is in comparison to 75.7 percent for Bulgakov's *Heart of a Dog* and 85.4 percent for Pasternak's *Doctor Zhivago*.[3] The number of those surveyed was not provided, but it is important to note that about two thirds of them had received some form of higher education and

---

[1] The terms are borrowed from Ricoeur, *Lectures on Ideology and Utopia*, 1.
[2] Novikov, "Vozvrashchenie k zdravomu smyslu," 215.
[3] V. Stel'makh, "Novye starye knigi," *Izvestiia*, no. 32 (January 31, 1989): 3.

about one third a high-school education. Thus, however they may be interpreted by their readers, both these works would seem to be entering the mainstream of cultural interest.[4]

The publication of so many dystopian novels in so short a time has contributed to a much-needed national discussion of issues of social change, particularly the transfer from a social order based on what Ferdinand Tönnies called *Gemeinschaft*, that is, a unitary, communal order bound together in part by the adulation of a charismatic leader perceived to be omniscient and omnipotent, to *Gesellschaft*, or a civic social structure built around voluntary organization and participation of responsible, knowledgeable citizens in their government. Despite misgivings that dystopias would not make popular reading because of their emphasis on the experience of the victim, these novels have lent weight to a broad shift of concern to the issue of citizens' rights. As the sociologist R. Galtseva put it, "utopia is sociocentric, anti-utopia is personalist."[5] The discussion shows a clear preference for a civil or "pravovoe" government, one founded on guarantees of civil rights and citizen participation.[6] As the critic M. Pavlova-Silvanskaia noted, the appearance of *We* was one symptom of the reawakening of political life after a "long lethargy."[7] What has been called the "post-utopian society" is to be founded on tolerance of pluralism, a focus on diversity, and a return to "sober" acceptance of social reality and a "common-sense" approach to solving problems.[8]

Vsevolod Revich, a reviewer of *We*, writes of a sense of liberation from the totalitarian state structure described by Zamiatin and argues that this kind of literature is a tool for combating both Stalinism and the resurgent Stalinist nostalgia in contemporary Soviet society.[9] Dystopias have given their readers a way to conceptualize and formu-

---

[4] For more on the general relevance of dystopian fiction for the general reader, see Natal'ia Ivanova, "Proshchanie s utopiei, ili Siuzhet dlia nenapisannogo romana," *Literaturnaia gazeta*, no. 29 (July 18, 1990): 4, 7.

[5] R. Gal'tseva and I. Rodnianskaia, "Pomekha—chelovek: Opyt veka v zerkale antiutopii," *Novyi mir*, no. 12 (1988): 220.

[6] Iuliia Latynina, "V ozhidanii Zolotogo Veka: Ot skazki k antiutopii," *Oktiabr'*, no. 6 (1989): 182, 187.

[7] M. Pavlova-Sil'vanskaia, "Eto sladkoe 'My,' eto kovarnoe 'My'," *Druzhba narodov*, no. 11 (1988): 259.

[8] Viktor Erofeev, "Pominki po sovetskoi literature," *Literaturnaia gazeta*, no. 27 (July 4, 1990): 8; see also Novikov, "Vozvrashchenie k zdravomu smyslu," 214.

[9] Vsevolod Revich, "Preduprezhdenie vsem," *Literaturnoe obozrenie*, no. 7 (1988): 45.

late the effects of totalitarianism on the individual citizen. As the literary scholar Aleksei Zverev writes in *Novoe vremia*, Orwell showed in *1984* "to what degree coercion is capable of turning a person not only into a slave but into a fully convinced supporter of the system of oppression."[10] Pavlova-Silvanskaia sees *We* as a powerful antidote to the current nostalgia for the unthinking faith and enthusiasm of the "cold, hungry, naked" 1930s.[11] She argues that people will still be yearning for a Benefactor for some time to come: "Comprehension of the fact that fragmentation of interests and the emergence of a pluralistic society are unavoidable, that of the 270 million 'we' there will inevitably be smaller 'we's' and unitary 'I's'—all this has a hard time penetrating mass consciousness and [mass] political life."[12]

An interesting aspect of the current discussion is an exploration of concepts of time that depart from those typical of utopian and anti-utopian thinking. Utopias tend to isolate the ideal future society from past experience, giving total authority to the future. They often express a yearning for a time when history—past or future—will no longer be relevant because there will be a complete absence of change. Anti-utopian thinking tends to revert to a prehistorical, pre-civilized "natural" state of being. The current "meta-utopian" thinking, by contrast, tries to reconstruct the links to the past, to live in the present, *and* to accept Zamiatin's notion of the future as a series of revolutions, each linked to the others. Of Zamiatin Pavlova-Silvanskaia writes: "Happily, now we dare fearlessly to say how right the writer was when his rebel I-330 insisted that revolutions are endless, and any argument about the finiteness of progress, about the last revolution, is [nothing but] a sweet bedtime story for children. Zamiatin is helping us today to grow up, to give up comforting illusions, merciful myths; he is teaching us the difficult courage to love life as it actually is."[13] Zverev adds that the great merit of dystopian literature has been to point out the gap between myth and reality: it undertakes to "reject myths, point out dead ends, and show the way to overcome them."[14]

---

[10] Aleksei Zverev, "Bez starshego brata ... O slozhnom cheloveke i neprostom avtore—Dzhordzhe Oruelle," *Novoe vremia*, no. 37 (1989): 40.

[11] Pavlova-Sil'vanskaia, "Eto sladkoe 'My,' eto kovarnoe 'My'," 261.

[12] Ibid.

[13] Ibid., 262.

[14] Aleksei Zverev, "'Kogda prob'et poslednii chas prirody ...': Antiutopiia. XX vek," *Voprosy literatury*, no. 1 (1989): 69.

Different perceptions of what culture and language should be are emerging in the debate about utopia. A chief concern is to overcome the "Aesopian" character of Soviet culture, that is, the weak, allegorical message of protest inherent in many utterances and the automatic habit of readers to read between the lines, to look for hidden meaning in any public utterance. In an interesting article, "The Language of Utopia," the critic M. Arapov argues that a discourse taken largely from thieves' jargon has taken root since 1918 and has even become the basis for the individual citizen's self-defense against an oppressive state. Here the obvious meaning is not the intended message. The real message can be understood only by a competent receiver who already shares the views and information of the sender. Arapov argues that such wholesale adoption of this kind of language is not healthy: "It is not normal when all verbal humor, all living, nonofficial speech, becomes 'criminalized,' when cockney becomes the model not for individual expressions but for a whole approach [to language]."[15] He proposes to put in its place a tolerance of open linguistic "pluralism," in which utopian ideals are offset by a critical irony.[16]

The pluralist concept of culture now emerging rejects the constraining Socialist Realist "method," which in turn harks back to the Godbuilders' utopianism, with its romanticized orientation toward the future, its adulation of a strong leader, and its ultimate distrust of critical reasoning and the force of spontaneous imagination.[17] Gorky, the creator of Godbuilding and the "father" of Socialist Realism, is now seen as the chief bogeyman. He is reviled for his general intolerance of ironic, dystopian thinking and his unthinking approbation of Stalinist utopianism. Critics point specifically to his very personal, angry criticism of *We*, his role as middleman in the decision not to publish *Chevengur*, and, especially, his endorsement of Stalin's nightmarish social experiments, such as the Belomor Canal Project.[18] By contrast, Voronsky, the editor of *Krasnaia nov'*, is now hailed as

---

[15] M. Arapov, "Iazyk utopii," *Znanie-sila*, no. 2 (1990): 70.

[16] Ibid., 67.

[17] Erofeev, "Pominki po sovetskoi literature," 8; for more background on this claim, see Katerina Clark, *The Soviet Novel: History as Ritual* (Chicago: University of Chicago Press, 1985), 147–55; Clowes, *The Revolution of Moral Consciousness*, 200–23.

[18] Evgenii Evtushenko, "Sud'ba Platonova," *Sovetskaia kul'tura* (August 20, 1988): 5; Zverev, "'Kogda prob'et poslednii chas prirody ...,'" 50. See also L. Saraskina, "Strana dlia eksperimenta," *Oktiabr'*, no. 3 (1990): 159–70.

the defender of all sorts of politically skeptical and artistically radical works, including *We*.[19] Surprisingly, critics also look to such unlikely figures as the Godbuilder Bogdanov for support of a pluralist concept of culture. For example, Arapov chooses Bogdanov as his model, claiming that the founder of Proletcult maintained a critical distance from his utopian projects in his novels *Red Star* and *Engineer Menni*.[20]

The best overall foundation for a pluralist culture is given by one of the new "antiauthoritarian" avant-garde, the novelist Viktor Erofeev. Erofeev contemplates not just a synchronic dialogue between different ideological outlooks within one era, but a diachronic encounter with voices from past epochs and other cultures. What he calls "post-utopian" culture

> opposes the 'old' literature first and foremost in its readiness for dialogue with any culture, even the most distant in time and space, to create a polysemic, polystylistic structure freely supported by the experience of Russian philosophy of the early twentieth century, existentialism in world art, the philosophical and anthropological discoveries of the twentieth century which have all been beyond the bounds of Soviet culture; it stands for adaptation to a situation of free self-expression and against the speculative journalism [encouraged by Socialist Realism].[21]

Although Erofeev sees only the tiniest shoots of this new literary culture just starting to appear, other critics are more optimistic, finding in the dystopian novel the point of departure for the resurgence of literary art.[22] While Novikov argues that the dystopian novel has already been perfected and cannot develop further, he claims that it has already enjoyed fruitful interaction with other genres, for example, Tendriakov's novel about writing history *A Potshot at Mirages* (*Pokushenie na mirazhi*), Iskander's political antifable *Rabbits and Boa Constrictors* (*Kroliki i udavy*), and some of the Strugatsky brothers' recently published work. Serbinenko sees the Strugatskys' science-fiction novels *Snail on the Slope* (*Ulitka na sklone*) and *The Ugly Swans* (*Gadkie lebedi; Vremia dozhdia*) as important examples of

---

[19] Revich, "Preduprezhdenie vsem," 46.
[20] Arapov, "Iazyk utopii," 68.
[21] Erofeev, "Pominki po sovetskoi literature," 8.
[22] Novikov, "Vozvrashchenie k zdravomu smyslu," 214.

such experimental literature.²³ All of these works take a critical distance from utopian thinking, but parody the classical dystopian novel as well. Unlike dystopian fiction, these works, which I have called "meta-utopian," do not reject the varieties of utopian imagination out of hand, but strive to expose their pathological, as well as productive, tendencies.

In addition to the currents of "constitutive," fresh thinking emerging in the utopian debate, we find in many quarters a "pathological" inability to go beyond an either/ormentality that denies all forms of utopia and that makes a fetish of anti-utopian cynicism. Many critics, it would seem, have ignored Zverev's thought that "in and of itself utopia is not a monster, not a homunculus, not the nightmare of the century; it is nothing but an attempt at predicting the future." He goes on to say that "it is characteristic of people to look into the future, to try to make out at least some vague contours."²⁴ Several critics remark on the pervasiveness of an anti-utopian belief that reduces all "realized" utopias to repressive versions of totalitarianism. Iulia Latynina reports that in the Soviet Union, anti-utopian skepticism has become a kind of idée fixe.²⁵ In an article entitled "Farewell to Utopia," Natalia Ivanova comments: "If we were to speak of a genre which has gripped our minds and our life, as well, of a genre toward which many writers hasten without regard for 'parties' or interest groups, this genre would be anti-utopia."²⁶

Frequently, all kinds of utopias are equated with the Marxist-Leninist-Stalinist one, condemned as enslaving myths, destructive of human rights, of the individual, and of memory and the creative imagination. The critic Mikhail Epshtein commented in a roundtable discussion on new departures in literary theory in *Voprosy literatury*: "Imagination is the chief among liberating forces that move humanity forward; but when such archaic instincts as the will to power or [the desire for] universal leveling are attached onto the imagination ... then imagination turns into utopia, sets limits for itself, stopping at some one, unshakable, and absolutely 'correct' vision of the future. Utopia is the suicide of the imagination: convening the masses of

---

²³ V. Serbinenko, "Tri veka skitanii v mire utopii: Chitaia brat'ev Strugatskikh," *Novyi mir*, no. 5 (1989): 248–53.
²⁴ Zverev, "'Kogda prob'et poslednii chas prirody...,'" 31.
²⁵ Latynina, "V ozhidanii Zolotogo Veka," 178.
²⁶ Ivanova, "Proshchanie s utopiei," 4.

people for the reshaping of the world, it transforms them into the gravediggers of their future."[27] For many, "utopia" has become the scapegoat for all kinds of ideological ills. Evgeny Evtushenko, for example, sees everywhere in society the signs of "utopian psychosis," of promises made but never kept.[28]

The dystopian novel—in which the "no place" of the ideally just and happy society is revealed as a "bad place," repressive, tyrannical, unjust, and miserable—has sometimes even been made into a template for a popular revision of Soviet history. Russians, as Ivanova argues, have been living and experiencing in their own lives the "genre" of utopia-being-realized, which indeed, in her view, is dystopia.[29] Evtushenko has called dystopias the "textbooks of anti-totalitarianism."[30] R. Galtseva and I. Rodnianskaia interpret Soviet history through literary texts, placing "realist" works such as Dombrovsky's *Department of Unnecessary Things* or Grossman's *Life and Fate* next to *We* or *1984*. They see parallel themes in both: the opposition of the rebel to the advocates of the New World, the abuse of history by the regime, the use of paradoxical slogans by those in power to confound logic and reason, denial of canonized religion combined with a quasi-religious affirmation of the mythos of salvation, the reduction of selfhood to nothing. While this kind of analysis is intriguing, it is dangerously simplistic as historiography. One asks whether history is being oversimplified yet again, in much the same way as it has been in utopian writing. Only now the goal is to prove a different point, to discredit all utopias as fundamentally a fixed, moribund form of social consciousness.

Potentially the most problematic aspect of this anti-utopian maximalism is a kind of apocalyptic or dead-end mentality. The literary scholar O. B. Sabinina claims that dystopian fiction itself embodies a nihilistic attitude toward both the present and the future, closing both off to new imaginative possibility.[31] While some critics, especially Zverev, emphasize that dystopian fiction leaves the reader choices to make and facilitates the "search for ways to overcome

---

[27] "'Kruglyi stol': Nereshennye problemy teorii literatury," *Voprosy literatury*, no. 12 (1987): 25.

[28] Evtushenko, "Sud'ba Platonova," 5.

[29] Ivanova, "Proshchanie s utopiei," 4.

[30] Cited in Novikov, "Vozvrashchenie k zdravomu smyslu," 215.

[31] O. B. Sabinina, "Zhanr antiutopii v angliiskoi i amerikanskoi literature 30-50-kh godov XX v.," *Vestnik moskovskogo universiteta: Filologiia*, no. 2 (1990): 51.

[dead ends]," many others underscore the dystopia's "sense of an ending." Zverev himself points out the ecological disasters of the atomic era and the potential for apocalyptic thinking. Ivanova certainly writes in a near-apocalyptic vein. Novikov calls the twentieth century the anti-utopian century and emphasizes that all utopian political dreams have ended in disaster. The philosopher Iury Davydov describes the dangers of unchallenged utopian dreaming and demagoguery in an era dominated by mass media.[32]

At times, this anti-utopian idée fixe looks merely like the other side of the same coin of a long-lived Russian utopian cast of mind: the same passion, the same need for enemies, the same demands made of writers and artists for works with a narrow didactic focus—the need for total authority, for "lessons," for a "moral," rather than an ability to engage in dialogue—the same claim to universality, the same teleology, but now directed against the fallen god of utopia. One wonders at times whether in the main it will lead anywhere but to a kind of blank nihilism, a total lack of faith in social values of any kind. What we find all too frequently is that pattern of which Lotman and Uspensky speak in "The Role of Dual Models in the Dynamics of Russian Culture," an age-old Russian ideological maximalism, an unwillingness to define a middle ground between extremes.[33] This "reactive" quality is epitomized in the title of a recently founded magazine, *Sodeistvie: Antiutopicheskaia, nonkonformistskaia, vnepartiinaia gazeta* (*Assistance: An Anti-utopian, Nonconformist, Non-party Newspaper*).[34] All of its descriptors are negative, as the magazine reacts against what has gone before rather than opening up new alternatives.

It should be noted in passing that signs that a more moderate, nonpolarized kind of thinking is penetrating to educated Russian society at large are also evident. Some participants in the recent discussion about Socialist Realism and Marxism-Leninism address the polarity between Leninist, Socialist Realist monumentalism and nationalist, Russian Orthodox, critical realist valuations, and seek other alternatives to it. In a series of roundtable discussions about Socialist Realism conducted under the auspices of *Literaturnaia gazeta* in 1988, writers and critics sparred over the value of Socialist Realism as a

---

[32] "'Kruglyi stol,'" 43.
[33] Lotman and Uspenskij, "The Role of Dual Models," 3–35.
[34] Cited in Ivanova, "Proshchanie s utopiei," 7.

"literary method."³⁵ The writer R. Kireev recognized in Socialist Realism "our old disease of monopolization," thus confronting another version of the same Russian maximalism. The literature professor Iu. Borev put the problem in terms of close parallels between the ideological opponents, Marxist-Leninist materialism and Christian otherworldliness: "In the theory and aesthetic practice of Socialist Realism could be found ... more than a little rosy futurology, transposing paradise from the other world to the near future."³⁶

Beyond the discussion among known writers and academics, a variety of voices have made themselves heard on issues that amount to a confrontation with Russian maximalist thinking. For example, there were several responses to an article in *Literaturnaia gazeta* by Iu. Kublanovsky entitled "On the Ruins of Utopia" that propose a return to a religious Orthodox culture, which would simply reinforce the Marxist-Leninist/nationalist-Orthodox polarity. One reader from Sverdlovsk asked whether there are no ways of making sense of the world other than dogmatic Marxism and dogmatic Christianity: "Is it really possible that there are no books other than the Gospel and *The Communist Manifesto*, the Bible and *Das Kapital*, and [no other] paths for Russia [to follow] other than Bolshevism and Orthodoxy?"³⁷ Such readers are surely ready to contemplate the kind of civil society and genuine cultural and political pluralism that Western Sovietologists kept trying to uncover in Gorbachev's Russia.

Despite such clear signs that cultural moderates are vocal, polarized thinking is prominent and powerful. And it is this polarized mentality that makes all the more urgent the recovery of a usable literary past that is organically related to the present. To some degree, it must be said, the critics and writers are themselves the victims of a certain historical amnesia that is characteristic of utopian thinking. In their haste to recapture and digest the dystopian experiments of the first half of the twentieth century and to find in them the seeds of literary and social renewal, on the whole they have in good utopian style severed themselves from more recent and very usable social-cultural precedents emanating from underground culture of the past few decades. Critics have largely overlooked the overwhelmingly rich, if hidden, corpus of meta-utopian literature from their own time, the

---

³⁵ See *Literaturnaia gazeta*, May 25, 1988, 3.
³⁶ Ibid.
³⁷ *Literaturnaia gazeta*, February 13, 1991, 14.

post-Stalinist era.[38] It is this oversight that makes the whole current discussion less productive than it might be. Instead of articulating a really different social consciousness, critics are often treading on old ground.

There is a certain tendency to dismiss the Thaw period as a time when fundamental utopian concepts were reinforced.[39] In fact, it was a time when increasingly, at least in unofficial writing, they were being called into question. In the late 1950s and early 1960s, Siniavsky-Terts and Daniel-Arzhak, the first writers of the young, post-Stalinist generation to publish beyond the borders of the Soviet Union, particularly irritated the authorities by using literary experiment to question the (utopian) ideological foundations of the Soviet regime. Throughout the Brezhnevian stagnation of the 1970s and early 1980s, the sociologist-novelist Aleksandr Zinoviev, the very popular novelist and translator Vasily Aksënov, and the satirist Vladimir Voinovich also dethroned the Soviet utopia through narrative play. Eventually, it is interesting to note, all of them ended in exile in Europe for their challenge to the regime. Most memorably, Aksënov was asked to leave for his attempt to publish ludic fiction openly within the Soviet Union in the anthology *Metropol'* (1979). Benefiting in part from the challenges laid down by these writers, other very popular authors, such as Fazil Iskander and Arkady and Boris Strugatsky, managed to continue their careers in the Soviet Union and publish their experimental work abroad.

It is worth noting, by way of contrast, that a parallel "post-utopian" cultural phenomenon known as "conceptualist" art has received significantly more attention, in both East and West. Artists such as Larisa Zvezdochetova, Ilia Kabakov, Vitaly Komar, and Aleksandr Melamid have become familiar to the Western world partly through the well-publicized Sotheby auction held in Moscow in 1988. Since then their work has been exhibited in several places in the United States and Europe.[40] As the art critic Margarita Tupitsyn puts it, conceptualists "proposed to view socialist realism and propaganda im-

---

[38] The tip of the iceberg has barely been touched with recent slight discussions of Iskander, the Strugatskys, and other writers who stayed within the bounds of Soviet writing, never going into exile. See Novikov, "Vozvrashchenie k zdravomu smyslu," 214.

[39] Latynina, "V ozhidanii Zolotogo Veka," 180; Ivanova, "Proshchanie s utopiei," 4.

[40] Margarita Tupitsyn, *Margins of Soviet Art: Socialist Realism to the Present* (Milan: Ginacarlo Politi Editore, 1989); D. A. Ross, ed., *Between Spring and Summer: Soviet*

agery not as mere kitsch or simply a vehicle for bureaucratic manipulation, but as a rich field of stereotypes and myths which they could transform into a new language, one able to deconstruct official myths on their own terms."[41] This art uses the common materials of everyday life—decorative objects, posters and other political icons, laboratory equipment, educational materials—to confront Soviet (utopian) claims to gender, ethnic, and class equality; liberty; technological progress; and the like.

The conceptualists have a strong sense of having come "after utopia." One of conceptualist art's most prominent practitioners, Ilia Kabakov, noted in 1989: "Our generation arrived on the scene after the utopia had been accomplished and after the cooling off of the nuclear explosion. Radioactive fallout has descended and we have rediscovered ourselves in a post-utopian world."[42] The conceptualists share the meta-utopian mentality of many of their literary contemporaries. They are aware of the ironies of the various utopian experiments of the twentieth century and they are seriously concerned to recuperate a nonutopian history, a "usable past." Still, although artists like Komar and Melamid reject utopian efforts to "abolish the past" and are in search of another usable past, they view themselves as the "children" of Socialist Realism. In a typically meta-utopian way, they retain a fascination with utopian thinking, both as fantasy and as ideology, at the same time that they parody its artifacts and its reasoning.[43]

It still remains something of an enigma that so far the most radical exemplars of the meta-utopian oeuvre have been left nearly unexplored even long after official censorship ceased to be a problem and when the utopia-bashing taste of the public was already recognized. Perhaps old habits die hard: whatever else one may say, the modernist literary "classics" are less threatening both to political leaders and to the public at large. As late as 1990, Voinovich recounted the foot-dragging associated with publishing his novel *Moscow 2042*.[44]

Conceptual Art in the Era of Late Communism (Cambridge, Mass.: MIT Press, 1990). I am grateful to Svetlana Boym for information about conceptualist art.

[41] M. Tupitsyn, "U-turn of the U-topian," in *Between Spring and Summer*, ed. Ross, 36.

[42] Cited in Elisabeth Sussman, "The Third Zone: Soviet 'Postmodern,'" in *Between Spring and Summer*, ed. Ross, 63.

[43] Peter Wollen, "Scenes from the Future: Komar & Melamid," in *Between Spring and Summer*, ed. Ross, 109–10.

[44] Public lecture at Purdue University, West Lafayette, Ind., April 1990.

It finally has appeared in two separate editions, one of them with a new, private Russian–West German publishing firm, Vsia Moskva, in an enormous run of 500,000 copies![45] Clearly the book publishers sense that this kind of writing (and this particular author) will bring in profits. Zinoviev's citizenship was returned to him during the summer of 1990, and his works are scheduled to appear. They have already begun to come out in small excerpts.[46] Deprived of the broad publicity accompanying the publication of modernist dystopias in Soviet "thick journals," Siniavsky's and Daniel's works came out during the summer of 1990 in a mid-sized edition of 100,000 copies. The critic N. Azhgikhina has noted that Siniavsky and Daniel have "returned" much less than others have, partly because their art is less accessible to readers. Although they are mostly known as early fighters for civil liberties, Azhgikhina reminds her Russian readers that "if there had been no works of Siniavsky-Terts and Daniel-Arzhak, mellow, ironic, scoffing at literary dogma, laughing at stereotype, few of those works that now are returning and are growing and developing on native soil would have been created."[47] Other, less confrontational meta-utopias by Tendriakov, the Strugatskys, Iskander—all authors who stayed in Russia—have indeed appeared and have enjoyed some slight critical discussion.

What meta-utopian writing offers is a sense of humor and perspective. It is far more ambivalent and self-ironic than its dystopian antecedents, both criticizing and coexisting with utopian ideals. The narrator or protagonist is frequently a writer of some sort—a novelist, historian, academic, or just someone writing a confession—who has a problematic attitude toward existing ideology. The process of writing exposes the limitations of ideologically "fixed" language. Inevitably the existing "utopian" ideology is revealed as a mere fiction among other fictions. Historiography, sociology, literary criticism, and fiction that are uncritically conceived, written only to bolster existing belief, are pilloried. What is reaffirmed here is the responsibility of the self-conscious, linguistically aware person to be resistant to all dogmatic thinking, to keep open the notion of choice.

---

[45] The other edition appears in an anthology edited by V. P. Shestakov entitled *Utopiia i antiutopiia XX veka,* published in a run of 100,000 copies by Progress Publishers. I am grateful to Ellen Chances for this information.

[46] See the interview with Zinoviev in Amurskii, "Ia—odinochka vo vsem," 14; and Kantor, "Siiaiushchaia vysota," 30.

[47] Azhgikhina, "Vozvrashchenie Siniavskogo i Danielia," 204.

The aim of the present study, then, is to bring to light the ways in which the underground has provided post-Soviet culture with a usable past to which living writers and critics are organically connected, that is, one that has sprung to life on the near side of the Stalinist abyss. Meta-utopian fiction stands as proof that play, creative imagination, historical memory, and a capacity for productive skepticism and critical thinking were not lost in the ravages of the Stalinist experiment. Ways to comprehend the vicious circle have been conceived within the vicious circle itself.

PART TWO

THE META-UTOPIAN EXPERIMENT IN FICTION: ELEMENTS OF LITERARY AND IDEOLOGICAL REANIMATION

*

* CHAPTER THREE *

Charting Meta-utopia

CHRONOTOPES OF DISORIENTATION

AMONG the canonical markers of utopian writing is the ambiguous location of the ideal society in space and time. Thus, a good point of departure for a discussion of meta-utopian fiction will be a definition of it in terms of its treatment of spatial and temporal dimensions. Moreover, the positioning of plot events in a matrix of space and time, what Bakhtin calls "chronotope," lays the coordinates for a sustained valuative framework.[1] Chronotopes can give a palpable sense of the ideological project central to meta-utopian fiction. This fiction is about liberation from spatial and temporal stasis. It is about the unfolding of a consciousness of ideological options, of moral choices in the midst of a static, monolithic cultural milieu. Meta-utopias expose the "utopian" time-space matrix in an effort to open up this closed zone.

There are several problems with conceptualizing spatial metaphors in meta-utopian writing. Utopian images of place treat the tension between what Fredric Jameson has called "text" and "geography," between fantasy and reality, and between antinomies in social life, such as equality and hierarchy, stability and unrest.[2] Following the work of Louis Marin on More's *Utopia*, Jameson compares spatial imagery in utopian fiction to that in mythic narrative: while myth mediates between irreconcilable, noncongruent loci, typically in a vertical plane, utopia accepts and "neutralizes" incongruities, typically in a horizontal plane.[3] While seeming to be an idealized blueprint for the perfection of an existing society, utopia actually combines

---

[1] M. M. Bakhtin, "Forms of Time and of the Chronotope in the Novel: Notes toward a Historical Poetics," in *The Dialogic Imagination*, ed. M. Holquist, trans. M. Holquist and C. Emerson (Austin: University of Texas Press, 1988), 85.

[2] Fredric Jameson, "Of Islands and Trenches: Neutralization and the Production of Utopian Discourse," in *The Ideologies of Theory: Essays, 1971–1986*, vol. 2: *The Syntax of History* (Minneapolis: University of Minnesota Press, 1988), 75–101.

[3] Ibid., 79.

oppositions in a "both/and" geography where, for example, equality and hierarchy or individual freedom and the demands of community coexist. Likewise, the text appears to map a single geographical referent, but by no means completely, at times appearing to map another referent. For example, in *Utopia* Utopia seems to refer to England, but at times the referent might be construed as Portugal or Ceylon. Text and geography are never mediated and remain incongruent. This nonmediation, in Jameson's view, has to do with the ideological function of utopia: it points out the failings of established ideology while singling out possible coordinates of a new one. While myth establishes a border between two states that the protagonist eventually crosses, utopia avoids defining spatial differences, for example, between a "here" and a "there." Although the utopian "there" can seem to be a separate place at some distance but still accessible from the intended reader's "here" through some sort of unspecified, uncharted journey, the utopian locus can also seem to be a shadow copy or an idealized design to be superimposed on "here."

While the idea of "neutralization" may explain the use of geography in Renaissance utopias and has some meaning (though not the one intended by Marin and Jameson) for the Russian meta-utopian chronotope, as a general rule, it in no way describes the "positive" utopian tradition in Russia that includes writers and thinkers as diverse as Chernyshevsky, Fedorov, Gorky, and Bogdanov. The Russian tradition, taken as a whole, resembles a religious psychology in its need for mythic mediation between noncongruent conditions. For example, personal dream and social reality are negotiated in *What Is to Be Done?*, death and life in Fedorov's theory of resurrection of the dead, the fusion of the isolated, conscious self with the life-giving, collective "we" in Gorky's *Confession* and Lunacharsky's *Religion and Socialism*. This tradition is strongly dualistic, positing a border (either vertical or horizontal) that must be crossed, not accepting the "sheer discontinuity" of Marin's spatial scheme of neutralization.[4] It is perhaps not by chance that a Slavist, Gary Saul Morson, finds a mythic model at the heart of the utopian narrative. In his discussion of utopian narrative structures, he points specifically to the allegory of the escape from the cave in Book 7 of *The Republic* as the basic utopian fabula.[5] It will be useful for our project to extend this obser-

[4] Ibid., 87.

[5] Gary Saul Morson, *The Boundaries of Genre: Dostoevsky's "Diary of a Writer" and the Traditions of Literary Utopia* (1981; Evanston, Ill.: Northwestern University Press, n.d.), 89.

vation about narrative form to the matter of chronotope. In Plato's story we find a hierarchical, vertical relationship between the lower world of the cave, with the imperfect, two-dimensional vision of reality that its inhabitants have, and the higher world of the open air drenched in sunlight, affording a fuller knowledge of reality to the person capable of adapting to the blinding light. The border between the two involves an epistemological shift, a transformation of consciousness marked by the sensation of blindness followed by the experience of fresh insight. This vertical border-crossing certainly applies both to Russian utopian thinking and to parodic, dystopian allusions to it in the architectural imagery contrasting basements and towers of *Notes from the Underground*, *We*, and even, to some extent, Platonov's *The Foundation Pit*. But, in addition, the dystopian novel envisions the reanimation of an elemental human self not as what Nietzsche in *Thus Spoke Zarathustra* would call a vertical "going down" or "going under," but as a horizontal "going across." Specifically, dystopian novels, starting with *We*, borrow the image of the wall from *Notes from the Underground* (and possibly Leonid Andreev's story from 1901, "The Wall") as a border to be crossed horizontally from a confining space to the open, unconstructed space of "nature."

Chronotope in meta-utopian fiction plays with the Russian utopian tradition taken as a whole (both positive and negative visions), arriving at a kind of neutralization of the spatial differences posited in myth. But this neutralization is not based on a notion of "sheer discontinuity," as it is with Marin. Rather, we find that the seemingly "ideal" locus is connected to the other and is just as bad as the other. There is no change in valence. In particular, meta-utopian works distinguish themselves from the chronotopes used in the utopian genre nearest to them, the dystopian novel. They demythicize the dystopian border, the notion of the wall, by underscoring the sameness of conditions on both sides and by stressing characters' sometimes comical lack of curiosity about the other side. For example, in *Liubimov* both the hamlet of Liubimov and the outside world of the Soviet province are viewed by their respective leaders and ideological proponents as the best of all possible worlds. The police in the provincial capital feel that Lënia Tikhomirov's alternative may be a threat to their own ideological well-being and take steps to invade Liubimov. In other words, the inward invasive movement here is, if anything, a denial of the outward, escapist movement in a dystopia. In a comic twist, the spy Kochetov, who is entrusted with finding a way to sabotage Tikhomirov's experiment, is very impressed with Tikhomirov's techniques of mass magnetism and hypnosis and writes a long letter to the outer world in support of Tikhomirov's improvement on Soviet ideology and techniques of political persuasion and control. He argues that Tikhomirov has mind-bending powers "more technological [sic] by comparison with our own utopia" (L, 365). He even suggests that Tikhomirov's methods should become a standard for political education everywhere. Thus, in meta-utopian writing not only is there no escape, but there is no substantial difference between the inside and the outside.

Voinovich's *Moscow 2042* is founded on the same motif of invasion of utopia. The Solzhenitsyn-like writer in exile Sim Simich Karnavalov intends to invade the postsocialist Moscow of the future to restore the city to its more "moral" medieval existence. He has himself frozen and stored in a Swiss bank vault until 2042, when presumably the Russian public will be ripe for revolt. Dressed as a medieval prince, he plans to invade Moscow and ride the crest of popular upheaval to power. In preparation for the takeover, the Karnavalov of 1982 commands Kartsev to smuggle a floppy disk containing his major works into the Moscow of the future. Both Kartsev's act of smuggling, which is quickly foiled, and Karnavalov's own invasion of the Moscow of the future are variations on the same motif that we found in *Liubimov*. Just as there is no essential difference between Kochetov and Tikhomirov, so Karnavalov's tyrannical mentality is merely a more intense version of the mentality of those already in power in the Moscow of 2042. Similarly, Karnavalov's new regime will impose the same autocratic rule that has always been in place, under the tsars, in the "preparatory" Soviet state established by Lenin, and now in the true "communist" society. Only now, as a true counterutopian, Karnavalov uses symbols of power and faith taken from the deep past of medieval Muscovy. Thus, the border motif that marks a transfiguration of consciousness in Russian utopias and dystopias is here discounted. The differences between the postsocialist Soviet state and Karnavalov's ideal are quite illusory: both regimes are at base the enactment of willful, self-righteous despotism.

In Zinoviev's two meta-utopian works, *The Yawning Heights* and *The Radiant Future*, the border serves only to show the hypocrisy of those in favor. Trusted official representatives of the socialist experiment are the only ones allowed to cross the border. While on the inside, they do everything to support official ideology and, thus, to further their own careers. On the outside all they do is complain and criticize the existing state of their own society, thus hoping to raise themselves in the eyes of Western skeptics.

The image of the border is central to the Strugatsky brothers' science-fiction novel *The Condemned City*. Here the characters find themselves in an urban wasteland illuminated by a light-bulb sun that is turned on and off at the appointed time every day. On one side their city is bordered by a high opaque yellow wall that people talk about but never try to cross. Although they have no idea how they reached this wasteland, they know that they are part of a social construct known as "The Experiment," an ecumenical and international community that embraces people from all countries and of all political ideologies and religious faiths. The only "wall" that impinges on their consciousness is a temporal one existing in their memories. All the characters have been driven to this wasteland by some terrible historical event from the first half of the twentieth century—collectivization, Nazi pogroms, the Chinese revolution—believing that nothing could be as bad as what they have left behind. Some were the victims of crimes, some the perpetrators, but none ever regrets or misses what has been abandoned, and no one thinks of trying to go back. The wasteland is, practically speaking, the only reality, and it is up to each character to define it according to his or her own predilection. A few, such as the American, Donald Cooper, see it for what it is and understand that what the settlers are building in the wasteland will be just a reenactment of the social forms of the recent past—for example, Stalinist state centralism, fascist oligarchy, or a stultifying welfare state. For characters such as Cooper the end is suicide. The chief protagonists, Andrei Voronin and Izia Katsman, come to a similar realization, but instead of committing suicide they choose to depart the "condemned city" to explore the surrounding deserts and are eventually shot by an unidentified assailant.

The same indifference to the border is operative in the Strugatskys' *The Ugly Swans*. Here the time-space matrix is a provincial spa town at some indeterminate time. It is like a point in space, a microcosm bearing no relation to any larger framework. No one ever arrives or leaves—a fact that never seems to bother anyone. This society does have some characteristics of a modern utopia, now old, degenerate, and functioning badly. For example, the responsibility for child-rearing appears to have been assumed by the state. The novel's protagonist, the writer Viktor Banev, remembers his own gloomy experiences in the same boarding school in which his daughter is now being raised. Family relations are porous. Children are removed early from the home, and husband and wife have only a tangential relationship to each other, each leading a life almost completely independent of the other. Public presence dominates over private life. Moreover, this society appears to function by itself. Hours spent working are minimal (except for those working in security and intelligence), and people spend their many hours of leisure drinking and carousing.

The one border about which everyone cares is an internal one: the fence surrounding the local leprosarium that has been inhabited for several years by superintelligent extraterrestrial beings, known as the "slimies." These creatures allegedly suffer from a degenerative eye disease and are completely enveloped in bandages. They are blamed for visiting upon the community a latter-day Flood, years and years of rain that have undermined the area's economic base as a spa. Moreover, they are suspected of hypnotizing the whole community and especially of brainwashing the children, in a move to establish a new kind of utopia that will be built in place of the old community. Here, as in *Liubimov*, the dystopian chronotope is reversed: the people on the outside feel threatened and try unsuccessfully to penetrate and neutralize the inner sanctum. But what actually happens is a circular, generational recurrence of a youthful utopian urge to remake the social world in one's own image. One notion of utopia is being replaced by another, and each new realization, it is implied, is equally suspect. Thus, here, as in other meta-utopias, the character of space and time coordinates, valueless in and of themselves, shifts as they are repeatedly reimagined and redefined.

Special note should be taken of Erofeev's *Moscow-Petushki*, which would seem to be dystopian in the sense that Petushki represents an escape to a paradise of personal pleasures from the oppressive dominance of Moscow and its Kremlin. There is, however, no real border here, and Erofeev comes to the meta-utopian conclusion that there is no difference between the two poles. All claims to social (or personal) transfiguration are false. The way Erofeev deals with geography and text, on one hand, and religious mythic thinking, on the other, is quite unique. Erofeev's novel is patterned clearly on Aleksandr Radishchev's eighteenth-century travel description *A Journey from Petersburg to Moscow* (1790). In Radishchev's work the narrator travels from the new capital, St. Petersburg, where, as one character says ironically, "there is much more enlightenment," to the ever-darker heartland of Russian towns and finally to Moscow.[6] He uses the various stops along the way as chapter headings, each to witness and expose a different evil of Russian society. As his observations become harsher his hopes and prescriptions for Russian society are more clearly articulated. He reserves two middle chapters for musing about the ideal society and finishes with an encomium to Mikhail Lomonosov, Russia's great Enlightenment man, as the bright light illuminating Russia's darkness.

Erofeev's novel undoes the notion of "progress," both physical and spiritual, that underlies Radishchev's travelogue. He starts with Moscow and moves toward a bright utopian destination whose name, "Petushki" ("Roosters"), playfully echoes Petersburg. Just as Radishchev's two end points are clearly identifiable points on the map, so Erofeev's protagonist, Venichka, claims that his paradisal destination is connected to Moscow by rail. It is implied that one can reach one place from the other by a linear progression. The chapter headings, which mark the part of the journey between two stations, support this claim. Even the place names seem to show some kind of "progress," even if backwards to a presocialist age and then to "nature." Just outside of Moscow the station names assert the power of Moscow, a utopia based on heavy industry, the industrial "workers' paradise." Among others we find Serp i molot ("Hammer and Sickle"), Novogireevo ("New Weight"), Zheleznodorozhnaia ("Railroad"), and Elektrougli ("Coal for Electricity"). Subsequently there is a release from the heaviness and darkness of these images as the station names reflect natural or old Russian images: Nazar'evo (recalls the Russian "Nazaret" or "Nazareth"), Pavlovo-Posad ("Paul's Quarter"), Krutoe ("Steep"), Usad ("Country Estate"), Omutishche ("Whirlpool"). It is only at the end of the journey that the last four chapter headings superimpose quite unambiguously the "map" of Petushki onto the map of Moscow. For example, "Petushki. Station Square" mimics the title of the second chapter, "Moscow. Kursk Station Square." The next title, "Petushki. Garden Ring" is an obvious reference to Moscow, as is the following one, "Petushki. The Kremlin. The Statue of Minin and Pozharsky." The final chapter makes the identity of the two complete: "Moscow-Petushki. An Unfamiliar Entryway." The fusion of the fantasy world and the familiar one makes

---

[6] Aleksandr Radishchev, *Puteshestvie iz Peterburga v Moskvu* (Leningrad: Khudozhestvennaia literatura, 1969), 24.

it clear not only that Petushki is a figment of Venichka's imagination but that the notion of a physical "progress" or journey toward some ideal place and the accompanying ideal of social progress and perfectibility are likewise imaginary. As long as it is held separate in Venichka's imagination, the town of Petushki does serve as a satirical double for Moscow and Soviet society. Venichka's vision makes virtues out of heavy drinking, loitering on the job, sexual promiscuity—all activities perceived as vices in Soviet society. Once even this topsy-turvy vision is gone, one is confronted with the only real "fact" about Soviet life—physical coercion—as Venichka is mugged, beaten, and finally "murdered."

Horizontal, utopian geography is kept quite separate from the vertical, mythic quest until the very end of this complex novel. Religious psychology and spiritual seeking are acknowledged as such and are consciously divorced from social fantasy. Disgusted with the various "feats of valor" of social enthusiasts, didacts, and engineers of human souls, the drunk Venichka rejects any notion of a good social imagination or the goodness of human will. Rather, he retreats within himself and creates a private relationship with "God" and the "angels." Toward the end he finds himself beset by darker supernatural forces as well—including Satan, the Sphinx, the bacchic Erinyes, and, quite incongruously, Mukhina's (utopian) statue of the worker and the peasant woman. Venichka envisions himself as Christ and several times throughout his narrative experiences martyrdom and resurrection. The dark and bright sides of Venichka's spiritual fantasy lead him to several conclusions about the power of social imagination. While he is suspicious of any idea of human perfectibility without the aid of some beneficent supernatural power, he does not reject anyone's social fantasies outright. In the spirit of Psalm 22, he embraces a notion of paradise created by God, not by human effort: "He is good. He leads me from suffering to the light. From Moscow to Petushki. Through the torments at Kursk Station to the light and to Petushki. Durch Leiden—Licht" (MP, 30). By contrast, the dark forces that accost him in the end are in a sense the epitome of anti-utopianism: they urge him simply to give up all social imagination, "to accept the darkness" (MP, 58).

Just as real and fantastic geography are merged by the end of *Moscow-Petushki*, so are religious and utopian discourses—the effect of which is to underscore the bleakness of a world in which there are neither borders nor differences. In the fifth-to-last chapter, "Petushki. The Platform," Mukhina's (utopian) statue of the worker and the peasant appears as the last in a series of dark visions. As with the statue of Peter in Pushkin's "The Bronze Horseman," here the social and the spiritual come together to create a nightmare. The worker hits Venichka over the head with his hammer and the peasant woman castrates him with her knife (MP, 68). Venichka now "wakes up" and thinks only about death. Like Ivan Karamazov, who hands back his ticket, he believes he will die, "without accepting this world . . . comprehending but not accepting it" (MP, 69).

Just as horizontal borders are made unimportant and the dystopian hope for escape is shattered, so meta-utopian fiction uses a variety of carnivalesque techniques to annul the mythic vertical border so important to Russian utopianism. Here the higher locus is exchanged for the lower—the "more" real with the merely real, paradise with the garbage pit, the spiritual with the visceral, the escatological with the scatological. The utopian higher locus, utopia as "paradise," is consistently exposed in meta-utopian fiction as a wasteland, a garbage dump, that is, nature made lifeless and absurd by too much human meddling. *The Condemned City* opens with a nocturnal scene of drivers in garbage trucks hauling garbage to a dump. In *Liubimov*, the narrator Savely Kuzmich stands by his new "tsar" and master, Lënia Tikhomirov, on his victory day on the heights above the town. As he describes the new paradise in all its grandeur, his chronicler's eye belies his utopian enthusiasm. His eye roves from the heights of the heavens down to the distant patterns of the fields and the river and downward to a still closer range, where he sees the "yellow coffin of the hospital," "the iron nakedness of the shrubbery," "the silvery strands of mud," an "empty lot full of trash" (L, 371).

Zinoviev in *The Yawning Heights* conducts the most sustained carnivalization of paradise. The oxymoronic title of the work gives the first hint. Here "gleaming" or "shining" (*siiaiushchii*) heights of the socialist paradise have been exchanged for "yawning" or "gaping" (*ziiaiushchii*) heights. "Yawning," of course, is an epithet more appropriate for an abyss or chasm or, indeed, for hell. From the first pages, Zinoviev plays with vertical metaphors central to the Bolshevik mythos, such as flying, airplanes, high-rise architecture, and especially hydroelectric dams, one of the major engineering feats of the Soviet period, in which whole heavy bodies of water are raised toward the sky, thus producing enormous power.[7] The key place, the spiritual center of Ibansk, is its Pilots' School, an institute of aviation that

---

[7] Stites, *Revolutionary Dreams*, 170–71.

is soon exposed for what it really is, a prison camp. The most obvious symbol of social progress in Ibansk is its public housing, that is, the familiar faceless high-rise apartment buildings that The Big Mouth describes as "identical in form but indistinguishable in content" (YH, 11), an absurdist paraphrase of the Stalinist formula for Soviet communism, "national in form, socialist in content."[8] These structures, like everything in this "utopia," repress individual identity, making a citizen wonder who he really is (YH, 11). And the greatest technological feat of which Ibansk boasts is the dam built across the river Ibaniuchka that, instead of bringing the river level *upward* and providing a source of energy and power for the city, makes the river flow sideways, flooding the surrounding potato fields (YH, 11).

Meta-utopian fiction devalues the utopian locus through the carnivalesque reversal of sacred and profane. While most meta-utopias, like their predecessors, utopian fiction and the dystopian novel, shy away from mention of the human body, three works, *Moscow-Petushki*, *The Yawning Heights*, and *Moscow 2042*, use images of private parts and various bodily functions in comic juxtaposition to the lofty ideals of utopia. In *Moscow-Petushki* Erofeev makes incomparable use of reversals of the sacred and the profane. He is particularly ruthless with Soviet messianism, utopia realized in communal living, and the joys of being a worker in the workers' paradise. Of particular interest here is Erofeev's treatment of communal living, the lofty "experiment" in equality that falls apart over an argument about going to the bathroom. Several years ago, Venichka tells us, he moved in with four other men. As Mark Altshuller shows, this scene echoes Rabelais's utopian episode "The Abbey of Thélème."[9] Everyone lives "in complete harmony [dusha v dushu]" and does as he wishes. When someone wants to drink port, all join in and drink with him. Equality and fraternity become a yoke around Venichka's neck when the other four accuse him of never going to the bathroom: "You don't walk on air.... Since you moved in, not one of us has seen you go to the bathroom even once. We can understand about number two. But not even number one, not even once" (MP, 14). Offended, they claim rather incoherently that Venichka sees himself as "Cain and Man-

---

[8] I am grateful to Bernice Rosenthal for insight into this allusion. Tangentially, for more information on how conceptualist artists parody this principle, see Tupitsyn, *Margins of Soviet Art*, 69–85.

[9] Mark Al'tshuller, "'Moskva-Petushki' Venedikta Erofeeva i traditsii klassicheskoi poemy," *Novyi zhurnal*, no. 146 (1982), 75–85.

CHARTING META-UTOPIA

fred" and a "lily." They complain resentfully that, in Venichka's view, "we are dirty animals," "we are like spit under your feet," and the like (MP, 14). They imply that he should get up and announce to the world what he is going to do, that he should live completely in the public sphere. Here, certainly, is equality at the lowest common denominator. When there is no room for private habits, even at the most basic level, equality becomes oppression.

Venichka similarly devalues the high ideals of liberty, equality, and fraternity by equating them with unemployment and with standing in line at the liquor store. He sings a double-edged "hymn" to the Soviet utopia: "Oh, freedom and equality! Oh, fraternity and dependency! Oh, the sweetness of not being held accountable! Oh, the most blissful time in the life of my people—the time from opening to closing of the liquor stores" (MP, 16). In Venichka's topsy-turvy world drunkenness is raised to the highest possible level in his (religious) reveries about the new (God-given) Eden, Petushki. Petushki is itself a lyrical celebration of the profane, of basic pleasures like copulation and drunkenness. Voices tell Venichka: "Petushki is a place where the birds never stop singing, day or night, where the jasmine never stops blooming, summer or winter. Original sin—perhaps it used to exist—doesn't weigh on anyone. Even people who don't dry out for weeks on end have a clear, bottomless look in their eyes" (MP, 19). Venichka elevates himself, in his drunkenness, setting himself beside the most beloved writers—for example, Schiller, Chekhov, Gogol—who, he claims, also drank. His drinking is like the stigmata of Saint Theresa: although both are tormenting, both are fervently desired. Finally, Venichka pontificates that one should "drink more, eat less" if one wants to avoid arrogance and "superficial atheism" (MP, 30). Thus Venichka crowns himself repeatedly until at the end he is again made to face the lowliness of his existence when he regains contact with the "real" world in the dark entryway.

Zinoviev, whose work is otherwise almost unbearably abstract, makes very good use of carnivalization. The name of the town in which the utopian ideology of "ism" is carried out, Ibansk, and the name shared by all its citizens, Ibanov, represent a comic conflation of perhaps the most common male name in Russian, Ivan, and an obscene word for copulating, *ebat'*. In addition, the river flowing through Ibansk, the Ibaniuchka, suggests something foul, perhaps nasty-smelling. A great deal is made of the privy, which here is known as the "sortir." Its French etymology, we are told by The Schizophrenic—who is proficient at creating etymologies—stems from the great sixteenth-century Utopian (almost certainly Rabelais, whose Gargantua invents a new way of wiping himself!) who "put forth the idea of erecting a special building in which everyone could freely take care of natural needs" (YH, 112). But in its realization "ism" revealed one of its greatest weaknesses, oversight of basic human needs. The Ibansk builders of "ism" forgot all about bathrooms as they designed their social experiment. When they erected the Pilots' School, for example, they omitted a bathroom and then had to add an extra outhouse soon thereafter (YH, 20). Later, when the Ibanskians undertook basic reforms, we are told, the outhouse was rebuilt in the least comfortable or practical way, out of steel and glass using modern (utopian) architectural design (YH, 10).[10] In the course of *The Yawning Heights*, the privy becomes an important location, in addition to the beer parlor, for intense ideological discussions. Indeed, it is rumored that the dissident sociologist, The Schizophrenic, is composing his sociological tract, the key "event" in this rambling book, while sitting in the outhouse.

Voinovich, perhaps following Zinoviev's lead, makes excrement a central ideological problem in the Moscow of the year 2042. In an absurd distortion of Lenin's original saying "From each according to capability, to each according to need," Kartsev learns the hard way (after he has done his morning ablutions and has gone to the canteen for breakfast) that "the primary product [food] is secondary, and the secondary product [excrement] is primary." People at the dining hall must turn in their waste in order to get a ration card for their food (M, 150). This, then, is the new way of discharging "ordinary needs." Although Kartsev is told that the excrement is a major item of export, he notes that all publicly served food smells suspiciously like it.[11]

Various details of Moscow life under the great Genialissimus inadvertently emphasize baser human nature. In an amusing reversal of the Soviet practice of using newsprint as toilet paper, toilet paper is printed with the daily news right on it. Many of the ubiquitous acronyms remind one of baser functions. For example, the Job Bureau, "Punkt kommunisticheskogo raspredeleniia po mestu sluzheniia

---

[10] For more on modernist utopian architectural design, see Hutcheon, *A Poetics of Postmodernism*, 22–36.

[11] The process of changing waste back into food is reminiscent of the researcher's dream at the Academy of Lagado in *Gulliver's Travels*. See Robert C. Elliott, *The Shape of Utopia: Studies in a Literary Genre* (Chicago: University of Chicago Press, 1970), 58.

kommunian," is known as "Pukomras." "Pukat'" is a relatively mild word for "to fart," while "mras" sounds something like *mraz'*, or "rubbish, dregs, scum," a pejorative term applied to people. "KK," that is, "kol'tsa kommunizma," or the rings of communism that correspond to Moscow's various rings of boulevards and bypasses, further emphasizes "kaka" as the essence masked by "utopian" ideology. The further one moves from the center, the deeper in excrement one finds oneself. The parallel to Dante's rings of hell, where denizens find themselves immersed in various horrible materials, is also implied. Finally, "Upopot" or "udovletvorenie povyshennykh potrebnostei," or "the satisfaction of higher needs," is reminiscent of the Russian word *popka* or "fanny."

Essential to the meta-utopian project is the refictionalization of the utopian locus, its return to the fictional status that it had until the Enlightenment when utopian thinkers began to avoid the "utopian" label and argue for the credibility of their dreams as realizable social goals.[12] *Utopia*, for writers like Terts, Erofeev, and Zinoviev, retains its original meaning as "no place." The difference between these writers and their Renaissance predecessors is that the concept of "no place," even as a dream of a total, perfect social existence, is wrongheaded and detrimental. Implicit in meta-utopian writing is the idea that personal imagination and memory are the two strongest and most constructive human faculties, traditionally repressed by collective myth and as yet almost completely unexplored in defining the terms of our social existence. A community, just as a person, is conditioned to live within the geography in which it pictures itself, its past, and its future. To become wholly committed to a single, unchanging image of one's social landscape is to give into ideological fixation and imaginative stagnation.

The most blatant technique for establishing the fictionality of utopian projects is the use of wish-fulfillment dreams by characters who in actuality have no political clout but find influence in the framework of their dreams. For example, in *The Yawning Heights* The Dauber (Mazila), a semiofficial painter who gets a commission to carve Hog's gravestone—in much the same way that his historical prototype, Ernst Neizvestnyi, sculpted Khrushchev's gravestone—is tempted by just such a wish-fulfillment dream at the moment when his career is balancing on the border between official recognition and

---

[12] Ricoeur, *Lectures on Ideology and Utopia*, 2–6.

the underground. He dreams that "ism," the official ideology of Zinoviev's fictional city of Ibansk, has been reconstituted in his image:

> He dreamed of a splendid city bathed in sunlight. Everywhere were The Dauber's sculptures. And just as he had dreamed of building them. Over there was The Truthteller's Street. At the head [of the street] was a hundred-meter-high "Prophet," and at its foot a two-hundred-meter-high "Orpheus." And what was this? Hog Square! In the middle of the square an enormous pedestal. On it a hairy hand giving the finger and an inscription: "dis generation, yo' mama, is gonna live in full ism." The Dauber's engravings were displayed in shop windows. They had understood despite everything, thought The Dauber happily. (YH, 220)

Such a dream, it becomes very clear, is a form of self-indulgence and nothing more. The Dauber is as susceptible to the allure of power and influence as those now in favor. The dream changes to something more like a nightmare as The Dauber's sense of sane self-irony catches up to him: he overhears a group of young girls and boys making fun of him and his work, just as he and his crowd had run down the officially recognized art of their elders, for example, The Artist and The Writer. One person's imagined utopia, thus, is another's prison, nothing more than an enforced restriction of the imagination.

In *Moscow 2042*, Voinovich's writer-protagonist, the unassuming Vitaly Kartsev, returns to the Moscow of the future as a "tourist." He is curious as to whether things have changed much. When he arrives, he hopes that life will prove not to be as primitive and brutal as it at first seems. His first night in Moscow, he dreams a dream with all the lightness and airiness of the protagonist's first dream in the antitotalitarian movie *Brazil*. At the same time, it travesties all kinds of utopian motifs. Kartsev dreams that his host, Smerchev, and he are strolling through the new Moscow. Everything is light and bright, bathed in a warm, artificial sun. Streets are lined with palm trees and tropical flowers and crowned with graceful skyscrapers and weblike galleries. Everyone is happy, intelligent, and physically beautiful. People are lightly dressed and walk with a wonderfully light, almost airborne step. Smerchev explains that scientists have come up with a way to decrease the impact of gravity. People never work here, and life is so interesting and enjoyable that they barely sleep. Kartsev's description conflates the Godbuilders' notion of the masses as God and Fedorov's notion of utopia based on resurrecting the dead: "I understood that I was in paradise, perhaps created not by God but by people. I understood that if these people had managed to make an artificial sun and to weaken the effect of gravity, there would be nothing surprising in the fact that they had learned how to raise the dead" (M, 145).

In keeping with his very practical, undreamy nature, Kartsev in his dream directs his attention to the concrete details of everyday existence. He notes that the streets are lined with food shops and, in an incongruously Gogolian vein, proceeds to list all the kinds of fish, caviar, cheese, fruit, vegetables, and drink offered there for free (there is no money in this dreamland). In an unseemly way, Kartsev starts to grab at all the free goods, which he cannot possibly hold or carry, spilling them all over the street. He is further upset and humiliated when he encounters his wife kissing Zilberovich, Karnavalov's majordomo, and then going to the baths with Smerchev. Like The Dauber's dream, this one ends by exposing the incongruity of the utopian fantasy with the realities of human nature.

A second way in which meta-utopias reestablish the fictionality of the utopian project is by representing utopia as a locus devoid of inherent meaning, a wasteland that is given contours only by the human imagination. One example of utopia as wasteland can be found in Terts's *Liubimov*. In this novella, the social experiment carried out in the sleepy hamlet of Liubimov by the bicycle repairman Lënia Tikhomirov is really only the enactment of a fiction concocted by a nineteenth-century nobleman, Samson Samsonovich Proferansov. This "character," himself a fantasy of the story's first narrator, Savely Kuzmich, has produced a book on magnetism and magic that gives Tikhomirov the idea of taking power and executing his utopian experiment by hypnotizing the local citizens. Tikhomirov goes on to create a "land of milk and honey," making his subjects believe that toothpaste is really pâté, Kharkov mineral water is really *spirt*, or 100 percent distilled alcohol, and river water is really champagne. He uses his powers of hypnosis to set up a magnetic screen around the periphery of the town to protect it from outside attack. Samson Samsonovich later intrudes into the story, functioning variously as Tikhomirov's "devil" (a comic variant of Ivan Karamazov's familiar) and as a second narrator. His ambition for Liubimov is to make the sleepy town into a "nebyvalaia utopiia," which translates ambiguously as either "wonderful utopia" or "fantastic" or "fictitious" utopia (L, 360). This ambiguity, of course, underscores the fictionality of the whole project. The whole fictional construct does indeed collapse when, among other things, it turns out that the citizens are not fooled in the slightest but are just playing along with Tikhomirov's whim, waiting patiently for the political edifice of yet another megalomaniac to crumble. The late Professor Proferansov eventually decides to take his book back, claiming that Tikhomirov is abusing his newfound powers (L, 352). The Liubimov experiment thus melts into thin air. Tikhomirov escapes his own (and Proferansov's) fiction, and everything returns to its former shabby condition.

In *The Condemned City* the wasteland—the squalorous, oppressive social conditions known euphemistically as "The Experiment"—is defined in whatever way people choose. Here people of all nationalities have gathered, but it is not at all clear what their goal is. The only thing that the participants share is a general disorientation and bewilderment as to how they arrived there. The Experiment thus becomes whatever each character perceives it to be. Andrei Voronin, for example, who sees himself as a Komsomol activist, imagines The Experiment to be a continuation of Stalin's communist experiment, the "establishment of the dictatorship of the proletariat in union with working farmers" (CC, 94). Unself-consciously mimicking a bombastic, Gorkyesque diction, he claims that The Experiment is a wasteland, a "chaos which we were called to put into order" (CC, 87). Donald Cooper, an American intellectual who eventually commits suicide, takes a more skeptical view. He repeats the "justification" that everyone has been given, that indeed becomes an empty, tautological refrain throughout the novel: "The Experiment is the Experiment" (CC, 69).[13] He believes that whatever experiment there may have once been failed a long time ago, and that society is continuing to exist only by inertia (CC, 95). Another minor character, the Polish Catholic Pan Iuda Stupalski, who was hung in 1944 for handing over hundreds of Jews to the Gestapo, argues that this place is really hell and that everyone here is dead (CC, 89). The Chinese settler, Wan, sees it as a kind of purgatory, a place to be endured and survived. Yet another Russian, the farmer Davydov, is sure that The Experiment, with its artificial sun and huge wall, is a huge "aquarium," set up by some extraterrestrial beings called Mentors to study human behav-

---

[13] For an interesting discussion of tautology in anti-utopian discourse, see Thomas Lahusen, "Inversiia utopicheskogo diskursa. O 'Zapiskakh iz podpol'ia' F. M. Dostoevskogo," *Wiener Slawistischer Almanach*, no. 20 (1987): 5–40.

ior. The Mentors themselves have a semi-Platonic, semi-Leninist view of the undertaking at hand: "Action above all. Each person in his place and each doing everything he can" (CC, 74).

Although each member of The Experiment must participate actively, periodically doing each job that needs to be done, from that of garbage hauler to that of councillor, very few have a real say in governing the society. The Experiment turns out to emulate a dictatorship by "councillors" rather than a real civil society. Thus, when Andrei later achieves the status of councillor, a position somewhat like that of the guardians in *The Republic*, he is reminded by his Mentor of his social duty: he is one of only twenty councillors and is responsible for the fates of thousands of simple citizens. The fictionality of the condemned city is reaffirmed in the final chapter of the novel when the whole adventure is revealed as the dream fantasy of the boy Andrei Voronin, who reawakens to "reality" in Leningrad at the height of the Stalinist Terror of the 1930s.

The chameleon-like antihero Izia Katsman clarifies the danger of utopian fictions, articulating a suspicion of ideological totalities of all kinds. He feels he cannot support any "system for transforming the world" (CC, 143). He continues: "I know of no such system and don't believe that one exists. Too many of all kinds of systems have been tried, and afterward everything has stayed much the same as it was" (CC, 143). He feels that Andrei is just the kind of person who could do the most harm in the service of such a dream. Andrei and people like him need something to submit to, and having been divested of all their beliefs, Izia believes, such people could now commit even worse acts: they "could begin to take revenge on the world for being the way it really is, because it does not fit any preconceived ideal" (CC, 144). What one ultimately has to confront is human nature—its need for such fictions, its unwillingness to deal with things as they are. In his own life, Izia has come to value most highly the concrete moral and aesthetic achievements of family and personal refinement. He has set up his own personal "temple" to culture, one in which no one else can be made to worship.

From the very start of *The Yawning Heights*, the fictionality of Zinoviev's city of Ibansk and its social experiment is given strong emphasis. The narrator tells us in his preface that "socism" (later simply known as "ism") is a completely imaginary order: "If by chance it did exist, it would be a pure figment of the imagination" (YH, 7). He goes on to define Ibansk as a "locality populated by nobody [nikem ne naselennyi naselennyi punkt] which in reality does not exist" (YH, 7). Nonetheless, the narrator believes, the events and ideas described in his book are interesting "as documentation of the mistaken notions about human nature and society of the ancient forebears of the Ibanskians" (YH, 7). Finally, the underground, dissident characters central to Zinoviev's work, The Schizophrenic (Shizofrenik) and The Big Mouth (Boltun), find comfort at times in the fact that they really are fictional characters and that there are distinct advantages to such a status, for example, that they do not have to deal with the unpleasant details of material life. They can, for instance, "talk about the disorderliness of life and not have to fix the faucet" (YH, 188).

Zinoviev also attacks the notions of the truth and reality of the utopian locus by making fun of its origins. As Lotman points out in *The Structure of the Artistic Text*, it is through establishing and emphasizing historical beginnings that documents such as the Old Russian *Primary Chronicle* (and, of course, the Old Testament of the Bible) legitimize their project.[14] Zinoviev plays fast and loose with notions of historical veracity and comes up at different moments with various, unrelated versions of the origins of Ibansk. In one version, Zinoviev parodies the notion of legend-made-history used in chronicles. In a manuscript recently discovered on a rubbish heap about the legendary founding of Ibansk by The Master (that is, Stalin), Ibansk is described with a Woody Allen–like, humorous illogic as an "imaginary village of the urban type which in fact was impossible because of a false premise, and if it were possible, then certainly not in Ibansk!" (YH, 223) It was founded when "The Master first led the forebears of the Ibanskians from the dark cave onto the radiant path and constructed for them a happy future" (YH, 223). In a later section of this deliberately achronological and fragmentary work, The Schizophrenic maintains that he thought up Ibansk: "Ibansk, with all its problems, solutions, and other tripe, was dreamed up by The Schizophrenic sitting in a Greasy Spoon [Zabegalovka] in the company of The Colleague, The Big Mouth, The Shouter, The Thinker, The Spouse, The Dauber, and all the rest. He did it after downing a half-liter of vodka and five rounds of beer without any snacks" (YH, 292).

Thus the meta-utopian notion of space envisions a wasteland the contours and significance of which are negotiated by the human

[14] Iurii Lotman, *Struktura khudozhestvennogo teksta* (Providence, R.I.: Brown University Press, 1971), 259–60.

imagination. Its emphasis on parody, carnivalesque play, and the fictionality and provisionality of all ideological constructs conversely underlines the importance, and indeed the responsibility, of fantasy in the process of shaping our social environment. So far, it is implied, utopians have imagined spaces that in their realized form end up as rubbish heaps, toilets, and wastelands. Similarly, how meta-utopias conceive of time reveals a great deal about the part that memory has to play and its relationship to imagination in formulating social plans.

If meta-utopian fiction dismisses the utopian locus as a "real" or "truthful" or "good" place, it also confronts the still more troublesome problem of time. Images of time here suggest a kind of thinking that has nothing to do with the temporalities typical of modern thinking. Meta-utopias challenge three concepts of time: Hegelian progressivist teleology, notions of time as evolution, and the "critical" historical mentality (to use Nietzsche's term from *The Use and Abuse of History*) that seeks deliverance from the past in a wholly different society of the future. One finds this last, apocalyptic mentality in Marxist-Leninist thought as well as in the mood of "future anxiety"—a fervent desire to break with an unbearable present combined with a fear of being inadequate to the future—characteristic of a great deal of Russian modernist art.[15] Nor do we find endorsed here what has been called "progressive-regressive" historicism, which rejects the near past for cultural and social models from the very deep past.[16] Such temporal consciousness has been identified in Nietzsche's concept of eternal recurrence, but it also informs certain kinds of utopian writing, for example, Gorky's *Confession*, as well as most counter-utopian writing, for example, Dostoevsky's "Dream of a Ridiculous Man" or Valentin Rasputin's *Farewell to Matyora*.

Of all preceding models of time, the circularity of Nietzsche's eternal recurrence seems best to describe one aspect of the meta-utopian view. Time in meta-utopian fiction certainly does not flow smoothly or progressively from past to future, nor does it jump from a past relegated to the dustbin of history across to a perfect future. Meta-utopias proceed from the assumption that the utopian "future" is already with us and has, indeed, become past experience, a past that

---

[15] For a full treatment of this term, see my *Revolution of Moral Consciousness*.

[16] This term comes from Ophelia Schutte, *Beyond Nihilism: Nietzsche without Masks* (Chicago: University of Chicago Press, 1984).

in no way suggests a more hopeful future. Thus, meta-utopian time is caught in a gridlock with the past, present, and future terribly entangled. In a way, this concept of time is analogous to a Möbius strip: the two sides of the strip seem different, just as past experience and future potentiality appear different, but turn out really to be contiguous. If utopia is first imagined as something for the future, an alternative to the flawed present, here it is already present or indeed past experience, something to overcome, but with no vision to overcome it. What all these texts confront is a bad present inextricably bound up with past and future.

Meta-utopian fiction thus offers us several scenarios that contradict each other and challenge temporal assumptions at the heart of existing ideological structures. Perhaps the worst scenario is that of the person who perpetuates the bad present in an effort to further his or her own comfort. This is the case of Zinoviev's Pretender (Pretendent) who lives solely by what The Schizophrenic calls "social laws" of self-protection and self-aggrandizement. He is paradoxically conformist in that he tries hard to climb the ladder of the bureaucratic hierarchy, to obtain for himself a more secure, comfortable position. Although he dreams of becoming director of the Ibansk sociological institute, he is ultimately assigned a post even higher than that of director of an institute but one that is a long way from Ibansk and without hope of upward or even lateral mobility upon return to Ibansk. When he goes to the "sortir" to take his revenge (by writing graffiti), he is subjected to a rather foul fate. There he discovers his fate, inscribed in graffiti on the wall, to live on in the bad present in which he has flourished so far and which he has visited on others. These graffiti, much like Dante's warning at the gates of hell, also become a warning at the opening to Zinoviev's hell, the hole in the privy through which one can fall and, indeed, disappear:

> Here [The Pretender] saw: right in front of his mug on the wall of the sortir the words burned: "Look around you, shithead [zasranets], before you sit down!"
>
> The Pretender looked around involuntarily and read on the opposite wall: "Everything that has been will be! Everything that will be is."
>
> The Pretender made an effort to understand, but didn't have time to because he fell into the pit [iama]. In the pit he was awaited by The Master himself, The Director, The Secretary, The Troglodyte, The

Hog, the new Manager, and even the Manager who would come after him. "Greetings, young, unfamiliar breed," said The Master to The Pretender. And grabbing him crossways, he engulfed him in a passionate kiss. "Help," The Pretender howled in alarm. But it was already too late (YH, 221).

In addition to condemning the perpetuation of what already exists, the meta-utopian sensibility undermines concepts of time inherent in the two enduring opponents of ludic art, realist narrative and utopian fiction—both of which make exclusive claims to be uniquely and correctly situated in time and thus oppose any aesthetic or philosophical challenge. Meta-utopias play with models of time, particularly by confronting standard notions of influence and causality and by deliberately confusing historical document and artistic text.

"Realist" literary texts lend themselves to particular deformation in meta-utopian narratives. Realist fiction traditionally defines itself as a historically accurate, or at least plausible, representation of past or present conditions. Classically, it lays an implicit claim to what the French post-Marxist Jean-François Lyotard calls the "enlightenment metanarrative" of social emancipation by serving the social goals of raising consciousness and inspiring audiences to self-liberation or emancipation of other oppressed groups in society.[17] This claim is certainly very strong, even dominant, in Russian literature at least since Belinsky and through the present day in the example of Solzhenitsyn. In *The Yawning Heights* The Truthteller (Pravdets), who is modeled after Solzhenitsyn, carries on a continual feud with The Double Dealer (Dvurushnik), an experimentalist writer based on Siniavsky-Terts, in an effort to defend his approach to art and politics. He claims to be the patriot and man of the people in this debate, blaming The Double Dealer for abandoning his people in their time of need and going into exile. The people of Ibansk, The Truthteller feels, are "sick," and it is the writer's job as "healer" to stay with them and bring them to new health. (YH, 367) He is rewarded for his populism with what The Big Mouth feels is an inordinate popularity in the cultural underground.

Much the same claims are made by Sim Simich Karnavalov (also modeled on Solzhenitsyn) in *Moscow 2042*. His multitomed lifework, *The Great Zone* (*Bol'shaia zona*), drums into its readers that their lives

---

[17] Lyotard, *The Postmodern Condition*, xxiii–xxiv.

are passing in a huge prison camp. Presumably it is intended to inspire revolt. When he goes to the postcommunist Soviet Union, Kartsev is meant to distribute hard copies of this work from the floppy disk entrusted to him. Actually, Karnavalov already has a secret following, the Simites, who write the letters SIM all over Moscow. The rubric of Karnavalov's adherents, "the Simites," can be seen as a rather unsubtle jab at Solzhenitsyn's alleged anti-Semitism, another indication of a realist writer's possible antipathy to genuine social emancipation and social progress.

Both works show realism to be temporally regressive in its vision of the future. It is counterutopian in its conservative answer to utopian fantasy. It lies somewhere in between Nietzsche's categories of "monumentalist" historicism, which borrows wholesale from previous models for the future, and "antiquarian" historicism, which strives simply to preserve the past in its exact form. This conservative historical mentality is blatant in the case of Karnavalov, who intends to return Moscow to its medieval form and preserve that form through a set of harsh regulations in the style of the very patriarchal sixteenth-century treatise on public and domestic etiquette *Domostroi*.[18]

The ideological conservatism of The Truthteller is somewhat more subtle. As Zinoviev's The Big Mouth puts it, The Truthteller is concerned with the "past and the future in the past" (YH, 207)—that is, the progressive-regressive project of designing society's future according to models constructed from a nostalgic vision of some remote past. This archconservative and ultimately unsatisfactory approach does not push beyond the vicious circle of paired ideologies with opposing symbols of faith that ultimately perpetrate one and the same closed, coercive, patronizing social behavior. The Big Mouth agrees with The Double Dealer that the revolution was "a very great benefit" (YH, 371) to the people and that The Truthteller is wrong in thinking that "ism" was forced upon them from above (YH, 409). What The Double Dealer (that is, Siniavsky-Terts) understands and The Truthteller does not is that the people of Ibansk are experiencing the "most terrible tragedy for a civilized people," the "tragedy of unrealized possibilities" (YH, 372). The ironic implication is that the Ibanskians really are not yet civilized. They have very little tolerance

---

[18] It is curious that one of the new independent newpapers of the "real" postcommunist Soviet Union bears the title *Domostroi!*

for art that tries to extend Ibanskian thinking beyond the vicious circle of "ism" and its critical double, literary "realism." The citizens of Ibansk are more or less incapable of comprehending the genuinely different ways of thinking of The Schizophrenic and The Slanderer, and the playful, allusive art of The Double Dealer—which nonetheless embodies the potential of the Ibanskians. What they appreciate, and perhaps what they deserve, are the "false and superficial ideas" of The Truthteller (YH, 441).

Meta-utopian fiction raises doubts about the possibility of a "utopian" realism that "premembers" the future, that is, an art that claims to trace the future as if it were already historical experience.[19] This contorted notion of historical experience is basic to Socialist Realism, for example. Voinovich's protagonist Kartsev insists at the start of *Moscow 2042* that he is a "realist," a label of which he becomes suspicious by the end of the book. The text *Moscow 2042* becomes the victim of a time loop: the reader is asked to interpret it both as a historical document and as a work of art, of creative imagination. What belies the legitimacy of artistic realism in this novel is the synchronic overlay of two mutually contradictory "realist" interpretations of the text. This novel about Kartsev's time travel to Moscow and his documentation of the downfall of the postcommunist regime both exists and does not yet exist. The Kartsev who arrives in Moscow possesses a consciousness, that is, a memory and imagination, shaped in 1982. This 1982 self views his art in general as a rigorous, objective documentation based on actual observation of social conditions; for him, his trip to Moscow is an opportunity to gather material for what he calls a science-fiction novel, with the emphasis on *science*. He cannot conceive of a plan for his work until he has lived experience. But for some of his readers, the Muscovites of 2042, his book *does* exist, written sixty years ago, and it is being interpreted not as a prophecy or a flight of fancy but as a reliable historical document of events yet to happen in the *future*. It is assumed that the text itself contains the truth and is equal to the events it describes. Thus, the rationale of the Muscovite rulers in pressuring him to edit Karnavalov out of the book is that if Karnavalov does not appear in the book, he cannot appear in history. The toppling of the regime by Karnavalov will not take place.

---

[19] This nice neologism is borrowed from Brian McHale, *Postmodernist Fiction* (London: Methuen, 1987), 65.

By the end, in total confusion, Kartsev abrogates his calling as a "realist" writer, with the social and moral imperative that goes with it.[20] He accepts that his reputation may be tarnished by his open flouting of literary realism, but he finds it simpler and more honest to conceive his work as a product of fantasy. His liberation from "future history" is brought about through his refusal to harness his work and his imagination to one or another ideological construct or group claiming political control. He will not wed himself to one single view of the future and offers no particular guide to his readers, hoping only that in the future "it will become easier to live." Interestingly, however, realist habits die hard: Kartsev claims that even such a fantastic work can and should have an impact on the thinking of political leaders, and he states that he hopes those in the Kremlin will see fit to read it and take it to heart as a possible warning.

Meta-utopian fiction also undermines the Marxist-Leninist (utopian) rejection of the past and search for salvation in the future, an attitude toward time well expressed in Nietzsche's concept of "critical" historicism. Here again we find a kind of time loop different from that used in dealing with realist time. In works such as Tendriakov's *A Potshot at Mirages* or Terts's *Liubimov* can be found a "historical" reassessment of those well-known futuristic fantasies conceived in the historical past that made predictions or laid plausible groundwork for future social development. These works confront the paradox of an imagined future that was enacted and has now become history. The essential paradox of realized utopia here is the incongruity of the future as it is imagined and the historical event embodying the fantasy. For example, Belinsky's prediction that people would be much happier and better off in a hundred years, that is, in 1940, rings very ironic to Tendriakov's narrator, Grebin, as he writes in the 1960s (PM, 69). Grebin later strains over the paradoxes inherent in a Renaissance utopia, Campanella's *City of the Sun*, that is recognized in official Soviet culture. The main problem is the injustice inherent in practiced equality. Grebin comes to the paradoxical conclusion that "realized" equality is very unfair, and that giving equal treatment to people who are inherently unequal in effort and intelligence results in ruinous social tension.

Terts in "What Is Socialist Realism?" delineates a constructive use of the past: to explain how the fixation on the future came about and

---

[20] Fanger, "Conflicting Imperatives," 117.

to free our conceptions of the present from ironclad preconceptions of the future. He finds three cultural-historical sensibilities in nineteenth-century Russia that contribute to Soviet worship of the future. One is the nineteenth-century anxiety over living in a time when a negative "femininity" predominated. By cultural femininity Terts appears to mean the failed social and spiritual archetype of the superfluous man with his "generous impulses" who is "unable to find a destiny" and who "presents a lamentable example of a purposelessness that is of no use to anybody." Terts's concept of cultural femininity is also marked by the worship of Woman as the Higher Purpose (SR, 185). A second historical sensibility is the displaced religious passion of such writers as Chernyshevsky for the just society. This passion is invested with great hope for the future of Russian society. And, finally, Terts finds Dostoevsky emblematic of a yearning for simple answers, for "simple faith." All of these sensibilities, Terts implies, conspired in a demand that art turn the reader's attention from a blank past and an unhappy present to a bright future. His attempt to unharness the future from the yoke of political authoritarianism and utopian dreaming consists of doing away with all "realist" and social-didactic requirements for literary art. Art especially should not have to be plausible: it may be ambiguous and "hypothetical." Above all, it should give free play to fantasy.

In *The Yawning Heights* Zinoviev goes further to diagnose the problem of present gridlock than he does to find a way to live in time. As The Slanderer puts it, the problem is "how to purge oneself of the future.... One is oppressed not by the past, but rather by waiting for the inevitable" (YH, 167). Like Terts, The Big Mouth is interested in "the future and the future in the past" (YH, 207). This phrase expresses well the meta-utopian concern with time: an important goal of this art is to explore the link between historiography and imagination, to explain how our image of the future was formulated, and how finally we can confront received notions of the future. In short, in meta-utopian fiction memory becomes a challenge to imagination, past experience—a challenge to future exploits. The drama of these works lies in reopening choice and imagination, not in forging a specific re-vision of the future. Creating a new totality, the meta-utopian would say, is a destructive enterprise.

Zinoviev implies that the time at which *The Yawning Heights* is being written, 1974, marks something of a turning point for Ibansk, although not the kind of historical "either/or" watershed of "critical" historical thinking. In one of the final sections, entitled "Communiqué from the Future," the narrator conveys a report from the year 8974 that large graveyards of bones were found on the outskirts of Ibansk. This number clearly plays with apocalyptic numerology: 8974 is 7000 years from 1974, the year when Zinoviev finished his book. According to traditional Christian chronology, 7000 is the number of years between the founding of the world and its end. What is implied here is a time of reckoning when Ibanskians will have to confront their past in all its terror if they are to escape the temporal gridlock in which they now exist.

The chronotopes offered in meta-utopian fiction are reminiscent of the drawing of the tower made by the Dutch artist M. C. Escher in which the guards seem to be progressing in some way, either ascending or descending stairs, but are really just going around in a circle. Movement within actual time and space is physically static, if mentally dynamic. Both dimensions become categories of the mind that is just beginning to redefine their nature. The first step taken in this fiction is the discrediting of two reigning ideas of time and space, the "realist" and the "utopian," and the more ambiguous departure from the apocalypticism of its closest "ally," the dystopian novel. Realism is founded on the idea of liberation, of progressive movement in geographical space and historical time toward a just, happy, and personally fulfilling future. In realist fiction specific places are clearly defined and separate from one another; by moving from one place to another the protagonist develops in some way. For example, in Tolstoi's work there is a strong, enduring contrast between the morally questionable city and the relatively idyllic countryside. In Dostoevsky there are clear boundaries between personal hells, heavens, and purgatories—for example, in *The Brothers Karamazov*, old Karamazov's house, the monastery, and the town proper of Skotoprigonevsk. Traversing these borders allows the character a chance to perceive him- or herself anew. Meta-utopian fiction undermines the easy optimism of the realist tradition by throwing into doubt the strength of such borders, by diagnosing past and future not as qualitatively different states but as part of the grid of a "bad present."

The traditional utopian time-space matrix consists of a "neutralized" notion of a perfect place and time that is discontinuous from but that can be mapped onto lived space and time. Meta-utopian writing sabotages this notion of perfection; time and space are symbolized by an image, not so much of a prison, as in dystopian fiction, as of an outhouse or even a rubbish heap. Having directed our attention so far to the ways in which meta-utopias move beyond utopian and dystopian chronotopes, we must finally ask whether there is a preferred locale that suggests a different social attitude. In dystopian fiction this locale is "nature"—a relocation away from the city and a rediscovery of the vitality and importance of one's irrational impulses. This locale is perceived to be a threat to total power and then destroyed by those in power, The Benefactor in *We*, O'Brien in *1984*, and so forth. Meta-utopias are never so radical, almost always establishing a personal space of one's own in the present time where one can be true to oneself and can resist the claims of mass ideologies. This space is most boldly and optimistically sketched in the earliest meta-utopia, Iuly Daniel's *Moscow Speaking* (1961), in which the protagonist has to face an "Open Murder Day." Having survived it and understood it for what it is, a political diversion, he redefines the public space, the whole city of Moscow, as a place that belongs neither to the party nor to the state but to the people who inhabit it, who walk in its parks and ride its subways. Moscow is properly "speaking" when one hears the voices of these ordinary people.

Other meta-utopias end more darkly and pessimistically—one is almost tempted to say in a "dystopian" fashion. *Moscow 2042, Liubimov*, and Aksënov's *The Island of Crimea* end with escape. *The Yawning Heights* and Zinoviev's second novel, *The Radiant Future*, end with suicide, *The Condemned City* and *Moscow-Petushki* with murder, and *The Ugly Swans* with an apocalyptic rejuvenation of nature itself as a quite militant younger generation undertakes to build society in its own particular utopian image. And yet in each of these a consciousness of personal resistance is never relinquished, as it is in dystopian fiction. And in each a chronotope of personal space is created. For example, *Liubimov* ends with an apostrophe to pockets as the minimal private sphere, a modern-day room of one's own, as it were, where one can "crawl in . . . and sit, daydreaming," where one can think, say, and do precisely what one likes (L, 422). In *Moscow 2042* claims for Kartsev's loyalty are made even after he leaves Moscow. It is not by chance that he is in his own home in Munich when he makes the final decision to listen first to himself and not to answer those claims.

Suicide and murder must always be put in quotation marks in meta-utopian art. In *The Yawning Heights* The Big Mouth signs up at a crematorium to have himself turned into ashes. Before this final event he and various others ruminate over what might be the key to solving all of Ibansk's social problems. In the light of recent events, it is curious that one of them, The Teacher, suggests that "glasnost" guaranteed by law is the answer, to which another answers in a Gogolian vein that Ibansk's problems are "banal" and this solution is "boring" (YH, 558). Thus, before it ever happened, Mikhail Gorbachev's answer to the Stalinist utopia is rejected out of hand. The Big Mouth carries on a different line of reasoning in a final conversation with himself. He decides that "truthfulness" (*pravdivost'*) is the sine qua non for the improvement of cultural and moral conditions in society: "From the point of view of humaneness the level of social development will be determined from now on by the degree of truthfulness which society permits" (YH, 560). Having come to that conclusion, he sets off for the crematorium. While The Big Mouth's death is an inescapable fact, his demise differs from that of dystopian protagonists in that, first, it is he who makes the decision and, second, he is unwilling to remold his psyche to fit the needs of the powers-that-be (as D-503 and Winston Smith do), but decides to remove himself entirely. The Big Mouth notes that even the cremation room carries an ideological message—which he resists. By the exit he notes the absurd sign: "AS YOU LEAVE, TAKE THE URN WITH YOUR ASHES"(YH, 560). Strange to say, even in the deathly chronotope of the urn with his ashes there is a certain expression of enduring personal presence and ideological resistance. Clearly, in death he loses his power to comply with these orders and thus one final time can resist the press of authority. Even the minimalist space of the urn containing one's remains is a slim reminder of the problem of personal space and its denial by the authorities.

The murders in *Moscow-Petushki* and *The Condemned City* are both problematic. Since Venichka is the most unreliable of narrators, there is no reason to believe that he is killed, just as there is no reason to believe that anything else actually happens outside his fantasy. His final statement rings absurdly if one accepts that it is spoken or written by a dying man: "And from that time on I have not regained consciousness and I never will" (MP, 73). This is rather the statement of someone who has chosen to fall silent and not to participate in the deformation of language and consciousness by totalitarian power. In *The Condemned City* the murder is in no sense a physical act. It marks the awakening of the boy, Andrei Voronin, from his meta-utopian dream (that forms the novel we have just read). And it also implicitly marks his awakening to a different perspective on the violent politics of Stalinist Leningrad of the 1930s in which the boy lives.

In both of these works the protagonists end in a strange space that borders on the public and private. Venichka is "murdered" in an entryway to an apartment building. Andrei wakes up in his bed in his family's apartment—a private space that was frequently and shamelessly invaded by public forces throughout the Stalin era, and beyond. Certainly both end by raising personal space as a social problem. The space-time imagery at the end of all these meta-utopias reiterates an insistence on private space and separate, personal consciousness apart from a notion of the self as tool of the reigning ideology. It is in this consistent reminder that the meta-utopian mentality finally differs from the dystopian.

In the lively discussion about utopia in the Soviet literary press since 1988, when Zamiatin's *We* was finally published, there is a strong (and, in my view, productive) tendency on the part of several contemporary Russian critics to interpret the utopian fixation on the future and obsession with perfection as a contempt for the here-and-now. Such critics as Zverev and Pavlova-Silvanskaia urge a sober vision of reality and a basic acceptance of things as they are. Without condoning apathy or stagnation, they support confrontation of real social problems and the devising of practical solutions while retaining utopian social ideals in some form.[21] Meta-utopian art urges no such alternatives or solutions. Nonetheless, it reveals a palpable acceptance of life, no matter how awful it has been made by utopian schemes. And, indeed, we find here a strong resistance to the apathy and stagnation that result from the suppression of historical perspective and imaginative play. Meta-utopian writing reasserts the inevitable relativism and interconnectedness of past, present, and future. It encourages the quest for insight into the relationship between the experience, process, and possibility that are all embedded in time.

[21] Ivanova, "Proshchanie s utopiei," 4, 7.

* CHAPTER FOUR *

Science, Ideology, and the Structure of Meta-utopian Narrative

THE MODERN Western tradition of utopian writing, rooted in More's *Utopia*, is very much the product of a "scientific" mentality that has emerged over the last five hundred years. Although this mentality has been variously characterized, one of its firm bases is the epistemological concern for verifiable ways of knowing and measuring reality. Tracing the beginnings of this way of thinking in the late Middle Ages and early Renaissance, the comparatist Timothy J. Reiss defines an "analytico-referential" discourse founded on repeatable acts of mediated perception of the world, enabled by some invented instrument or mechanism.[1] Reiss draws particular attention to the discovery of magnetism, the concomitant invention of the compass, and the invention of the telescope as symbols of the new thinking and its technological and social consequences. In his much-discussed book *The Postmodern Condition: A Report on Knowledge*, the French post-Marxist thinker Jean-François Lyotard stresses the overwhelming claim of this "scientific" epistemological mode to truth, based on a commitment to verification.[2]

Although the ideological interestedness of scientific thinking has been repeatedly exposed, perhaps most famously in Nietzsche's *The Gay Science*, this kind of knowledge is extremely resistant to other cognitive modes or any ideological system, such as religious belief, political programs, or folk wisdom. It discounts all of these, which Lyotard calls "narrative knowledge," because such knowledge is transmitted unexamined from teller to listener and acquires credibility only through the process of repeated telling. Lyotard explains: "The scientist questions the validity of narrative statements and concludes that they are never subject to argument or proof. He classifies

---

[1] Timothy J. Reiss, *The Discourse of Modernism* (Ithaca, N.Y.: Cornell University Press, 1984), 31.

[2] Lyotard, *The Postmodern Condition*, 24.

them as belonging to a different mentality: savage, primitive, underdeveloped, backward, alienated, composed of opinions, customs, authority, prejudice, ignorance, ideology."[3] Lyotard argues that science, in its hostility to other ways of knowing, implicitly claims for itself absolute reliability as truth. In his historical account Reiss maintains that the scientific thinking at the heart of modernity gradually "occulted" or discredited medieval "theological-feudal" discourse, with its emphasis on inspired mediation between incongruent spheres, on faith, on intuition, on identity of the transitory self with a concept of eternal, absolute being.[4]

One important aspect of the relationship between science and ideology lies in the following paradox: in order to have an impact in a society in which the vast majority of people are not experts engaged directly in "pure" research, scientific thinking and its tangible results must lend themselves to some form of narration and, thus, to engagement in ideological discourse. Science must make of itself the hero of some sort of saga, whether a voyage of adventure or discovery, an epic about social or spiritual emancipation, or a story about created wealth and welfare. Both Reiss and Lyotard agree that science has legitimized itself through stories of empowerment of the disenfranchised, of social justice and personal betterment—all of which belong to what Lyotard calls the Enlightenment "metanarrative" of emancipation, which in turn is one of the bases of modern ideology. Lyotard sees two main branches of the liberationist scientific narrative. One is extensive, concerning the promise to enlighten and empower whole nations through the spread of scientific knowledge. The other is intensive, promising personal insight into the nature of the world by the acquisition of verifiable, repeatable knowledge. Reiss emphasizes the historical concurrence of the development of scientific thinking with the emergence of socioeconomic and juridical groups that had been wholly unaccounted for in medieval discourse. These groups, newly empowered with the notion of an instrumental will and a more rigorous, questioning approach to knowledge, were capable of independent ideological growth.[5] Here is a discourse that allows an individual new power through "objective" knowledge.[6]

---

[3] Ibid., 27.
[4] Reiss, *The Discourse of Modernism*, 88. Reiss refers to the soul as the image and mediation of God.
[5] Ibid., 54.
[6] Ibid., 361.

It should be added that scientific rationalism has found extensions in two kinds of narrative that have done a great deal to enhance its legitimacy. One is the post-Enlightenment tradition of social and political thought that promises freedom for individuals through the establishment of a better, more rational and accountable social order. The other is aesthetic realism, particularly in its classical form in the nineteenth century, that is founded on the idea that art makes thinkable a just social order by raising social consciousness through exact, naturalistic, scientific observation of people in their own social setting. Thus, narratives of scientific rationalism include epics of social liberation, science-fiction voyages of discovery and conquest predicated on technological superiority, and *Bildungsromane* charting the hero's process of acquiring deeper social consciousness through scientific education. In some cases, as in Turgenev's *Fathers and Sons*, the protagonist's experience with scientific research is applied by analogy to human society.

Utopian fiction since More—from Bacon to Chernyshevsky to H. G. Wells, Bellamy, and Bogdanov—turns on the tension in modern thinking between stasis and change, being and becoming, description and fabula, in short, between science and ideology. Having started as self-proclaimed fantasy about "no place," this kind of fiction has become increasingly obsessed with the legitimization of its project as rational, plausible, and even performable. As a result, utopia continually calls into question its own character as fantasy, as a form of play.[7] And, indeed, it seems deliberately to diminish its narrative and dramatic qualities in favor of exact, "objective" description. Only later, in conjunction with other forms such as science-fiction adventure, the Soviet Socialist Realist novel, or programs and histories of social liberation does it actually change from being a description of the ideal society to being a story about building that society.

Meta-utopian fiction draws attention to the vexed character of narration and plot construction in utopian writing and, in particular, its applications of the master plot of liberation through rational knowledge. True to its nature as parodic art, it takes as its central theme the very forms in which the plot of emancipation is most frequently expressed.[8] As in dystopian art, its point of departure is the rather stag-

---

[7] For an interesting treatment of the contradiction between utopia as play and as real-life performance, see Michael Holquist, "How to Play Utopia: Some Brief Notes on the Distinctiveness of Utopian Fiction," *Yale French Studies*, no. 41 (1968): 106–23.

[8] This definition of parody is based on the work of Viktor Shklovskii in "Parodiinyi roman," in *O teorii prozy*, 177–204.

nant social state of "having-already-been-liberated," although, in distinction to dystopian narrative, the meta-utopian protagonist does not believe that he or she lives in a state of liberty. This position enables meta-utopias to challenge exclusivist scientific claims to the truth and the commitment of science to liberation and enlightenment. How components of narrative such as event, fabula, and plot are treated reveals a great deal about the mentality underlying meta-utopian fiction.

The notion of a plot "event" in meta-utopian art would almost certainly be questioned by Iury Lotman, who defines an event as an encounter or crossing of a "semantic threshold" that results in some transformation of character or condition.[9] Meta-utopian art contains no such transformative encounters. It thus continues a Russian tradition of nonaction, such as we find in *Notes from the Underground*, Goncharov's *Oblomov*, or Chekhov's plays, in which action in the classical sense transpires offstage. The observation of Anton Zimin, one of the ideological spokesmen in Zinoviev's *The Radiant Future*, that Soviet history is best understood as a series of "futile discussions" epitomizes the concept of "nonevent" in meta-utopian writing (RF, 47). There is, of course, the protagonist's account of a development of his or her own consciousness, but this development is something that has taken place at some point in the past. In contrast to the moral and metaphysical searching apparent in *Notes from the Underground*, the process is already completed at the time of narration.

The incidents that do transpire are reduced to the status of mere anecdote and do nothing to change anyone's mind. In *The Yawning Heights*, for example, the eventual incarceration of the dissident sociologist The Schizophrenic (Shizofrenik) for writing and circulating "anti-Ibansk" manuscripts, the infighting over who will become the next director of the institute, and even the suicide of Zinoviev's main protagonist, the intellectual The Big Mouth (Boltun), at the end of the book are reduced to the equivalent of a one-line announcement on the back page of a newspaper. By contrast, the efforts of the semi-underground painter The Dauber (Mazila) to realize his artistic talents gain resonance only because The Big Mouth responds to The Dauber's experience and work in a critical essay, fragments of which, in turn, are reproduced in *The Yawning Heights*.

Perhaps the real "event" in meta-utopian fiction happens in the larger framework of the response of a reader to a text. In his book

---

[9] Lotman, *Struktura khudozhestvennogo teksta*, 280–89.

Postmodernist Fiction Brian McHale argues that the dominant concern in modernist art is epistemological, that is, modernist art concentrates on the nature of consciousness and how we know the world we inhabit. Postmodernist art, by contrast, builds on an ontological base, focusing on defining existence in this world and what can be done in this world.[10] Meta-utopian art spans both areas of concern. The most radical exemplars of meta-utopian fiction address primarily epistemological concerns of the reader, involving the reader in an opportunity to meditate on the nature of society and the axiomatic valuative constructs informing social consciousness. We will see that popularized meta-utopian narratives, on the contrary, are generally concerned with ontological problems, that is, what can be achieved in this world.

What actually occurs in meta-utopia—and this contributes to the impression that "nothing happened"—is their parody of conventional fabulas and exposure of the values embedded in them. Plot becomes a subject for moral or aesthetic discussion rather than a moving force for the narrative. Analysis of this parody of narrative structures must focus on the master plots and metanarratives that are exposed and the degree to which they really serve the ends that they claim to serve: emancipation and truth.

Meta-utopias expose utopian plots of liberation in two ways: through absurdist reduction and by reversing the movement of the traditional liberation plot from enslavement to freedom and from ideology to science. One of the fabulas most frequently mentioned as a foundation for utopian plot is the allegory of the cave in Book 7 of Plato's *Republic*.[11] Here Plato's philosopher leaves the cave where people are chained in such a position that they see not real figures but their moving shadows illuminated on the cave wall, like the two-dimensional figures on a Greek urn or puppets in a shadow play. The philosopher then enters a higher world illuminated by the blinding

---

[10] McHale, *Postmodernist Fiction*, 6–11.

[11] Morson views it as the master plot for the utopian tradition. See Morson, *The Boundaries of Genre*, 89. The Ghanan writer Ayi Kwei Armah invokes this allegory in his anti-utopian novel *The Beautyful Ones Are Not Yet Born* (1968), 79–80. See also Lyotard, *The Postmodern Condition*, 29. Lyotard mentions ironically that scientific legitimation is often found in the "allegory of the cave, which recounts how and why men yearn for narratives [that is, received, unquestioned information] and fail to recognize knowledge. Knowledge is thus founded on the narrative of its own martyrdom" and not on that epic heroism often claimed for their project.

light of the sun. Having learned to perceive reality, he returns to the cave to disabuse his fellow humans of their false notions of the real. But his eyes are unused to the darkness within the cave, and he cannot perceive and identify the shadows as well as the prisoners can. Since he has lost credibility, what he recounts about the upper world is dismissed as fantasy. The relationship between the philosopher and the cave-dwellers is paralleled by that of the narrator-protagonist and his or her readership. The narrator of utopian works, such as More's *Utopia*, Defoe's *Robinson Crusoe*, Bellamy's *Looking Backward*, or Wells's *Modern Utopia*, experiences a different, better social order, the superiority of which he then tries to convey to his incredulous readers.

Ironically, meta-utopian fiction heartily affirms the status of Plato's cave as "reality" but destroys any notion of a "higher" world, except perhaps the private world of a moral consciousness that resists ideological coercion. All allegedly higher worlds are obscured by the strongly implanted "cave" psychology—reactive, narrow-minded, resentful of change—forged over millenia of living in isolation. As a result, a plan that might have been brilliant as a dream of a better human existence becomes worse than life in the cave when it is realized. It becomes another cave, as it were, deformed by the illusion that it is actually a higher, more light-filled realm. In short, it is nothing more than a deception.

In *The Yawning Heights* Zinoviev exposes the Platonic fabula as a key narrative strategy in utopian writing. He reduces it to an absurd "history" of the exploits of The Master (Khoziain)—obviously a foil for Stalin—found in fragments of an unpublished manuscript found on a trash heap:

> In [the fragments] was an account of the fabricated events from the reign of The Master—the legendary founder of Ibansk. According to this legend, The Master first led the forebears of the Ibanskians from the dark cave onto the radiant path and constructed for them a happy future. Having done this and having conquered all his enemies and friends, his hubris increased, and he started to punish the rest. This made everything much better. In his waning years he suddenly saw the light and pardoned all the survivors. In honor of this sad event they gave him a new name, The Hog [Khrushchev], and decided to erect a monument. But they thought the better of this idea just in time. Around the monument grew Ibansk—a fabricated

village of the urban type which was in fact impossible because of a false presupposition, and, if it were possible, then not in Ibansk. (YH, 223)

Here everything but the cave is made absurd and illogical. What distinguishes this reference to the Platonic utopian master plot from a dystopian parody of it (in which "return" to the cave would be viewed as a positive step) is the effort to see the effects of primordial "cave" psychology on the "utopian" mentality. In addition, civilization and its benefits are not rejected as they are in dystopian novels. Indeed, in their quest for civil society Zinoviev's protagonists would only like a higher level of civilization, with some measure of personal autonomy and genuine social responsibility. Thus, meta-utopian art redefines the place of the thinking, conscious, moral individual within the developed situation; it emphasizes her right to sabotage, parody, ironize, and finally reject the enforced utopian picture of that situation and reframe actuality in more honest and productive terms.

Of all meta-utopian works, *The Yawning Heights* is the most radically experimental in form, and also the most difficult to read. In its very stasis and narrative entropy it most strongly calls into question the suppositions of the Platonic master plot. Here there are no thresholds, no paired opposites of dark/light, low/high, interior/exterior. Everything is dark, low, interior, even if it disingenuously claims to be the opposite. Indeed, here the mythic fabula of transferral from one realm to another is finally reduced to wordplay. The ideal world of Plato's scenario, the "radiant heights [siiaiushchie vysoty]," are transformed with a single pun into the "yawning heights [ziiaiushchie vysoty]," that is, not "heights" at all but the abyss of hell. The only choice one really has is to behave according to the dark, low "laws" of human social behavior or to resist them. In defining and resisting them is really to be found the only "light."

In *Liubimov*, Terts exposes the liberation story as a magic trick, the function of the power of hypnosis. The effect is to turn the canonical plot about enlightenment, truth, and justice into one about the fallibility of "science," about ideology and authority. The new chosen leader of the town of Liubimov, the bicycle repairman Lënia Tikhomirov, divulges his utopian aims to his "chronicler," the town librarian Savely Kuzmich Proferansov, who has recorded them in the text we now read:

Why are we badly off, or, better put, why are we not well enough off? Because each person thinks [only] about how to fill his pockets. Because in our splendid society the slaves to routine and the bureaucrats, the cheaters [ochkovtirateli], thieves, fashion plates, bigamists, and decadents have unfortunately not yet become extinct. But now we won't even need prison to correct all of them and turn our earth into one single garden. I will inculcate into each person the correct way of thinking, I will teach them to respect labor and love their country. I will teach them to raise the level of their material and cultural life limitlessly. (L, 355)

Tikhomirov envisions himself as the great leader who gives earthly life meaning, the philosopher-king who leads his people out of the "cave" of avarice and dishonesty. Yet soon thereafter it becomes clear that he has power not through the force of his own character, or the compelling nature of his insight into the higher world, but only by grace of another, wholly fantastic presence, that of the nineteenth-century "ancestor" of both Savely Kuzmich and Tikhomirov, Samson Samsonovich Proferansov.

Proferansov is a bogus "scientist," the translator of a work of very dubious value on magnetism. He returns in the twentieth century to enact his plan for the good society. His goal is to "return to the earth its lost love," to overcome alienation through the creation of the ideal community (L, 396). The godforsaken backwater in which he wishes to carry out his utopian scheme is called, significantly, "Liubimov," or "Beloved-town." Endowed with superhuman powers of hypnosis (presumably related in some way to his theory of magnetism), he takes control of the pen of Savely Kuzmich and directs through him the process of plot construction. He also uses him intermittently (and most unreliably) as a mouthpiece for his views on history, science, technology, love, and morality.

Proferansov treats the philosopher-king, Tikhomirov, as his marionette, merely an "actor" in his scheme. Tikhomirov first comes to Samson Samsonovich's attention when he falls hopelessly in love with the local schoolteacher, Serafima Petrovna Kozlova, and wracks his brain trying to come up with a way to win her affections. Samson Samsonovich makes contact with Tikhomirov when his book on magnetism, now used as attic insulation in Tikhomirov's house, falls on the young bicycle repairman. When Tikhomirov acquires his magical powers, he gains the ambition to become the liberator of

Liubimov and lay the town at Kozlova's feet, thus bringing her to agree to marry him. Thus, he fulfills Samson Samsonovich's dual purpose of returning love to the earth and creating its social embodiment, utopia.

It is worth remarking in passing that Proferansov's thinking plays on the tension that traditionally obtains between scientific and ideological thinking. It is "scientific" in that it bases itself on the verifiable, reproducible phenomena related to magnetism, which in the early nineteenth century was, indeed, assumed to be a science. Here Terts emphasizes the relative truth-value even of science that traditionally claims to stand beyond ideological frameworks, to be "meta-ideological." Proferansov's thinking is "ideological" in that it contemplates the distinct social application of a scientific theory to the task of altering and "improving" human nature and social consciousness. To begin with, Proferansov believes that the utopian dream might be scientifically verifiable and realizable. In this oxymoronic juxtaposition of dream and rigorous observation Proferansov anticipates a confusion at the center of Marxism-Leninism.

Proferansov's bid for absolute authority over the narrative turns out not to be defensible: he is unable to control and remake human nature to suit his plan. As in other meta-utopias, here, too, protagonists are unwilling and unable to part with a "cave" psychology, even in their effort to realize utopia. Despite Proferansov's efforts to control his consciousness through magic, Tikhomirov will not free himself of the very human instinct to "fill his pockets": he papers the walls of his bridal suite with hundred-ruble notes and bilks his citizens of their possessions. Finally, disillusioned with his experiment, Samson Samsonovich relieves Tikhomirov of his extraordinary powers. As in *The Yawning Heights*, the liberation fabula functions not as a blueprint for action but as an epistemological scheme to be contemplated. The very notion of emancipation is falsified in the reiteration that one can never change human nature's core of petty self-interest and desire for self-preservation.

By focusing on the authority relationships between his three main characters, Terts exposes scientific claims to pure rationality and truth as little more than mystifications foisted on and perpetuated by willing listeners. In *Liubimov* all three major characters are in some way "scientists." Savely Kuzmich is a "historian." As the town librarian and chronicler, he is committed to telling the "truth," providing an "objective" eyewitness account of historically significant events (that is, moments of liberation). Tikhomirov is a technological genius and inventor, a naive, simple man ingenuously seeking a way to create a perpetual-motion machine that could free people of the necessity of finding new sources of energy. Proferansov at first resembles an early-nineteenth-century scientist, a dreamer working on projects on the edge of what might once have been called "scientific" concerning in particular the forces of magnetism and mesmerism.

None of these characters, as it turns out, is free of social restraints. As participants in a narration, each is decisively influenced by the others. Each undermines the authority and credibility of the others so that everything about this narrative soon becomes doubtful, mentionable only in quotation marks. Instead of reading a saga of liberation through science, we are muddling through a "saga" about "liberation" in which "science" leads the way. The question then becomes: Which "scientist," if any, can be believed—the planner, the technician who puts the plan into practice, or the observer who chronicles the event or writes up the "lab report"? For example, as historian, Savely Kuzmich has the power to recount and reshape events, to give them the resonance and meaning that he deems appropriate. However, one abuse of narrative autonomy is soon replaced by others. Savely Kuzmich's narrative consciousness is taken over and his narrative power is appropriated by Proferansov to build his own utopian tale. And somewhat later Savely Kuzmich's authority is claimed by Tikhomirov, who wants him to reproduce the liberation of Liubimov not as he perceives it as objective observer but as Tikhomirov wants himself to be portrayed in it. Tikhomirov, meanwhile, turns out to be the marionette controlled by Samson Samsonovich. Finally, however, Proferansov himself is daunted by the intractability of human nature, expressed in Savely Kuzmich's toadyism and Tikhomirov's corruption in the face of total power. In the end no one has the power to impose his vision of reality, with the result that each character, with his particular story, recedes into silence. Without any story there, of course, can be no legitimization of science and no social liberation.

Voinovich's *Moscow 2042* and the Strugatsky brothers' *The Condemned City* play on a second plot type: the utopian–science-fiction voyage of discovery and liberation.[12] It should be noted that, at least

---

[12] It is interesting to note that some of the conceptualist artists also play on Soviet claims to scientific and technological perfection. Il'ia Kabakov's amazing three-

in Stalinist science fiction, liberation means conquest: the voyagers are traveling from an already enlightened society to bring enlightenment to some cosmic backwater. Nonetheless, voyages in utopian writing—for example, in Bogdanov's *Red Star*—typically move from a state of ignorance, from "enslaved," limited consciousness, and from ideology to knowledge, enlightenment, science, and utopia. Voinovich's and the Strugatskys' two meta-utopias reverse this voyage.

In *Moscow 2042*, the narrator, Vitaly Kartsev, returns to a "utopia" that he has escaped from once already and knows to have failed, only to find that it claims to be still more technologically and socially advanced than before. In fact, its citizens are even more stupid and ignorant and live in even greater squalor than before. Voinovich pokes fun at other science-fiction motifs. Instead of worshiping rocket travel as a means of freeing oneself from time and space, Kartsev focuses on the concrete problems associated with it. For example, time travel is prohibitively expensive, costing, at the lowest possible price that the travel agency can offer, well over four million German marks! It takes the budget of the American CIA and the funds of an Arab terrorist group to finance this trip. Once in the vehicle that transports him to the Moscow of the future, a machine suspiciously like an ordinary jet, Kartsev observes his companions on the flight, many of whom are terrorists, radicals, and spies. As they near Moscow, Kartsev sees in the sky near his window something like a room with a bloated, fishlike figure in it. It turns out that this person is his old schoolfellow, the KGB agent Leshka Bukashov, who had instigated the August putsch and who later became known as The Genialissimus, the focal point of a new cult of personality. Doubting the wisdom of his genuinely revolutionary schemes, his comrades have had him incarcerated and put into orbit. They have erected in his place a carefully crafted, godlike persona embodied throughout Moscow in street names and statues in honor of The Genialissimus and in endless volumes of his works.

---

dimensional work *The Man Who Flew into Space from His Apartment* (1980–1988) particularly plays on utopia and the science-fiction plot in a humorous way in which the object is to escape utopia. The work is like a stage set showing a room clearly in a communal apartment, a utopian setting in the Soviet context. The room has a bench, shoes, a jury-rigged catapult, and a gaping hole in the ceiling. The accompanying narrative is a kind of news report about a lonely inhabitant of a communal apartment who propelled himself into outer space to join up with a "stream of energy" flowing through the cosmos. The text is cited in Ross, *Between Spring and Summer*, 25–27. For more on Kabakov, see Sussman, "The Third Zone," 63–65.

Claims to technological advancement are travestied here at every opportunity. Everything in Moscow is built cheaply and looks as if it might fall apart at any moment. Plastic and cardboard are used in the most outlandish, inappropriate places. For example, a monument to The Genialissimus is erected in plastic to replace the statue of Pushkin in Pushkin Square. Kartsev's companion, Iskra, has a plastic locket around her neck. The attendant at the House of Love wears glasses with cardboard frames.

Even more trenchant is Voinovich's treatment of computer technology, which, instead of increasing the flow and availability of information, destroys it. For example, writers in the postcommunist Soviet Union can work through Bumlit (Bumazhnaia literatura) or "literature written on paper," in which works are printed on paper only after being hacked apart by censorship committees. Or they are free to write anything they like through Bezbumlit (Bezbumazhnaia literatura), or "literature written without paper." Here they are given a computer without a monitor or a printer into which they type anything they wish to express. A central computer preserves everything that is written, but for public purposes edits out anything that is not deemed suitable and consolidates everyone's writings into one big text. Obviously this massive computer serves only to bolster ideological oppression.

Voinovich's mockery of technological advancement comes to a climax in his encounter with "Supik," a robot who is supposed to be able to perform every task to perfection. Supik's inventor, Edik, turns out to be another old schoolfellow of Kartsev's who has survived and even grown younger all these years by discovering and separating out of the human body the elixir of life and the elixir of death. The picture of the mad scientist, Edik subverts any notion of science as an activity intended to emancipate humanity. In the name of creating the "new man," Edik conducts sadistic physical and psychological experiments on live humans. He dreams of taking over the world by controlling the sources of the two elixirs, by giving his enemies the death elixir and himself a steady dose of the elixir of life.

"Supik" (a nickname for "Superman") was meant to be the image of the "new man" and is both Edik's greatest success and his greatest failure. Much like the character Robinson Crusoe in Ilia Ilf's and Evgeny Petrov's story "How Robinson Was Made," Supik is the victim of creation by committee. When Edik first made him, he was all-powerful, talented in every way. He could write poetry, play Beethoven on the piano, prove difficult mathematical theorems, shoot a gun with perfect aim, and quote *The Communist Manifesto* in full! (M, 264) But then he had to pass through various censorship committees and was deprived of all his wondrous powers. When Kartsev sees him, he has become an "edited superman [otredaktirovannyi supermen]," little more than a moron capable only of washing bottles in a laboratory. Supik plays an important role in the plot, since it is his example that finally convinces Kartsev to resist the changes to his book that are being forced upon him.

In *The Condemned City*, the voyage motif is reduced almost to nothing and the movement of consciousness from a state of enslavement to a state of enlightenment is made into a circle. The settlers of the unbearable wasteland of The Experiment have all come from ruined realized utopias of the twentieth-century world—Stalinist Russia, Maoist China, Nazi Germany, the American Dream. Here as in other meta-utopias, action takes place mostly outside the narrative. The settlers have no idea how they arrived in The Experiment. Instead of finding salvation, they are confronted with the circular fate of repeating the same disastrous political and social practices they thought they had left behind. The result for thinking, conscious people is insupportable, a welfare state created through coercion in which no one except a very few at the top has any say in the conduct of social and political life.

The utopian ideological thrust of Stalinist science fiction is reduced to the status of a delusion of the novel's main character, Andrei Voronin. Personally he seems a parody of the positive hero type. He is hopelessly single-minded, simpleminded, and dictatorial, traits that irritate even his closest acquaintances. He seems unable to understand what is clear to more refined sensibilities. Physically he is youthful and strong. There is even a touch of humor in this otherwise quite humorless parody when Andrei (who is otherwise rather abstract and disembodied, like most meta-utopian protagonists) stands in front of a mirror and admires his naked body, with its rippling muscles. His worldview imitates the belief of Stalinist science-fiction protagonists that they were born in utopia to bring enlightenment to other societies and other planets. Andrei supposes that he was put into The Experiment in order to liberate it and build communism.

Events bear out the misguidedness of Andrei's beliefs as he unwittingly joins forces with neofascist settlers who take over the rule of the city and impose a totalitarian government, an unfree environment in which everyone is materially well-off but otherwise oppressed, unable to question existing power or consider other political alternatives. He realizes that he himself, although a high councillor in the state, much like a Platonic guardian, helps no one and has settled for a narrow, comfortable existence. Thus, the terms of the liberation master plot are reversed—liberation/escape becomes enslavement, knowledge disguises ignorance, welfare hides despair, change merges into stagnation.

The most radically experimental meta-utopian texts, particularly *The Yawning Heights*, *Liubimov*, and *Moscow-Petushki*, confront the paradox in the fundamental rationale of utopian thinking since the Enlightenment, the use of science to transcend ideology, only to be co-opted by a new set of vested interests and values. We have seen how science invested with a strong personal agenda, such as Proteransov's psychosocial theory of magnetism in *Liubimov*, are exposed as wholly unrigorous, fantastic, and politically harmful. Most meta-utopias—for example, Tendriakov's *A Potshot at Mirages*, *The Radiant Future*, or Terts's literary-critical essay "What Is Socialist Realism?"—expose the intimate relationship between science and ideology, reality and fantasy, by using as raw material for their narratives "scientific" writing, such as written tracts, essays, and descriptive analyses that might in another context pass for rigorous, academic, social-scientific, or critical-humanistic discourse.[13] By interpolating this scientific material into a fictional narrative, authors of meta-utopian works highlight its ideological qualities.

The most obvious example of this process is *The Yawning Heights*. Here Zinoviev may on first impression appear to be arguing for the

---

[13] It is interesting to note that some meta-utopias are so close to nonfiction that on occasion they have indeed been mistaken for such. Although, for example, it would be very difficult to categorize *The Yawning Heights* as any known fictional genre—even if Zinoviev insists that it is a "sociological novel"—it is certainly a work of fiction. See Amurskii, "Ia—odinochka vo vsem." It comes as a surprise to find Zinoviev not even listed in one of the major, recent Russian literary encyclopedias, Victor Terras's *Handbook of Russian Literature* (New Haven: Yale University Press, 1985). The function of such handbooks is *de facto* to codify what "literature" and "fiction" are. Another recent dictionary of literature, Wolfgang Kasack's *Dictionary of Russian Literature Since 1917*, does list Zinoviev but faults him for being "without artistic talent" and for writing works without sustained plot lines! Zinoviev is seen not as a strong experimentalist but as a sociologist producing "one of the sharpest and most pertinent sociological analyses of Soviet society." See Kasack, *Dictionary of Russian Literature Since 1917*, trans. M. Carlson and J. T. Hedges, with revisions by R. Atack (New York: Columbia University Press, 1988), 487.

existence and superiority of a "pure," that is, ideologically untainted, science. He weaves a large amount of ideologically "unacceptable" scientific material into *The Yawning Heights*, contrasting it with the discourse of acceptable, "official" science, thus exposing the challenge that rigorous, "scientific" thinking poses to ideology. *The Yawning Heights* comprises both serious scientific manuscripts and parodies of scientific writing, two by The Schizophrenic and one each by The Slanderer and The Big Mouth. The first by The Schizophrenic is a serious sociological study, "Sociomechanics," that examines "social laws" governing human social behavior and the way that the utopian state interacts with those fundamental laws. Since it cuts too close to the bone to be officially published, this work is later recycled and sees the light of day as a book on the social behavior of rats. The other of The Schizophrenic's manuscripts is a cultural-historical study of the adventures of cadets from the Pilots' School, where the "new man" was supposed to be formed. Here the focus is on the conversations that go on in the outhouse and on life in the guardhouse, where the delinquents among the cadets are incarcerated. Included in these fragments of analysis are bits of a "ballad" by a Cadet Ibanov about survival in the guardhouse and at the front. The Slanderer's notes have to do with the relationship between science and ideology, and The Big Mouth's manuscript gives a socioaesthetic analysis of the art of The Dauber.

In his manuscript The Slanderer directs his attention to the claim of Ibansk ideology to the status of science and the ways in which it legitimizes itself by clothing itself in scientific terminology. He notes:

> Ideology and science are mutually exclusive phenomena. I don't mean to say that they are mutually hostile. Enemies can live in peace and even at times look like friends. I mean only that these phenomena are qualitatively different. Science builds on ... intelligibility, precision, and clarity of language. Ideology builds on senseless, diffuse, and ambiguous linguistic formations. Scientific terminology does not require interpretation. The phraseology of ideology requires interpretation, association, reading between the lines, and so forth. Scientific assertions assume the possibility of their confirmation or disproof or, in the most extreme case, the proof that they are unresolvable. Ideological statements cannot be disproven or confirmed because they are meaningless. (YH, 163–64)

The Slanderer continues: "The expression 'scientific ideology' ... refers to an ideology that sucks the juices of ... science and disguises itself as science. But ideology as science in the sense of a properly scientific approach is nonsense [nonsens]. It has origins and goals completely different from those of cognition" (YH, 164).

The Slanderer points out here that ideologies are neither provable nor disprovable, since they are not based on rigorous thinking and have no rules of the game by which their truth-value can be tested. In this sense, ideologies of the twentieth century are in no way distinguishable from the world's great religions:

> Ideological doctrine contains doctrine about the world in general, doctrine about people, and doctrine about human society. I emphasize, doctrine and not science.... If one formulates the essence of ideological doctrine in a preliminary, concise fashion, it boils down to the following. The world, people (that is, you), and society (that is, a system [consisting] of a large number of similar "you's," with all their weapons, means of existence, etc.) are all ordered in such a way ... that the society in which you live is the best of all imaginable societies. The authorities grasp profoundly (more profoundly than anyone else) the laws of the world, people, and society and are ordering your life in full harmony with [these laws]. They are doing the very best for you.... And your life is splendid. Splendid thanks only to the wise authorities who are guided by the most correct theory, etc. In short, here we find all the attributes of divine wisdom, goodness, insight, etc. But here is one special detail that deserves our attention. And that is that the twentieth century is in no way better in terms of the [ideological] conditions of human existence than those times that produced such great ideologies as Buddhism, Islam, Christianity. (YH, 179)

These arguments would seem to support the traditional contention that science in and of itself is ideologically disinterested in that it strives relentlessly to uncover "truth," and is thus better than ideology that is as knowledge unreliable and deceptive. While this point is treated seriously, other aspects of the relationship between science and ideology come into play. Zinoviev implicitly gives a good deal of weight to ideological discourse, even more than he gives to scientific discourse as such, and he distinguishes between kinds of ideological discourse. For example, the critical analyses of Ibansk society and culture that are central to the various manuscript fragments are important, but not in and of themselves. They gain significance and life in a communicative network, when they are read, discussed, and debated by their readers, when they change someone's evaluation of the institutions, people, and events with which they live.

Zinoviev would very likely agree with the anthropologist Clifford Geertz, who proposed a redefinition of ideology as the pervasive symbolic formulation of cultural and social values. On the relationship between ideology and science, Geertz has this to say:

> Though science and ideology are different enterprises, they are not unrelated ones. Ideologies do make empirical claims about the condition and direction of society, which it is the business of science . . . to assess. The social function of science vis-à-vis ideologies is first to understand them—what they are, how they work, what gives rise to them—and second to criticize them to force them to come to terms with (but not necessarily to surrender to) reality. The existence of a vital tradition of scientific analysis of social issues is one of the most effective guarantees against ideological extremism, for it provides an incomparably reliable source of positive knowledge for the political imagination to work with and to honor.[14]

The Big Mouth acknowledges the greater importance of the interaction between ideological discourse and science than of some notion of a disengaged science for the refinement of social consciousness and particularly for the creation of his preferred model of social personality—the active, responsible citizen in the context of civil society based on the contrast of many ideologies. He writes: "It is not science and technology that make a person into a citizen: it is art, morality, religion, ideology, the consistent experience of resistance" (YH, 253). The basic problem, in his view, is to "mold the human herd animal [chelovek-skot] into a citizen [chelovek-grazhdanin]," that is, to inculcate into her "honor, conscience, a striving for freedom of will and choice, for freedom of movement, for freedom of creativity" (YH, 253). The question is which art, moral code, religion, and so forth can achieve this goal. The Big Mouth suggests that debate between all kinds of ideology is part of the answer. What is bad is ideological fixation, the untested faith in one system of values over all others. Toward the end he argues for a notion of glasnost *avant la lettre*

---

[14] Clifford Geertz, "Ideology as a Cultural System," in *The Interpretation of Cultures: Selected Essays* (New York: Basic Books, 1973), 232.

(which, as we have seen, is soon rejected by others): "All my life I have affirmed one thought: open public debate is essential, [as well as] its guarantee by law and, as a result of this [condition], the beginning of the moral improvement of society. Here in Ibansk actual life goes on in the form of deals and punishments behind the scenes. What comes to the surface is just the fluff of deception. Because lice-people, rat-people rule here" (YH, 556).

While Zinoviev uses scientific material to expose the close interworkings of science and ideology, Terts in *Liubimov* exposes scientific thinking as a kind of fantasy. His goal is to emphasize the central place of imagination in structuring forms of signification that we call "reality." Terts's work achieves its resonance in part by approximating the characters, tone, and narrative technique of the Socialist Realist novel to those of another ideologically saturated genre from another era, the medieval saint's life.[15] The "faith" of this modern saint's life is science, and the paradise to be gained lies not beyond life but in the future of earthly society. In the hagiographic tradition, the homegrown technological genius Tikhomirov is pictured as a young boy whose interests lay apart from those of typical boys. He spent his childhood inventing and tinkering with mechanisms, building a one-person submarine out of tin cans. Later he supported himself by overhauling bicycles so that he would have the means to pursue his life's dream, the invention of a perpetual-motion machine. True to modified Socialist Realist convention of the post-Stalinist era, *Liubimov* places the village higher than the city in its own playful way, suggesting that the brain of Russia, ignorant and backward as it may be, can be found away from urban centers, with their hidebound intellectual bureaucracies.[16] Thus, Tikhomirov's visionary qualities are not appreciated by the narrow minds at the Academy of Sciences in Moscow who, by ignoring his plans for the perpetual-motion machine, "hindered the approach of the future" (L, 348). The figure of Tikhomirov as scientific thinker, inventor, and creator of the utopian future belies claims that scientific truth is based on rigorous investigation and wholly verifiable results. And it is precisely Tikhomirov's dreamerlike qualities that make him appealing.

---

[15] This subtext for the Socialist Realist novel has been thoroughly discussed in Clark, *The Soviet Novel*, 46–67.

[16] Katerina Clark, "Political History and Literary Chronotope: Some Soviet Case Studies," in *Literature and History: Theoretical Problems and Russian Case Studies*, ed. G. S. Morson (Stanford: Stanford University Press, 1986), 230–46.

Terts points out the unreliability of truth-claims of science also by drawing attention to scientific anachronisms: concepts that once were thought to describe reality and in contemporary science have been discounted, but that ironically have just enough currency in the odd, fantastic world of politics and mass psychology to seem truthful. Such is the theory of magnetism, which was quite popular in the 1830s and to which Samson Samsonovich subscribes, but which has long since been discredited. And yet we are confronted with another of Terts's clever paradoxes, which make *Liubimov* such an intriguing ideological puzzle: although the anachronism of magnetic theory is operative here on the level of Terts's challenge to natural science, it does ring true when it is applied to social behavior as a metaphor for mass hypnosis and the cult of personality.

As much fun as Terts has with natural science, it is historiography as the science of defining, documenting, and interpreting social reality that is subjected here to the most consistent ridicule. The narrator-librarian-chronicler Savely Kuzmich professes to be a confirmed "realist" in his aesthetic views. He lives by this aesthetic taste to the extent that he continually confuses history and art. For example, he tells Tikhomirov that he, Savely Kuzmich, has inherited from his ancestors "the whole power of art, the main historicist trunk" of the family tree (L, 352). As he enumerates the books that Tikhomirov borrows from the library, he confuses historical figures and literary characters, writing that Tikhomirov "borrowed from me only literature on the subject of great people: Copernicus, Napoleon, Chapaev, Don Quixote" (L, 352). In the style of the proponents of Socialist Realism, who demanded of writers both an exact account of contemporary events and a fantastic, utopian interpretation of them, Tikhomirov as "tsar" also confuses fiction and historiography. In the same way that Stalin commanded Russian writers, Tikhomirov commands his chronicler Savely Kuzmich "tirelessly to study reality in its inexorable development and to give each fact its truthful reflection" (L, 371). Here Tikhomirov gives an unreasonable command to provide a true eyewitness account of an obviously benighted, squalorous little hamlet and still show the coming of utopia: "inexorable development" points to the main fiction of historical determinism driving Marxist-Leninist "science," whereas "truthful reflection" suggests a clear, balanced, and, if such is possible, unbiased description of events.

In his account of what he calls Tikhomirov's "scientific revolution," Savely Kuzmich borrows anachronistic narrative styles, once considered to be reliable and truthful, but clearly fantastic to a contemporary reader. We have already mentioned Savely Kuzmich's use of hagiographic form. He also employs techniques from medieval epic and chronicle writing. On the day of the revolution, Tikhomirov appears in his "steel-colored" suit with a golden halo around his head as a modern-day saintly prince (L, 341). As in "The Igor Tale," his battle with the incumbent mayor, Tishchenko, develops through the antagonists' progressive transformation into pairs of animals, Tishchenko the pursued and Tikhomirov the pursuer. First they change into crow and hawk, then fox and borzoi, but then, incongruously, a bicycle and a motorcycle! This series of events is unacceptable even for Savely Kuzmich's uncritical mind, and he discounts it as mere "folklore" in the style of a bylina about Ilia Muromets. Nonetheless, he does not question the main element of fantasy: that Tikhomirov magically strangles Tishchenko and hypnotizes the security forces into handing over their arms to him and supporting his bid for power. Even here the epic narrative mode is maintained: Tikhomirov appears as a monumental figure, a "bronze statue" that is then carried on the shoulders of his new bodyguards in a triumphal march (L, 346). Savely Kuzmich even pirates Pushkin's poem "The Memorial" ("Pamiatnik") as a celebratory panegyric to the new tsar.

One of the ways that historians legitimize their claim to be engaged in a form of science is by providing verifiable sources of information. Academic historiography typically comes armed with batteries of footnotes and commentary that can be as substantive as the primary argument itself. Terts's narrative experiment offers an ingenious parody of these tactics. The first narrator begins using them to comment on and document his primary narrative, but soon loses control and gets tangled up and confused. The footnotes become a way of introducing other narrative perspectives into the text. The elder Proferansov first makes his voice heard through these footnotes. Savely Kuzmich, confused, thinks he is hearing some sort of voice from the "underground." Soon he loses the primary narrative to his ancestor. The attempted air attack on Liubimov from the provincial seat of government is depicted visually through the contrasting placement of the footnotes (the ground) and the primary text (the air) on the page. Somewhat later, the spy Kochetov, who is charged with penetrating Liubimov's magnetic defenses, makes his way into the story through the footnotes.

Savely Kuzmich's account of Samson Samsonovich's life near the end of *Liubimov* parodies a popular form of historiography, personal biography. Here, as before, history and fantasy are hopelessly entangled as Savely Kuzmich violates conventions of historical chronology, cause and effect, cultural congruence, and the philosophical-materialist assumptions that underlie modern historiography. What emerges is a collage of various intellectual fashions and sentiments during the century between the Decembrist revolt and the 1920s. For example, Samson Samsonovich belongs as a grown man to the "Lovers of Wisdom" circle of the 1820s and corresponds with the older L. N. Tolstoi. He reads Goncharov and Turgenev "in the original," but translates an Indian tract on hypnotism into his native Russian! He is compared to Robinson Crusoe in his lonely existence on his estate and yet is the "father" of the Russian intelligentsia. Finally, he continues his efforts to "return to the earth its lost love" and to create an earthly utopia well beyond his death (it is never specified, of course, when he died). Ultimately, as Savely Kuzmich points out, there is no inner connection between all these facts (L, 399). Samson Samsonovich's biography finally unravels as nothing more than nonsense that lulls the dethroned Tikhomirov to sleep (L, 399).

In *Liubimov*, as in other meta-utopian fiction, the narrative perspective is dialogical, using every means to undermine the monologism of reigning ideological authority. But here dialogism is emphasized by its conspicuous absence: attention is continually focused on the voice of Samson Samsonovich, whose presence directs the events of the narrative—that is, until the end, when he deprives Tikhomirov of his hypnotic powers and the whole narrative falls into chaos. Through Samson Samsonovich Terts parodies the notion of the omniscient narrator at the heart of all monological texts from medieval chronicles to political decrees to conventional academic, scientific writing. As Proferansov's presence fades, Kochetov sneaks into the narrative, much as Samson Samsonovich did in the very first pages, only to reassert the monologism of Soviet ideology. By contrast, Tikhomirov escapes his assigned role and, avoiding speech, retreats to his own private space. Savely Kuzmich, always the survivor, realizes that he has been caught in a form of "idealism," in contradiction to the Soviet "materialism" that has been imposed from above. He wants to deny all responsibility for what he has written and yearns for the same passive oblivion from which he emerged at the beginning of the story.[17]

---

[17] See Michel Aucouturier, "Writer and Text in the Works of Abram Terc," in *Fiction and Drama in Eastern and Southeastern Europe: Evolution and Experiment in the*

Finally, Erofeev in *Moscow-Petushki* parodies scientific precision and logic to undermine the notion of human perfectibility that is at the heart of Soviet utopian ideology and then to sabotage science as a tool to predict the future. Venichka is fired from his job as foreman when his superior finds some charts in his desk. Worried that his workers had bought and drunk up all available supplies of the eau de cologne "Freshness" ("Svezhest'"), Venichka had made the graphs to show workers' drinking habits over a month. Some reflect a chaotic jumble of peaks and valleys, while others are as regular as a picket fence. Venichka points out: "One looks like the Himalayas, the Tirol, the Baku oil fields, or even the top of the Kremlin Wall, which I, by the way, have never seen" (MP, 18). He goes on: "Another had a predawn breeze on the Kama River, a quiet splash and a bead of lamplight in a watery ripple. A third shows the beating of a proud heart, the song of the stormy petrel" (MP, 18). This third example, it should be noted, refers to the overbearing regularity of the trochee in Gorky's "Song of the Stormy Petrel." The last chart describes the regular drinking pattern of the toady Andrei Blindiaev, "member of the CPSU since 1936 and a tattered old fart" (MP, 17), who finally hands Venichka's charts over to the authorities, an act that leads to Venichka's dismissal. None of the three charts shows any "progress"—for example, an increase or decrease in alcohol consumption—but all suggest the pervasiveness of sodden workers in the workers' paradise.

Another graph is used by one of Venichka's many voices, a "traveling companion" on the train to Petushki, to describe the correlation between his consumption of liquor and his mood. The morning is the precise opposite of the evening: "If I am obsessed with Eros in the evening, my morning repulsion is exactly equal to yesterday's dreams" (MP, 39). He provides a sine curve to demonstrate the rise and the subsequent fall in mood.

Like the drawings in Laurence Sterne's *Tristram Shandy*, these charts may be seen as foils for the plot of *Moscow-Petushki*. While the claim is made at the start that this narrative is about progress from the dark hell of Moscow to the light-filled pleasure garden of Petushki, these graphs suggest cyclicality in people's lives at best and

---

Postwar Period, ed. H. Birnbaum and Th. Eekman (Columbus: Slavica, 1980), 3. Aucouturier argues that Savely Kuzmich ends up nonetheless being "responsible" for the text, which is "reduced to the level of guilty fantasy, the product of a subversive imagination."

complete stagnation at worst. It is not by chance that Venichka compares his graphs to places rather than to movements. Finally, it is important to realize that accurate, "scientific" detailing of the patterns of people's lives belies the rosy picture of life communicated by Soviet propaganda. It suggests a narrative quite different from the narrative provided by the authorities; this narrative is thus silenced.

Venichka discredits the predictive claims of science in his ingenious "study" of the hiccup. He starts his project with the thought: "How much that is exciting is promised by experiment in narrowly specialized fields! For example, hiccuping" (MP, 29). Venichka claims that this field is a truly "Russian" area for research. His goal is to find some pattern in hiccuping that will allow him to predict when the hiccup will end. He "proves" that hiccuping is entirely without pattern, ending as unexpectedly as it begins, and gloats that "you won't be able to predict or prevent it, just as you can't predict or prevent death" (MP, 30). Venichka then draws broad conclusions that use the "findings" of his study to challenge the claims of socialist ideology to the status of science and its claims to predict the future: "They say that the leaders of the world proletariat, Karl Marx and Friedrich Engels, studied thoroughly the pattern of social formations and on this basis were able to foresee many things. But in this case they would be powerless to foresee even the tiniest thing. You have entered on your own whim the realm of the fateful—resign yourself and be patient. Life will put to shame both your elementary and your higher math" (MP, 30). Venichka suggests that we are "deprived of a free will" and live "in the power of the arbitrary," and not only in our physiological functions (MP, 30). He concludes that God does exist just because he is incomprehensible to the rational mind and that we ought simply to bow to his will!

A final issue in our discussion of narrative form concerns the possibility of a subgenre of meta-utopian literature. It would be difficult to classify these works under the rubric of any single "genre," because their essential quality is antigeneric: that is, they parody all kinds of prose genres.[18] Meta-utopias parody utopia, dystopias, counter-utopias, and the related genre of science fiction. In addition, some works, such as *The Yawning Heights*, parody nonfictional writing, while *Liubimov* plays with every conceivable prose novel genre, including the historical epic, the spy novel, the gothic novel, the love

---

[18] Morson, *The Boundaries of Genre*, 115–18.

story, the Socialist Realist novel, biography, and the realist novel. What is perhaps most important in this body of writing is the reintroduction of what Bakhtin calls "novelness," that is, the bold challenge to literary and fictional boundaries presented through the use of nonliterary and nonfictional material and through the carnivalesque play with fixed genres and ideas. The goal here is not necessarily to redraw borders and to give priority to specific alternative values, although this is sometimes a concern, but to reassert the force of intelligent interrogation of and play with ideologies. The chronicler Savely Kuzmich writes at the end that "all this," meaning both the Liubimov experiment and his narration of it, "is just an enchantment [chara] and nothing more" (L, 399). Meta-utopian fiction, like all ludic art, is a play with fantasy—indeed, an enchantment—that challenges a discerning reader to probe the ways in which all of our most cherished and "real" values are ultimately fictions.

Meta-utopian narrative thus makes plot into an ideological problem. It reduces conventional utopian plots to a sideshow in order to highlight in them the incongruous "ideological" and "scientific" impulses in the utopian mentality, the opposing impulses to become and to be, to change and to preserve, to do and to observe, to believe and to criticize. Ultimately science, like any other cognitive practice, cannot function effectively in the world without becoming "interested," without allying itself with some set of values and goals that are held by some group within society. The meta-utopian project hinges in part on the insight that unexamined action rebounds on itself: liberation ultimately turns into enslavement, and science eventually becomes ideology.

* CHAPTER FIVE *

The Meta-utopian Language Problem, or Utopia as a Bump on a -log-

> The results of philosophy are the uncovering of one or another piece of plain nonsense and of bumps that the understanding has got by running its head up against the limits of language.
> —*Wittgenstein*, Philosophical Investigations
>
> You'll keep bumping up against the same old words.
> —*Bitov, "Notes from around the Corner"*

THAT LANGUAGE and consciousness are intimately bound up with one another is a commonplace. How they interact is harder to ascertain. Post-Saussurian literary theorists claim perhaps too much for the priority of language over consciousness.[1] Philosophers concerned with this issue, such as Nietzsche or Wittgenstein, also acknowledge the impact of language on consciousness but stress the restrictions that linguistic structures and functions put on thinking. For example, in *Tractatus Logico-Philosophicus* Wittgenstein writes: "*The limits of my language* mean the limits of my world."[2] Perhaps these restrictions are best characterized by tautology, the ultimate, absurd limit of language, an indication of the inability of language to probe beyond itself. As Wittgenstein puts it, "What we cannot speak about we must pass over in silence."[3] He sees it as the task of philosophy to seek out those limitations, to expose and scrutinize the

---

[1] See, for example, Viktor Shklovskii, "Sviaz' priemov siuzhetoslozheniia s obshchimi priemami stilia," in *O teorii prozy*, 24–67, especially 35, 60; Lotman, *Struktura khudozhestvennogo teksta*, 16; Terry Eagleton, *Literary Theory: An Introduction* (Minneapolis: University of Minnesota Press, 1983), 60–61, 63, 71.

[2] Ludwig Wittgenstein, *Tractatus Logico-Philosophicus*, trans. D. F. Pears and B. F. McGuinness (London: Routledge and Kegan Paul, 1974), 56.

[3] Ibid., 74.

"bumps" that thinking gets as it probes the linguistic cage in which it is encased.[4]

Nietzsche looks at language in its primary social function as a great leveler and a major enforcer of conformity: "Given the best will in the world to understand ourselves as individually as possible, 'to know ourselves,' each will always succeed in becoming conscious only of what is not individual but 'average.'"[5] For him, other, more private and radical kinds of consciousness are repressed when language is used in its primary function. In contrast to some literary theorists who claim language as the great liberator from fixed consciousness, he argues that change in language does not necessarily predicate shifts in consciousness. Unarticulated intuition and perception precede language in any shift of consciousness. Nietzsche queries, "What is originality? *To see* something that has no name as yet and hence cannot be mentioned although it stares us all in the face." However, Nietzsche is quick to acknowledge the central role played by linguistic innovation in the process of making a shift in consciousness widely accepted: "The way men usually are, it takes a name to make something visible for them. —Those with originality have for the most part also assigned names."[6] This observation puts Nietzsche close to the modernist belief that invention in language could bring about invention of new consciousness.

Meta-utopian fiction as a whole addresses the complex relationship between language and consciousness. It particularly takes to task the utopian hope embedded in twentieth-century efforts to find in linguistic invention a thread leading to social self-transcendence. Writers such as Siniavsky-Terts, Zinoviev, Voinovich, and Petrushevskaia sense the limitations of language particularly keenly. They are tempted by the "wisdom" of silence, to use Bitov's term, yet experiment with alternative voices. In *The Yawning Heights* Zinoviev gives considerable attention to the language problem. The Big Mouth argues that the logical assumptions underlying existing language need to be reexamined, insisting that "the condition of language is an

---

[4] Ludwig Wittgenstein, *Philosophical Investigations*, trans. G.E.M. Anscombe (New York: Macmillan, 1962), 48e.

[5] Friedrich Nietzsche, *The Gay Science*, trans. W. Kaufmann (New York: Vintage, 1974), 299.

[6] Ibid., 218.

indicator of the condition of a society's higher culture" (YH, 141). Language, as it is now used, is hackneyed and rigid, "put together under the influence of Ibansk literature of the past century and Western culture also generally of recent centuries" (YH, 141). The Big Mouth insists that, "if we are to speak more or less rigorously about our present problems and in some small measure understand each other," language must be "reworked" (YH, 141).

That said, the general thrust of meta-utopian wordplay is more skeptical than, for example, Zamiatin's dystopian language experiments, which were based on the optimistic (and ultimately utopian) idea that really new language and really new consciousness were within our grasp. It was, indeed, possible to create the language and style adequate to new "reality." Political, social, and cultural revolutions, in Zamiatin's view, were advanced by revolution in language and consciousness. The meta-utopians' view of language hews somewhat closer to that of a writer who mourned the impossibility of realized utopia, Andrei Platonov. Platonov is relentless in the use of wordplay that draws attention to the abuse and petrification of language in its ideological, and particularly utopian, usages. Platonov, in Joseph Brodsky's apt phrase, "drives language into a semantic dead-end and, more precisely, . . . reveals in language itself the philosophy of the dead-end," that is, utopia.[7] Paradoxically, utopia as a static system kills dynamism and difference, that is, the possibility for meaning. By destroying language it destroys consciousness itself. In a palpable way utopian speculation helps to measure the linguistic cage in which we reside. It exists at the outer limit of the ability of language to mean, at the point where the word's attachment to a functional referent becomes suspect. In this Wittgensteinian sense, then, utopian thinking hits against the limits of words and is, indeed, a "bump on a -log-." In the sense that utopian existence is monological and stagnant, denying all difference, and thus quells all spiritual growth—in the sense that realized utopia is intellectually "lazy"—it is also a "bump on a log." This is Platonov's insight, and it is certainly reiterated and supported in meta-utopian writing. But in meta-utopian writing there is no mourning for realized utopia, but neither is there a denial of utopian thinking. Rather, we find a paring back of the claims of utopian thinking on language and a resolute endorse-

---

[7] Andrei Platonov, *Kotlovan* (Ann Arbor: Ardis, 1973), ix.

ment of sensual, concrete meanings and of linguistic humor, that is, the ability of language to mean in many ways.

An important model for the meta-utopian critique of language is clearly Orwell's *1984*. Here the utopian notion that neologism and unorthodox uses of style and syntax bring with them genuinely new and better social consciousness is consistently undercut. What is known as "newspeak" is revealed as a series of abstractions and oversimplifications of language—euphemisms, reversals of meaning, and oxymoron—that simply dislodge all meaning, making language absurd. The rulers of Oceania have in mind to make a sustained critique of public life impossible. The result, Orwell implies, is an emptying-out of language as a vehicle for making sense of the world.

Language use in meta-utopian fiction is motivated by the knowledge that we still face the same old realities of human nature that utopia had undertaken to transform. Indeed, utopian pretentions have brought to the surface and reinforced the negative traits in a particularly virulent, nasty form by lying about human nature. Thus, in meta-utopian art there is a tendency to unmask utopian language and its claims to have created new consciousness. In order to revive a Russian language stiff with stock ideological phrases, absurd from overuse, these writers resort to a number of techniques: critical analysis, puns, play with euphemisms, stylistic parody, and reduction of language to its most concrete, palpable meanings—that is, liberation from its overly abstracted and sententious qualities. This chapter will examine these techniques and then consider the ways in which meta-utopian writing moves away from utopian false optimism and the dystopian dead end of silence. The next chapter will then describe what might be called a meta-utopian mentality.

Among the most pervasive of techniques used throughout this body of fiction is parody of those stylistic attributes of utopian language that in the long run sap its vitality. Key among these are hyperbole and euphemism. Although he feels that Bolsheviks in the early years of the revolution did indeed use language in a way that excited the imagination, Terts in "What Is Socialist Realism?" comments on the use in monumental Stalinism of the 1930s of a particularly classical, eighteenth-century kind of hyperbole. Instead of *gosudarstvo* (state) one would commonly encounter *derzhava* (power, as in "Great Power"), instead of *muzhik* (peasant), *khleborob* (cultivator of bread), instead of *vintovka* (gun), *mech* (sword, saber).[8] He finds this a heavy, pedantic, deadening style.

In *The Yawning Heights* Zinoviev remarks on the silly euphemisms created from Latin roots chosen in favor of more lively Russian words. He comments that such a familiar and colorful Russian term as *stukach* (stool pigeon, petty spy) has become defamiliarized as *informator* in the lingo of the "experiment" (YH, 18). Latin roots often appear to have a kind of magic, an extra power about them that Zinoviev is quick to diffuse. For example, he claims, one must have permission from higher authority to use such ideologically loaded Latinate words as *perspektivy* (promise, prospects for the future) (YH, 17). In his commentary on ideology and science, The Slanderer (Klevetnik) argues that Latin roots give a false impression of being "scientific," making the notion of a Marxist utopia seem real and rationally founded, a notion he calls "monstrously ungrammatical" (YH, 195). As he puts it, "If instead of the expression 'the exploitation [ekspluatatsiia] of man by man' you say 'the use [ispol'zovanie] of man by man,' you will see right away the terrible nonsense of all the blather on this account. Can a person live without using another person for some purpose or other?" (YH, 195). Ironically, by emphasizing that "use" is an evil and by rejecting any legitimate, ethical notion of use, the Ibansk experiment has created a society in which people in search of "success" and "happiness" not only use, but abuse and try to destroy each other.

The Schizophrenic makes fun of Stalinist acronyms that act as euphemistic screens for a very ugly reality. He indulges in a field day of false etymologies as he describes the origins of one of the central loci of *The Yawning Heights*, the guardhouse at the Pilots' School, itself a "utopian" euphemism for the gulag prison system. Playing on the Soviet term *gulag*, which stands for *gosudarstvennoe upravlenie lagerei* (state authority for labor camps), this guardhouse is known as *guba*. It is to be remembered that *guba* means "lip" in "real" Russian. According to The Schizophrenic, people originally believed that *guba*

---

[8] SR, 205. There is an odd discrepancy between the English translation and the two existing Russian editions. The word *soldier* is discussed in the translation but appears in neither Russian edition. See *Fantasticheskii mir Abrama Tertsa* (New York: Inter-Language Literary Associates, 1967), 439; *Tsena metafory ili prestuplenie i nakazanie Siniavskogo i Danielia* (Moscow: Kniga, 1989), 453. For more comment on Soviet hyperbolic style, see Terts, "The Literary Process in Russia" (1974), trans. M. Glenny, in *Kontinent* (Garden City, N.Y.: Anchor/Doubleday,1976), 101.

came from the Latinate term for the unit of governance, *guberniia* or "province." Then it was "discovered" that the term came from the allegedly Tatar term *gebe*, which is related to the Russian verb *gubit'* or "to ruin" (YH, 17).

Within the confines of the *guba*, prisoners also come up with amusing "etymologies" that play with the distance between incomprehensible foreign cognates and abstract Russian terms, on the one hand, and concrete Russian roots, on the other. For example, it is decided that the Russian word for graffiti, one of the favorite pastimes of the inmates, is *stenografiia*. *Steno-*, to their minds, refers to the Russian word for wall, *stena*. One of the inmates suggests that originally the Russian word for artist, *khudozhnik*, comes from *khudo*, which means "the bad" or "ill fortune." (YH, 103)

Voinovich is another expert at undermining utopian claims to sociolinguistic innovation, again by identifying *innovation* with *euphemism*. The regime that has held power in Moscow since what is known as the August revolution has proclaimed that all Russian prior to that revolution is really just "preparatory" or *predvaritel'nyi* language. All prerevolutionary "classics," among which Kartsev's works are numbered, now have to be translated into the new, "real" Russian because people are forgetting how to read the old. The new, openly religious ideology, now forged by a latter-day Mikhail Suslov, Father Zvezdony or "Father Star" (relating presumably to the five-pointed pentagon, a symbol of the five-pronged, post-Soviet ideology), is a goulash of very familiar Stalinist stuff, consisting of adulation of the makers of the August upheaval and traditional Russian Orthodox pageantry and rituals. Along with it comes a new "language." For example, a whole battery of words pertaining to rites of ideological indoctrination are formed on the root *zvezd-*, relating to the emblem of the new regime, the pentagon. As soon as a child is born, she goes through a "starring ritual [obriad zvezdeniia]" (M, 190). When one makes obeisance to the "Supreme Pentagon," the ruling oligarchy of the post-Soviet Soviet Union, the verb used is *perezvezdit'sia* or "to re-star oneself" (M, 305). It becomes obvious that the root *zvezd-* has merely replaced the older root, *krest-* or "cross," implying that the new ideology is nothing more than a rather transparent verbal trick meant to hide a retooling of some familiar Orthodox rituals and some age-old political values. Another example that confirms this theory is the verb *otzvezdit'sia*, which means the same as *otkrestit'sia* or "to disown" or "to refuse to have anything to do with."

The Muscovite world, just as Zinoviev's Ibansk, operates on hopelessly vacuous but nonetheless threatening logic. We have commented in our discussion of meta-utopian chronotope on the scatological implications of such acronyms as KK (Kol'tsa kommunizma) and Pukomras (Punkt kommunisticheskogo raspredeleniia po mestu sluzheniia kommunian). Other absurd but strangely salacious acronyms are Bumlit (Bumazhnaia literatura), Bezbumlit (Bezbumazhnaia literatura), Meobskop (Mesto obshchestvennogo skopleniia), and so forth. By contrast, acronyms designating more colorful places such as the acronym for the toilet, Kabesot (Kabinet estestvennykh otpravlenii), are still more abstract and euphemistic.

The main vehicle for negotiating one's material existence in this society is not money. Legal tender for food is what is known euphemistically as "vtorichnyi produkt," that is, "secondary produce" or excrement. Food is known as "pervichnyi produkt" or "primary produce." Such absurd slogans as "Primary produce is secondary, and secondary produce is primary" hang on all the doors of public eating halls, the only place an ordinary person can get something to eat in Moscow, short of producing the food himself. As we know, this slogan means that one has to hand in a container of one's bodily waste in order to receive food. What is more, food itself turns out to be made of the very same stuff.

Zinoviev takes his mimicry of the absurd logic of Ibansk writing and sloganeering to relentless extremes. As The Schizophrenic says, linguistic chaos is an expression of social chaos, the condition of language is emblematic of the condition of society (YH, 73). Zinoviev's treatment is founded on the logical contradictions inherent in oxymoron. Thus, The Pretender, who wants to be the next director of the institute, is said to play a "prominent, unremarkable role" in the Ibansk experiment (YH, 30). In a parody of academic style, The Schizophrenic says that his tract claims "exhaustive incompleteness and strict asystematicness" (YH, 17). One of the chief mottoes of the Ibansk experiment is that "everything obsolete and outmoded should be nipped in the bud [vse ustarevshee i otzhivshee nado dushit' v zarodyshe]" (YH, 111). Another example of absurd logic concerns the use of the word *but* (*no*), which in normal syntax marks a contrast. Here it does not, again underscoring the illogic of official thinking. For example, the narrator describes the new neighborhoods around Ibansk as having houses that are "identical in form *but* indistinguishable in content" (YH, 11; emphasis added). And The Artist (Khudozhnik), the officially acceptable counterpart to The Dauber (Mazila), receives a prize for painting "ancient" frescoes that "depicted the heroism in labor of the freedom-loving descendants [potomki], their warlike everyday existence, and the outstanding figures active in the cult of that distant *but* completely forgotten era" (YH, 10; emphasis added). It is also worth remarking here that this last example emphasizes the absurd temporal logic of Ibansk, in which future and past are confused and the future is mentioned in terms implying memory, that is, in terms with which one would speak of the past.

Meta-utopian prose effectively pares back hyperbolic, utopian language and its inhibitive effect on thinking through parodic quotation and misquotation of its main literary perpetrator, Maksim Gorky, the "stormy petrel" of the revolution and the "father" of Socialist Realism. What is addressed here is not Gorky the truly complicated historical personality, but Gorky the model of the socially and morally engaged Russian writer whose literary-political role has shifted from that of self-proclaimed social and moral conscience to that of court poet, and who has crossed the fatal boundary from political opposition to legitimization of a repressive political force that itself was once repressed. Gorky's discourse of utopian dreaming discloses a strange defenselessness with respect to authoritarian behavior. In *Rabbits and Boa Constrictors* Iskander devises a parody of the Gorky type in the figure of The Poet at the court of the Rabbit King. Using the form of an animal fable, Iskander's novella deals with the conflict between ideologies. The Spartan boa constrictors, with their crude ideology endorsing brute force, hunt the more clever, psychologically complex rabbits, who rely on their wits to live. The rabbits' mentality is essentially utopian: oppressed in their present existence, they need to believe in a better future in order not to succumb to their "natural" fate as the victims of the snakes. The rabbits are ruled by a king who legitimizes his hold on power with the utopian symbol of the Cauliflower, that is, the promise of future stability, welfare, and happiness. Soon, however, it becomes clear that the king also defends his power from all challengers through a psychology of fear (of the boas) and suspicion (of fellow rabbits), buttressed by a Byzantine network of propaganda and terror.

The Gorky look-alike among rabbits is the court Poet, whose moral conscience is co-opted by the Rabbit King's promises of lasting fame and material comfort. Like Gorky, who sported the image as the stormy petrel (*burevestnik*) of revolution, The Poet loves to write about storms. When he wants to write about the one real storm of his life, the political betrayal of a great fellow rabbit, he finds he lacks the courage to speak out against repression. The philosopher-rabbit, Thoughtful (Zadumavshiisia), poses a real challenge to the power of the throne, exposing the king's reliance on fear to keep his citizens subdued. For his trouble he is secretly betrayed by an informer to the boa constrictors, who eat him. On learning of this betrayal, The Poet feels the pangs of conscience and wants to leave the court in order to write as his conscience dictates. Perhaps more in keeping with Pushkin's biography, The Poet's wife, who enjoys the comfortable life, keeps him at court.[9] The Poet fails to write this final storm poem. He falls silent, leaving behind him an archive full of stormlike rhythms but without the appropriate words, form without the needed moral substance. The rhythms are appropriated by the Rabbit King to generate poetry in praise of himself and to harangue citizens who are in arrears on their tax payments. Thus, Iskander stresses the image of Gorky as a writer who "sold out," who did not follow the promptings of his conscience and thus lost the power to use language meaningfully.

Other writers view Gorky as one in a long line of Russian "realist" writers enamored of a utopian dream, who self-righteously and disingenuously preached their own version of the "truth," never acknowledging the fundamental abuse and distortion of language that they were perpetrating. Such a view is most strongly developed by Terts. In "The Literary Process in Russia" (1974) Terts alludes to Gorky's challenge thrown down to American journalists in 1932, "Whose Side Are You On, Masters of Culture?":

> The danger threatening modern Russian literature—banned literature, of course (the other literature is not worth considering, since artistically it is about two hundred years out of date)—is of assuming the role of a sort of whining complaints book, supposedly to be perused by the leaders (who don't give a damn anyway), or to be stored away in a cupboard until the advent of those better times when people will have learned to live by the light of truth. This attitude is one of the chronic failings of the nineteenth century.... We are again

---

[9] It should be noted, however, that Gorky's first wife, E. Peshkova, had a great deal to do with bringing the writer back to Stalinist Russia and with keeping him there. See, for example, V. F. Khodasevich, "Gor'kii," *Sovremennye zapiski* (Paris), no. 70 (1940): 131–56.

faced by the eternal Russian dilemma: Where is your allegiance, you professional purveyors of culture? Whose side are you on? Are you for truth, or for the official lie? When the question is put like that, the writer obviously has no choice but to answer proudly: for truth! . . . But in proclaiming oneself to be on the side of truth, it is worthwhile remembering what Stalin said when some brave members of the Union of Writers asked him to explain once and for all what socialist realism was. . . . The leader replied: "Write the truth—and that will be socialist realism!"

The point has been reached where we should fear the truth, lest it hang round our necks again like an albatross.[10]

In Terts's view, Gorky and the crusading tradition of literary "realism" and political utopianism to which he belongs have actually created a kind of moral "newspeak," a language made absurd through contortions and reversals in word usage. Anything that one says is "truth," so long as one stands on the "right" side and professes the "right" values.

Meta-utopian writers are quick to parody Gorkian truisms that were not credible to begin with and have been so overquoted in Socialist Realist culture that they have been completely emptied of meaning. Particularly two phrases (lifted, it should be said in all fairness, from textual situations that actually give them an ambiguous coloring) have gained the status of commonplaces. One is the exclamation of the irreverent renegade Satin in *The Lower Depths*: "Man! That has a proud ring to it!" And the other is the narrator's eulogy to the brave, if suicidal, Falcon in "The Song of the Falcon": "To the madness of the brave we sing our song." Both of these sentences have become a shorthand for a romantic, utopian reverence for a new kind of human, "Man," with a capital "M," that while seeming to reaffirm the best in human nature, a sense of dignity and honor, actually devalues human nature taken as a whole. This new "Man" is endowed with a consciousness so superior to ours that it seems insane and motivates social acts, utopian projects that in their realization really are insane. In "What Is Socialist Realism?" Terts sarcastically points to the enactment of the first five-year plan, with its reenslavement of the peasantry, as an example of the "madness of the brave."

The same phrase, comically misquoted in *Liubimov*, motivates Lënia Tikhomirov to undertake his magical utopian project. The

[10] Terts, "The Literary Process in Russia," 103–4.

whole misbegotten "experiment" is part of Tikhomirov's attempt to win the heart of Serafima Petrovna Kozlova, the local teacher of foreign languages, a member of what the narrator Savely Kuzmich calls the "quite thick layer of intellectuals" in Liubimov society. She certainly considers herself progressive, even radical, in her social views. In his first declaration of love Tikhomirov offers to paper their bedroom walls with three-ruble notes and to install automatic doors, if only she will be his wife. Serafima Petrovna snubs him, alluding to Gorky as a way of reaffirming her "high-minded" social values: "And keep in mind: I have only contempt for wealth and money, but I value ambition in a man. 'The madness of the brave is the wisdom of life,' as Maksim Gorky said" (L, 350). Here she alludes to a concept of ambition discussed in Gorky's early story "The Reader," but she misunderstands Gorky's high valuation of honor, or *chest'*, and low estimation of ambition, *chestoliubie*, or an empty love of honor that leads people to do what will make them admired by others.[11] To punctuate her profession of faith, she throws down the challenge that she will accept nothing less than the whole town of Liubimov at her feet! Serafima Petrovna's misquotation from "The Song of the Falcon" shows her fundamentally empty philistine views. "Wisdom of life," in Gorky's early romantic view, is certainly the opposite of the madness of the brave, referring rather to a passive submission to existing conditions. Thus, Serafima Petrovna negates the romantic bravado of Gorky's phrase, and her high-mindedness is exposed as half-educated vacuity. But Tikhomirov does not know that, and soon he finds an answer to her megalomaniacal ambitions.

Both the Strugatsky brothers and Terts refer to Satin's speech in *The Lower Depths* in a way that belies its overtly affirming message. *The Ugly Swans* is built on the struggle between generations. A younger generation, raised in the morally dishonest atmosphere of a local boarding school, rejects the erstwhile utopian aspirations and achievements of their elders, putting forth their own youthfully arrogant, intransigent program for social renewal. In a debate with the novel's protagonist, the writer Viktor Banev, they quote Gorky's "Man! That has a proud ring to it!" as a piece of silly, even contemptible sentimentalism typical of their parents' generation: "You've been beaten on the head, excuse the expression, and you persist in repeat-

---

[11] For more on this point, see my discussion in *The Revolution of Moral Consciousness*, 192–93.

ing that man by nature is good, or, even worse, that the name 'man' has a proud ring" (US, 73). The young reject moral anesthesia, the peaceful nihilism with which their parents live, proposing instead a new world that, as Viktor sees, is founded on the same old shortcomings of the utopian impulse: a total rejection of the past and intolerance of other views. Neither side, thus, is "right." Nonetheless, the students, with their moral freshness and vitality, succeed in undermining whatever credibility Gorky's overused utopianism may have once had by pointing out the incongruity between intention and enactment.

Terts clearly has the most sustained quarrel with Gorky as a still-potent model of the socially engaged writer who vociferously affirms the veracity of his literary art. In *Liubimov* he cites Satin's words to show the distance between stated faith in humanity and actual scorn for real people. On accepting his new post as "tsar," Tikhomirov grants amnesty to all the prisoners. He exhorts them: "Be people! Don't steal, don't murder, don't falsify documents and don't do other crimes that demean your high human dignity. . . . Remember: man— that has a proud ring to it!" (L, 373). Of course, the freed prisoners hurry to get drunk on the water that has magically been turned into 100 percent alcohol. What is more, Tikhomirov, who professes to have such high hopes for humanity, mimics Stalin in his own enactment of a social project much like the infamous construction of the Belomor Canal. Gorky hailed Stalin's cynical use of highly educated, political prisoners, alleged "enemies of the people"—forced labor that ended in countless deaths—as an example of the remolding of human nature that must precede true communism. Tikhomirov boasts that in a year Liubimov can be outproducing two small, wealthy European competitors, Belgium and Holland. With this end in mind he hypnotizes the local citizenry into digging drainage ditches in the fields around Liubimov. He exhorts them: "Hold your heads higher! Step more boldly! Smile more merrily! Remember this: no one is forcing you to work! You yourselves want to outfulfill the quotas by 200 percent. . . . You feel a surging in your hearts, a tireless energy in your muscles. You are yearning to plunge your feet into the mud" (L, 379). Thus, Terts, like the Strugatskys, stresses the hypocrisy of such high-minded professions of faith, the contradiction between word and action that undermines the ability of the word to mean anything at all.

In *Moscow-Petushki*, Erofeev misquotes from a variety of bulwarks of Soviet culture, always applying them to the virtues of overtippling.[12] But his main and consistent target is Gorky, who emerges as a false moralist. He introduces Gorky obliquely when he recommends Aleksandr Blok's "Nightingale Garden" to his fellow cable-fitters as a poem of current interest whose hero is "fired from work for drunkenness, whoring, and absenteeism" (MP, 17). He buttresses his own opinion by citing Lenin's comment about Gorky's novel *Mother*: "A very timely book ... you'll read it to great personal advantage" (MP, 17).

Gorky is associated with sanctimonious toadyism and false optimism. When Venichka draws up his charts of his workers' drinking habits over a month, he finds that the self-righteous Aleksei Blindiaev has a chart that resembles the "beating of a proud heart, the song of the stormy petrel" (MP, 18). Blindiaev is the same person who informed the authorities about these charts, an act that resulted in Venichka's termination.

Gorky is such an important figure here because for all his falseness, he is still a formidable voice of moral conscience capable of making Venichka feel guilty. Women are the very abused and very elevated "other" in Venichka's monologue. Women's private parts are the very essence of Venichka's paradise, about which Venichka waxes most lyrical. And yet a woman is reduced to a bottle of liquor.[13] One voice suggests also that women exist only to take away men's empty liquor bottles and give them full ones (MP, 41). While Erofeev is quite modest in his scatological descriptions—for example, in the argument he has with his roommates about going to the bathroom or his descriptions of his fellow males, except those that deceive him, like Blindiaev—he is consistently hostile in his treatment of women. He does not distinguish between the deceptive and nondeceptive. All are *bliad'* (whore) or *gadina* (vermin). It is assumed that women deceive and that they will abuse a man at any possible opportunity. Only in the single case of the "heavenly queen" or "she-devil" does Erofeev become lyrical. Against this sexist carnival Gorky reminds Venichka: "The measure of any civilization is the way it treats women." This

[12] See Al'tshuller, "'Moskva-Petushki' Venedikta Erofeeva," 80–81; Svetlana Gaiser-Shnitman, *Venedikt Erofeev: "Moskva-Petushki" ili "The Rest is Silence"* (Bern: Peter Lang, 1989), 145.

[13] I. A. Paperno and B. M. Gasparov, "'Vstan' i idi,'" *Slavica Hierosolymitana*, nos. 5–6 (1981): 387–400.

thought sounds both true and quite inadequate to the task of addressing the deep hostilities basic to human nature (MP, 41).

Venichka's argument with Gorky continues as he meditates on the question about whether women really only exist to exchange a man's bottles for him or so that men can respect them. He imagines going to the Petushki store to hand in his empties and get a refill. The store manager owes him a ruble for the exchange. He does not trust the woman to give him the change and imagines her wondering, "Shall I give the vermin the change or not" (MP, 41). Along with this feeling of enmity, the Gorkyesque conscience in him is awakened in an incongruous and silly way as a kind of magnanimous nobility:

> What arises before my senseless gaze? The island of Capri [where Gorky lived just after the revolution] arises. The century plants and tamarinds are growing, and under them sits Maksim Gorky, his hairy legs [showing] from under his white trousers. And he shakes his finger at me: "Don't take the change! Don't take the change!" I wink at him . . . "OK, I'll have a drink but what am I going to munch on?" And he says: "Never mind, Venia, you'll survive without it. And if you want to eat, then don't drink." So I leave without any change. (MP, 41)

Feeling sorry for himself, Venichka accuses Gorky (much as Maiakovsky and others did in the 1920s) of judging a situation he is in no position to judge, moralizing from a position of comfort and well-being on his sunny island. Gorky is the false moralist.

Finally, as a clever way of delineating the meta-utopian human condition, Zinoviev parodies the social views expressed in Gorky's Stalin-period article "A Conversation about My Trade" (1930–1931). In this essay, which purports to explain the making of a Socialist Realist writer, Gorky claims that he developed his social morality, summarized by the phrase "Support the rebellious person," in conscious opposition to what he says is Nietzsche's repressive social "master" morality, "Push the falling person down" (YH, 320–21). The artist, The Dauber, says that in Ibansk society the weak have learned to stand on their own by enforcing mediocrity and conformity. The Big Mouth comments that it is not a promising sign for society when the "strong" people with initiative need all the help they can get. Indeed, he thinks up a new motto for those who stand up for their own ideas and resist the oppressive status quo. In English his motto sounds something like: "Hel-l-l-p the little strong guy! [Pomogi-i-i-te sil'nenkomu!]" (YH, 261). The intonation of this statement is at least as important as its semantic quality. The protracted diction of "hel-l-l-p" suggests the utterance of someone who is already falling or drowning and threatened with immediate ruin.

Through such mimicry of Gorky meta-utopian authors succeed in toppling a standard of utopian discourse and verbal "creativity" that has long oppressed the irreverent experimentalists among Russian writers. In his place they set a notion of the writer as a player of verbal games, an expert at creating fictions, who nonetheless, as Terts says, may "refuse to tell lies" and is doubly aware of the deception at the heart of authoritative claims to "truth."[14]

In his article "The Literary Process in Russia" Terts defines the central language problem to which meta-utopian fiction addresses itself: the confrontation with the bipolar, either/orthinking at the heart of utopian ideology. He argues that "communism" (which could easily be transcribed as "utopia" in Terts's critical oeuvre) and its popular rival, "realism," are linguistic mirror images of each other. Both make highly self-righteous claims to "truth" and, although both may once have, neither in the present day commands the linguistic power to define adequate moral and social values. Terts's major criticism of so-called realists is their use of negative forms of "communist" expression: "Why take as the yardstick of your own value something which you find worthless? How can you define yourself in relation to a negative? We shall never break away from 'realism-communism' if we are constantly glancing back at those words. We don't say: 'I'm an anti-liar!' or 'I'm anti-beast, anti-mass-murderer.' If you are a human being, why do you need to go on proving every day that you have long since evolved beyond the animal state?"[15] Terts thus focuses on the relationship between utopian thinking and realist style.[16] At its heart lies an irresolvable paradox of the classic type:

A: "B is lying."
B: "A is telling the truth."

Here each statement undermines the veracity of the other with its assumption of its own truth-value and its reference to the truthful-

[14] Terts, "The Literary Process in Russia," 104.
[15] Ibid., 105.
[16] Besides "The Literary Process in Russia," see "Solzhenitsyn kak ustroitel' novogo edinomysliia," *Sintaksis*, no. 14 (1985): 16–32; and "Chtenie v serdtsakh," *Sintaksis*, no. 17 (1987): 191–205.

ness of its opponent. Assuming that A is correct and that B's statement, that A is indeed telling the truth, is a lie, then we immediately reach a contradiction: A is telling the truth, and A is not telling the truth. The same holds for an analysis of B's veracity. The point is that in this particular situation the issue of truthfulness cannot be resolved.

Terts clearly belongs to a series of twentieth-century literary theorists who find the claims to truthfulness inherent in literary realism to be problematic. Roman Jakobson in "On Realism in Art" (1921) points out that since the term *realism* was coined, each ensuing style claiming to be realist has questioned the truthfulness of preceding styles that also claimed to be realist. By undermining the credibility of earlier styles, the new realism attempts to establish its own credibility as the most realistic and truthful style.[17] In other words, it assumes the position of A in the paradox above with respect to "realist" predecessors who take the position of B. By comparison to the new, fresh, "truthful" way of writing, these predecessors seem hackneyed and artificial and, thus, seem indirectly to support the claims of the newcomer to greater believability. Thus, as Jakobson argues, "realism" is at best a relative concept, strongly conditioned by historical context. Its claim to truth can never be verified and is justified only by the intuitive response of the reader.

If we substitute *realism* for A and *art* for B in the paradox above, we come to something like the problem that Terry Eagleton finds with the concept of literary realism.[18] Namely, realism effaces its own character as an aesthetic object, placing itself close to the unknowable "thing-in-itself," reality, and undermining other kinds of art, particularly nonrepresentational, fantastic, or abstract art.[19] Meanwhile, given the proliferation of realisms since the nineteenth century—social and socialist, mystical, romantic, critical, psychological, magical, and so forth—even fantastic, nonrepresentational art has bought into the realist mythos, claiming some higher truthfulness for itself.

It is in this context that Terts's ingenious play with realism can best be appreciated. The paradoxical relationship between realism and

---

[17] Roman Jakobson, "On Realism in Art," in *Readings in Russian Poetics: Formalist and Structuralist Views*, ed. L. Matejka and K. Pomorska (Ann Arbor: University of Michigan Press, 1978), 38–46.
[18] Eagleton, *Literary Theory*, 136.
[19] Ibid., 135–36.

other forms of fantasy with regard to their claims to truth is well illustrated in *Liubimov* where Savely Kuzmich travesties the canonical realist and Lënia Tikhomirov—the creator of phantasmagorias. The "author" who turns both of them into actors in a tale about making utopia into reality, Samson Samsonovich, most importantly contains the paradox within himself, in that his dreaming, romantic mentality and his efforts at a scientific, "realist" diction undermine each other.

Savely Kuzmich, with his utter artlessness, represents what Terts suggests literary "realism" *really* is: a loyalty to "facts" so radical that Savely is incapable of ordering his material in any way suited to achieving some desired effect upon the reader. His very first judgment about art is a condemnation of fantasy:

> One thing spoils everything—when a writer suddenly lets go with his fantasy. You are sitting there, agonizing, and perhaps you have chills running down your spine, and he, as it turns out, has dreamed all this up in his head. No, if you start writing, then write about what you have seen yourself or at least have heard about from trustworthy sources. So that the reader's spirit, traveling along the pages, will not spoil its invaluable vision in vain, but will get reliable and useful information for its own inner development. It, the spirit, that is, wants to live and grow wealthy [bogatet'], with its eyes sucking from the book someone else's warm blood, and not just empty air. (L, 338–39)

Obviously, Savely Kuzmich undermines his own faithfulness to the facts when he does not differentiate between observable reality—events that are accessible to the senses—and a sphere that is accessible only through symbol, that is, the realm of mind and spirit.

Much like Gogol's narrator in *Dead Souls*, Savely Kuzmich has no idea how to order, describe, and evaluate events. He becomes indignant at details and events that continually force themselves into his narrative, and he soon loses control over his material. He starts his account:

> ... One day I come out onto the small porch and see...
> No, wait. It's too early for that. In the first place, why "I"? and why "I come out"? What is this bad habit of inserting oneself into everything! And, anyway, it wasn't I who came out at that point onto the small porch, but he, he, Lënia Tikhomirov—our chief bicycle mechanic. In the second place, all these details, they really get in the

way. If a small porch made an appearance, then that means I have to describe it—how it was, the small porch—high or low, did it have carved columns, and, if so—and on and on, and you don't even notice how you get to telling about something quite different. (L, 340)

Savely Kuzmich hits upon the technique of footnotes used in one of his favorite models for "truthful" writing, academic historiography. He decides to put all "secondary" details in the footnotes "for ease of reading," and ends up instead putting his own opinions as well as important elements of the plot there. Most importantly, it is through Savely's footnotes that both the self-proclaimed author of this fantasy, Samson Samsonovich, and the fantasy's most admiring audience, the Soviet spy Kochetov, enter the narrative. Instead of serving as a measure of veracity, the footnotes become emblematic of the degree to which Savely Kuzmich loses control over his enterprise.

Being a "realist," in this sense, suggests having no design, no guiding idea, and no control over one's material. It does, dangerously, suggest a willingness on the part of the writer to become a cipher in someone else's project, much like The Poet in Iskander's *Rabbits and Boa Constrictors*, who prepares empty forms but lacks the courage to use them to express his own views and feelings, with the result that the Rabbit King uses them for his own propaganda.

This lack of control leads us to remark on a third characteristic that defines a realist, a total allegiance to some notion of "objectivism." Objectivism in Savely Kuzmich's case means a refusal to evaluate people and events. Much like a medieval Russian monk who would claim to be an empty vessel waiting to be filled with God's word, Savely Kuzmich insists that he is a "self-writing pen [samopishushchee pero]" (L, 339). Although his overt goal is to assure the reader of his total objectivity, it soon becomes clear that his attempts to remove his own opinions from his story have another motivation: the instinct for survival. Savely Kuzmich knows the dangers involved with writing. As he puts it, "Reading is a far cry from writing" (L, 340). A person can sit and read "in peace and quiet, in safety" (L, 340). Writing involves being called to task, taking responsibility for what one writes. It is safer to keep one's thoughts to oneself. He prefers to go fishing or sit in a steam bath. As we know, what finally decides his fate as a writer is Samson Samsonovich, who emerges as a new voice from the text and enlists Savely Kuzmich as his mouthpiece, thus relieving him of personal responsibility for what he writes. Subsequently, Tikhomirov hypnotizes him and commands him to write a heroic account of his exploits. Savely Kuzmich is left with no choice but to write down the "irresponsible words [bezotvetstvennye slova]" (L, 340) that come to him.

Both Samson Samsonovich and Lënia Tikhomirov are dreamers who live only in the "subjective" world of their fantasies. Each appropriates the veil of credibility that literary realism enjoys in order to legitimize his own wholly unreal utopian fantasy as "reality." A key to Samson Samsonovich's imagination is his embarrassment at its ontological stature and his determination that it be "real." This romantic spirit disguising itself as realism provides the context for a further elaboration of the paradox discussed earlier:

> Realism (scientifically verifiable description): "Romanticism (creative imagination, intuition, flight of fancy) is lying."
> Romanticism: "Realism is telling the truth."

In his 1830s self, the protean Samson Samsonovich stands ideologically on the brink between metaphysical romanticism, which is in the process of being discredited, and a utopian, social radicalism in which the dreamer can find a more acceptable outlet. When he first takes over the narrative from Savely Kuzmich, in chapter 3, his style mixes a clumsy, self-conscious, "realist" attention to detail and a reliance on "scientific" objectivity with a romantic inclination for the mystic and mysterious, for experience that is not immediately accessible to the senses. His description of the dawn brightening over Liubimov shows him groping for the "right" words: "I arrive in this city [Liubimov] in the early, early dawn, when the sun has not yet risen over the monastery wall, and everything is covered with a gray stratum of air, a shroud, mist—better put, when any object is giving off its last nocturnal warmth and the glimmering that enwraps its coarse dark skeleton in the likeness of a shaggy cocoon" (L, 359).

Proferansov's romantic predilection for phantasmagoria is directed into what for the middle of the nineteenth century would have been a more acceptable channel in revolutionary ardor. He gives himself over to imagining the last dreams that Liubimov's citizens might have before waking. But here he goes on to make a political, rather than a metaphysical, point, something again that would seem more "scientifically" acceptable. People sleep soundly before dawn, he claims, because "in sleep things become firm as they lose strength in the waking world" (L, 359). He imagines the townsfolk running wild and a peasant "performing world revolution for the *n*th time" by raping a governor's daughter. Such are the "acts of insurrection" that one could never perform in the stagnant, oppressive atmosphere of the real Russian countryside, but in which one can indulge during sleep.

The point of all these remarks is that "scientific" social experiments and "real" utopia are oxymorons. The mentality out of which nineteenth-century Russian utopianism emerged, Terts implies, was strongly romantic, but a romantic mentality embarrassed at itself and needing a new justification. The yearning for transcendence, to explore the realm beyond the senses, beyond the threshold between life and death, became laughable in the context of newly emerging scientific positivism. Still, the urge to rise above the merely human condition survived. The issue of creative fantasy is implied in Samson Samsonovich's narratives, in the sense that the life of the fantasy, the dreamworld, is first devalued here. The imagination as such is feckless, considered a poor surrogate for "real" social action and social change.

The discourse of realized utopia emerges in the stalemate created by the realism-romanticism paradox. It stakes territorial rights to both reality and fantasy and blurs the differences between them. Its key characteristic is its exclusive claim to truth, expressed in linguistic "monologism" and social authoritarianism. Utopian discourse here enforces a closed, unitary language system that permits no challenges to itself. It eventually becomes susceptible to absurdity in its very inability to change and its inadequacy to the multiple semantic possibilities inherent in language. The limitations thereby placed on creative play are obvious. At every opportunity Terts takes special pleasure in undermining the credibility of this singular, coercive utopian voice.

Samson Samsonovich's authoritarianism becomes immediately apparent when he emerges from Savely Kuzmich's footnotes, as if in answer to the chronicler's plea for some "objective" authority to guide his writing. In his bid for total linguistic control of the narrative he reduces Savely Kuzmich's already very fragile hold on style and narrative order to total gibberish (L, 356–58). Here is no room for a creative "other," as poorly as Savely Kuzmich might fill that role!

As Nietzsche suggests, the purpose of language as a communicative medium is to enforce conformity of social consciousness. Utopian discourse in *Liubimov* fulfills this purpose with the major difference that social and linguistic conformity here is generated from above by a single personality. For example, Samson Samsonovich in his nineteenth-century self enters the sleepy hamlet of Liubimov early one nineteenth-century morning and exhorts the sleeping townspeople to "arise." He imagines Liubimov as a "wonderful utopia" led by a commander full of passionate enthusiasm. His exhortation insists incongruously that these very people would be "liberated" by despotic rule:

> If [Liubimov] were to be fattened up, given liberty, a signal, and a reliable little person in a visible position, you'd find out what would happen next. . . . But what indeed would happen next? How this city could surprise and give joy if one were to say to it: "Arise, you've slept enough! The day of your glory has arrived! Here you have enough power to turn your dreams into real life. Here, quench your thirst for a kind and powerful tsar. I'll give you the commander endowed with insensitive power that you've been dreaming of for three hundred years" (L, 360).

No one responds because everyone is in his or her own monological world, a private dreamworld, the last few moments of sleep. Proferansov's coercive thinking is an outgrowth of that linguistic mode, and, as such, it gets the nonreception that it deserves. As a closed system that fabricates its own meaning, authoritarian speech needs no interlocutors.

Tikhomirov's authoritarianism is an echo of Samson Samsonovich's, acquired when he gains magical power from his predecessor's tract, *The Psychic Magnet*. To begin with, when he has not yet discovered Samson Samsonovich's book (or, more accurately, been discovered by it—it falls on his head from the rafters where it has been serving as insulation) and does not yet hold power, Tikhomirov seems a dreamer, harmless enough. In distinction to a rather acerbic fellow citizen, the naturalist Dr. Linde, who thinks that "man is a monkey without a tail" (L, 348) and is irredeemable, Tikhomirov wants to believe in the perfectibility of human nature. His dreaming is imbued with authoritarianism, however, as he starts to imagine *how* to make human nature better. As he learns the techniques of magnetism put forth by S. S. Proferansov, he starts to experiment on the narrator Savely Kuzmich, to whom he confesses his social dreams, and whom he then hypnotizes and turns physically upside down. The earth, he says, can be turned into a "flowerbed" (L, 355).

It is his intention to fill the role of the strong leader, to teach people "the right way to think," to teach them "to respect labor and love their native land," and "limitlessly to increase their material and cultural level" (L, 355). This last sounds very unorthodox, much like a call to enrich oneself, until Tikhomirov points to his volume of Engels and clarifies that he means "material" as it pertains to matter, that is, in Engels' sense that consciousness is the highest level of matter. Thus, Tikhomirov shows himself to be bound by the framework of Marxist-Leninist thinking: people are not meant to become richer and more prosperous, something that might be a basis for real freedom, but merely more "conscious."

With Tikhomirov's celebration of his ascension to power and his marriage to Serafima Petrovna, the problematic relationship between utopia, realism, and creative imagination reemerges in a more concrete form. Tikhomirov exposes his intolerance of free creative fantasy and subordinates literary "talent" to his political will. He tells Savely Kuzmich not to drink so much, to sober up and turn his mind to chronicling the development of the perfect society: "Your task as a writer, as the city historiographer, is tirelessly to study reality in its steadfast development and to give to each fact its truthful reflection. Be our mirror, our Lev Tolstoi, whom the people justifiably nicknamed 'the mirror of the revolution.' Look about you, penetrate the surrounding life and then reflect it fully in your historical memoirs" (L, 371). Tikhomirov demands that his chronicler not use fantasy, imagination, or powers of interpretation but produce an exact eyewitness account, something that includes the personal details of a memoir and the epic facts of a city chronicle. Writing should be a "mirror," reflecting events. The following description of Liubimov on the day it becomes "utopia" gives an excellent practical exercise in this antiaesthetic theory. Throughout "realist" detail belies the monumental glory of "realized" utopia. Savely Kuzmich, who is still clearly drunk, to judge from his eye that roves almost uncontrollably between sky and ground, combines clumsy description of the celebrations and pompous apostrophes to Tikhomirov with completely candid vignettes of the squalorous landscape surrounding them:

> The city lay beneath them like a tattered blanket, mussed [perebu-torennoe] and thrown into Bacchic disarray. Red flags and tablecloths, raspberry-colored jumpers quilted by the breeze, argued with the winter crop's green color of the village tiller of the soil [khlebopa-

shets], which from the heights of the heavens wedged into the narrow gully, splitting into two the iron nakedness of the shrubbery. (L, 371)

Savely Kuzmich abandons pompous, high-flown turns of phrase for a breathlessly long list of details about the Liubimov landscape rendered in colloquial language:

> And if we also take into account the bottle-colored bends [izluchiny] and sleeves of the river, molded here and there by teeming city-dwellers, and add to that the curvatures [iskrivlenie] of small streets, dead ends, backyards, and a small church tilting to one side with a collapsed cupola and masses of crows, the faded graveyard with its petty [melkii] crosses and the yellow coffin of the hospital with the thickset dark-brown prison, an empty lot full of trash and a solitary byway, glimmering at liberty [na razdol'e] with silvery rivulets [zmeiki] of undried muck, plus the elm in the pasture, the fences, the hullaballoo of the dogs, plus the slightly crazed accordion, the shaggy smoke from the chimneys and over the smoke—the round-maned clouds speeding like horses—if, I repeat, we put all this together and shuffle it enough, we get the picture that opened before our astonished public. (L, 371)

The grandeur of the victory celebration is completely, if unintentionally, sabotaged by the "realist's" eye for ugly detail. As his attention wavers between the distant and the near, the high and the low, heavy, archaic hyperbole becomes incongruously mixed together with substandard idiom and inappropriate personifications of nature that call forth a spirit of ill-will, poverty, deathliness, and physical deformity. The details fail to be synthesized into the celebratory "picture" that Savely Kuzmich insists he is creating. Subverted by their observer's overanxious efforts to form a picture, they remain flat, a mere list. Two notions of "objectivity"—the rigor of detailed, dispassionate observation and the conviction that one is witnessing an event of world-historical importance—are at loggerheads in Savely Kuzmich's diction: "This is a picture worthy of the brush of a painter. . . . The age-old dream of the people has come true, been realized. Here it is—the land of milk and honey! Here it is—the Kingdom of Heaven, which, scientifically speaking, would be better termed a leap into the radiant future. Never before in the history of humanity has there been such concern for the living person" (L, 371).

Throughout meta-utopian fiction such monological discourse is exposed as a linguistic dead end. Particularly so-called literary realism is shown to cancel its own character as aesthetic construct and to deny the credibility and veracity of all such constructs. Its aversion to the fantastic, and, indeed, aesthetic values as such, is powerful enough to compel the most egregious phantasmagorias, of which Samson Samsonovich's and Lënia's utopian dreams are clear examples, to seek legitimacy by claiming that they too represent a form of realism. All dialogue between ideological opponents—proponents of art as representation and proponents of art as play—is sealed off because these opponents no longer acknowledge themselves as such. The field of signification thus loses its middle ground, in which debate and negotiation between differences can take place and fresh sense can be created. Thus flattened, language becomes vulnerable to total control by a single voice strong enough to impose its own definition of "reality," as insane as that definition may be.

In his article "The Literary Process in Russia," Terts takes one more step to undo the conviction that literary realism is somehow an antidote to utopian thinking run amok. Gorky's utopian-communist Socialist Realism and Solzhenitsyn's nationalist critical realism are not real alternatives but rather two similar quantities involved in a "looking-glass war," to borrow John Le Carré's term for the cold war. More importantly, they are both allies in the real war against art-as-play, the kind of art with a really different concept of language and truly critical outlook able to expose the vicious circle in which all realisms are caught.

There are three alternatives to demands for blind faith. One is to resort to silence in order to resist what Terts ironically calls the "truth," a monological distortion of language and meaning. The option of "wise" silence, which Bitov acknowledges but resists, is the solution of the townspeople of Liubimov as they wait patiently for Tikhomirov's experiment to run its course. Silence is also the solution for Savely Kuzmich and Tikhomirov, both of whom retreat to a private, unlanguaged world after Samson Samsonovich retracts his magical powers.

Another possibility is to insist on the "concrete," nonmetaphorical (if such is possible) use of language. Writers such as Bitov in "Notes" or Petrushevskaia in "The New Robinsons" refuse to attach to linguistic signs any abstract meaning. In Chapter 10 we will discuss how Petrushevskaia uses language as a kind of "return to one's senses."

Images are linked at most to concrete and private sensory perception. The author claims to speak for no one but herself, and images used are not allowed to become magnified into universal, abstract ideas. And, finally, a strongly meta-utopian alternative is to apprehend the chinks in the armor of monological modes of social valuation and to incite dispute and dialogue between them. Meta-utopian writers hint at something like the dialogism that Bakhtin sees as the heart of the novel. No "teaching" or orthodoxy is allowed to stand unchallenged. Within what Bakhtin calls the "speaking person," whether of the protagonist, the narrator, or the cited passage that resonates throughout the text, there emerges an ambiguity, a skepticism that is ruinous of the monological, authoritarian faith that utopian consciousness typically involves.

It is interesting to note that this alternative is most commonly suggested by its marked absence. For example, in *The Condemned City* the failure of dialogue is striking. All conditions point to the possibility of debate between characters of the most varied ideological backgrounds. A central concern of this novel is the crisis proportions of the language problem, the *lack* of real dialogue, the *lack* of ability among the characters to articulate their own ideas and to understand those of fellow citizens. Despite the fact that everyone shares the same language, no one is really able fully to articulate his own view or to understand another point of view. This *kosnoiazychie* or lack of articulation is particularly evident in the protagonist, Andrei, who is unable to penetrate anyone else's way of thinking and, as a result, cannot scrutinize his own from a critical distance. The result is a repetition in The Experiment of some conflation of the two great Western utopian monologist systems, Nazism and Stalinism, to create peace, order, and welfare, but without meaning. The lack of dialogue has as its worst effect the suicide of some characters and the deepening silence of others.

The problem of dialogue is most forcefully presented in *The Yawning Heights*. We have seen how language in Ibansk society has become absurd, losing its logic and its ability to mean. However, this play with words and logic abates considerably in the various social and aesthetic tracts by Zinoviev's four chief protagonists where the linguistic and social chaos of Ibansk is scrutinized and serious debate goes on. Dialogue is salvaged from the cacophony of illogic in these characters' various projects and efforts to make sense of their environment and to respond to the others' serious challenges to social and linguistic absurdity.

What emerges is a picture of two basic kinds of social structure that could be compared to Ferdinand Tönnies' concept of *Gemeinschaft*, or a primitive community of feeling centered on some all-powerful leader, which informs the structures of both Ibansk society and The Truthteller's alternative to it, and *Gesellschaft*, or a civil society organized around voluntary networks and organizations and supported by the notion of the rights of individual citizens. As The Schizophrenic implies, "socism," or simply "ism," which was meant to produce the ideal human being in an ideal social setting, is in fact based on very primitive social organization and reinforces the crudest human motivations, which he calls "social laws." As it is somewhat cryptically put in the very first pages of the book, "Socism is an imaginary social order which would come into being if individuals were to behave toward one another within society in complete accordance with the social laws" (YH, 9) The "social laws," as The Schizophrenic later explains, are monological, aphoristic statements of the type: "Give less and take more," "Less risk and more advantage," (YH, 38) and "For one social individual the greatest danger is another social individual superior to him in potential" (YH, 101). The result of these social laws, ironically reinforced in "ism," is "hypocrisy, violence, corruption, bad management, lack of personal answerability, irresponsibility, shoddy workmanship, impudence, laziness, disinformation, deception, drabness, the system of privileges, etc." (YH, 40). "Ism" thus produces a cloying mediocrity and conformism, where exceptional individuals are discouraged from distinguishing themselves from the group.

One of the main claims of the Ibansk experiment in "ism" is to be progressive. The Schizophrenic insists that this claim is a contradiction in terms. Real progress emerges only in civil society, a society that curbs the force of the "natural" social laws. Social institutions, such as moral and legal codes, art, religion, the press, public opinion, and so forth, are completely lacking in such a primitive society. In Ibansk society there is no force to counter natural impulses.

The Schizophrenic's fate is proof of his theory that the "ism" in which he lives is, indeed, a monological system. His theory is denied open debate. He is castigated for stepping out of line by his colleagues who support "official" ideology. He is labeled a "deviant from the norm" for his theory. Official criticism boils down to the opinion that The Schizophrenic does not "like" "ism," and, therefore, that he is an enemy. Finally, he is put into a mental hospital. His theory is discounted as an empty abstraction. In his own defense, The Schizophrenic says that it is the people who step out of line who are most civilized. These people represent a "protest and defense against the norm" (YH, 117). About his theory he says that, on the contrary, his concept of the social laws is much more "real" and durable than the "ism" that his ideological opponents consider to be "reality" (YH, 116).

In conclusion, we need to consider whether this play with language has really produced new consciousness or alternative ways of thinking about society. Has a kind of "meta-thought" emerged, a larger framework that allows one to become conscious of the effects of one's acquired social values? Or does meta-utopian writing merely reemphasize the linguistic dead end that Platonov implied was the fate of utopian thinking? It seems to me that meta-utopian fiction implicitly reasserts the importance of the paradox raised by Dostoevsky, Berdiaev, and Huxley. It is well summarized by Anton Zimin, one of the characters in Zinoviev's *The Radiant Future*: "I believe that the brightest dreams and ideals of humanity, when they are realized in concrete form, produce the most disastrous consequences" (RF, 185). As the underground man says, ideals are to be striven for, but not to be achieved. It is in the quest for meaning, the conscious balancing and judging of the multiplicity of meanings that inhere in language, and not in the enforcement of one interpretation and one fossilized consciousness, that meaning itself can be found. The paradox and wordplay of meta-utopia continually reassert this vital aspect of language, the denial of which turns consciousness quickly into dogma, into fixated consciousness.

As Anton puts it, the real function of all ideological formulations, including utopian schemes, is to give social groups a way to defend themselves against the worst conditions facing them. Yet if one does not become aware of the terms of these formulations and how they affect one's attitudes and behavior, one has merely confined oneself to another prison house. One's best defense is a complex mentality including what Terts would call hypothetical thinking, a sense of irony, parody, and a strong will to search out the paradox in one's condition. Such an approach allows one to do what The Slanderer in *The Yawning Heights* calls "clearing oneself of the future" (YH, 167), that is, separating ideology from its claim to absolute truth and regaining the necessary perspective of one's own personal judgment (YH, 168).

The kinds of consciousness that emerge in this writing rely very much on paradox. For example, as Terts suggests, to be truthful one has to challenge the "truths" enforced in unitary systems. To be "good" one needs to take an oppositionist stance to the reigning ideology. As The Slanderer says, "if you want to be a friend—become an enemy, such is the sad fate of any decent person who dares to do good" (YH, 212). The good person must develop in herself the "constant experience of resistance" (YH, 253), that is, of being "other" to the existing system, but without becoming herself or causing others to become what Zinoviev calls "anti-citizens," merely hostile or cynical forces in society.

This attitude leaves more questions open than it answers. The *form* of the future is very unclear. What is undeniable is the move on the part of wordplay in this fiction to bring out an ironic consciousness in its implied reader. The sociologist Zinoviev sees this reader in terms of the thinking, self-conscious citizen in the context of a civil society. Although other writers are less explicit, all write and use language in such a way as to develop a consciousness of difference not only in the literary sphere but also in the intellectual, social, and political spheres. The particular goal of meta-utopian writers is to find the linguistic cracks in ideological façades and to create places for personal consciousness and language in the monolith of public language. Those who recognize and defamiliarize monologism can open the way to a multiplicity of voices and social consciousnesses that permit coexistence and dialogue between many perspectives and modes of valuation.

* CHAPTER SIX *

Meta-utopian Consciousness

A CONSIDERATION of consciousness provides an appropriate end point for understanding the interaction between aesthetic experiment and ideological critique in meta-utopian fiction. In its challenge to exclusivist modes of social imagination and practice there emerges in this art a different mentality characterized by an insistence on balancing public and private modes of discourse, a love of ideological play, and an acknowledgment of the thinking, discerning person. The meta-utopian consciousness is built on a distinction between apparent ideological differences (for example, the looking-glass war between modes of realism) and significant valuative oppositions and choices (for example, between didactic and ludic art, between *Gemeinschaft* and *Gesellschaft*, and the like).

Meta-utopian characters exist by dint of the ideological cross fire in which they stand and the extravagance of which they highlight. To use Bakhtin's formulation, they are "precisely the image of a language," that is, each character is first and foremost a voice representing some system of values: a "speaking person" who assumes a critical position on the border between the reigning ideology and its acknowledged opponents, casting them in a new light, exposing the vicious circle of signification in which they coexist, and making possible the emancipation and regeneration of language and of meaning.[1]

Characters in meta-utopian fiction appear in the most varied of guises. Some, such as Daniel's protagonist Tolia Kartsev in *Moscow Speaking*, or the writer Viktor Banev in the Strugatskys' *The Ugly Swans*, bear a strong resemblance to their counterparts in realist fiction, with individual names and individual social and psychological identities. Most meta-utopias, however, reduce external attributes to a minimum, the better to focus on the "speaking person." Erofeev's protagonist shares the author's name and exists only as a voice that then spins new voices and personalities from itself.[2] All of Zinoviev's

---

[1] Bakhtin, *The Dialogic Imagination*, 336.
[2] Paperno and Gasparov, "'Vstan' i idi,'" 397.

characters in *The Yawning Heights* have the same last name, Ibanov. They are distinguished, if at all, only by epithets, such as The Big Mouth (Boltun), The Slanderer (Klevetnik), and The Colleague (Kollega). Iskander's rabbits, Thoughtful (Zadumavshiisia) and Resourceful (Nakhodchivyi), in *Rabbits and Boa Constrictors*, likewise have only an epithet that identifies them as a psychological or social type. At first glance these epithets seem a rather flimsy way of distinguishing them from each other. Soon, of course, it becomes clear that it is their voices that set them apart. Anonymity is another technique used in this fiction that throws emphasis onto the speaking voice. For example, Petrushevskaia's narrator in "The New Robinsons" never discloses her own name or those of her mother and father. She thus makes of herself and her family a kind of everyperson and everyfamily. On the other hand, she identifies herself by the way in which she crafts her own language to resist imposed political values and convey her own values.

What all meta-utopian protagonists share, and what makes them meta-utopian, is their inquiry into ideological structures that profess their own exclusive truth-value, that insist on their "naturalness" and deny their basic fictionality, and, finally, that resist all self-referentiality and all kinds of speculation, experiment, and play. Three such targets have emerged in our discussion. One is classical Russian "realism," with its affinity for scientific "truth." Another is the Soviet-Stalinist utopian imagination, with its implied belief in itself as the ideal society. And, finally, the third is nationalist "critical realism," which posits its archconservative vision of monarchy and peasant patriarchy as the answer for the future. Meta-utopias challenge the seemingly progressive valuations inherent in realism—the notion of the centrality and uniqueness of personality, the notions of free will and self-determination, and the stable, trustworthy interaction of the self's separate, private world with a public sphere the events of which are knowable and explicable through cause and effect. While realism thus defined may not seem hostile to the play of imagination, such works as Voinovich's *Moscow 2042* and Zinoviev's *The Yawning Heights* will emphasize how dominant metaphors in realist fiction belie its claim to progressivism and humanitarianism.

In an effort to go beyond the bounds placed on consciousness by both realism and utopianism and to open up other possibilities, meta-utopian art focuses on the very act of writing as an experience of self-objectification, of seeing oneself as "other," central to the making of one's own consciousness. With the exception of the

Strugatskys' *The Condemned City*, the protagonist in each of these works engages in some sort of writing, whether a personal chronicle of events or some kind of academic, expository prose, and thus comes to hear the particular tonality of his or her own voice. Uncovering one's own consciousness certainly involves some sort of confrontation with utopian ideology and the more subtle and seductive values underlying realism as they emerge in one's own thinking as well as in one's social milieu.

How, then, is a meta-utopian consciousness different from a dystopian one? Rather than broadcasting ominous "warnings" about the effects of realized utopia, meta-utopian fiction makes dark fun of the idea at the heart of the Western utopian tradition of the perfectibility and rationality of human nature, the possibility of a perfect fusion of personal and collective interests, and the fundamental goodness of a rational social order. Perhaps more unexpectedly, meta-utopian protagonists often challenge the parodistic early-twentieth-century response to utopian solutions, "dystopian" fiction that despairs of all forms of social imagination. Most meta-utopian works, indeed, are narrated from a point of view *within* the utopian experiment by a person who has become conscious of its shortcomings, that is, from a "dystopian" point of view. But although many of these characters find themselves dissidents in their own society, in something like the position of a D-503 or Winston Smith, their response to their surroundings is significantly more self-conscious and deliberate. Almost all of them live with what in dystopian fiction is the welcome rediscovery of human nature. But while *We* or *1984* rediscovers strong, life-giving, and even noble impulses in human nature, meta-utopias show human nature to be fundamentally ugly, dishonest, and grasping. These inclinations have been made much worse by the experience of being denied and repressed in realized utopia. In contrast, what is genuinely cultured and civilized is judged generally to be good. As is apparent, for example, in *The Yawning Heights*, the utopian experiment put into practice is revealed as an arena not for the elevation and perfection of human nature, but for the continuous enactment of the worst elemental drives of greed, gluttony, status-seeking—in short, of narrow self-interest.

Despite the difference in the nature of their social values, meta-utopian and dystopian protagonists do share a fundamental quality that Northrop Frye has pointed out in dystopian characters: these characters, like their precursors in ancient menippean satires, represent and are defined by their ideological positions.³ At base, they have little or no palpable, "plastic" being: they are little more than voices perpetrating a certain evaluation of the world. In this sense, meta-utopian characterization owes a debt to the first part of Dostoevsky's *Notes from the Underground* in which one can perceive the speaker only through his agonized verbal gestures. What makes meta-utopian characters fundamentally different from their antiutopian and dystopian forebears is their awareness of several possibilities for evaluating and living in one's social environment and the assumption of personal responsibility in choosing among these possibilities.

Perhaps the clearest archetype of the meta-utopian protagonist is not, strictly speaking, a fictional character but a voice that exists on the border between fiction and literary criticism. I have in mind the persona of Abram Terts, Andrei Siniavsky's literary pseudonym. The name was borrowed from the Jewish underworld figure from Odessa and chosen for its very implication of challenge and sabotage of official authority. As he mentioned in a recent interview with *Literaturnaia gazeta*, in choosing this pseudonym Siniavsky was consciously opposing the tradition of such Soviet stalwarts as Maksim Gorky and Demian Bednyi, who opted for the "beautiful, significant pseudonym."⁴ In contrast, Siniavsky's goal was to shock, not to beautify but to "deflate." It is significant that Siniavsky has published some critical essays under his own name, reserving the pseudonym Terts for his fiction and for the essay "What Is Socialist Realism?" and the books *Walks with Pushkin* and *In the Shadow of Gogol*, which challenged valuative assumptions and established and defended an alternative "tradition" of experimental play at odds with the social and moral calling of the mainstream Russian literary tradition.⁵

Particularly in "What Is Socialist Realism?" Terts's voice comes across as that of a semifictional protagonist who is undergoing a dramatic crisis of consciousness. As such, he embodies in a relatively pure form techniques of characterization central to meta-utopian writing. If meta-utopian characterization is extremely reductive, depriving character of all its considerable "realist" assets and leaving it

---

³ Irving Howe, "The Fiction of Antiutopia" (1963), in *The Decline of the New*, 72.

⁴ T. Putrenko, "Pushkin—nash smeiushiisia genii," *Literaturnaia gazeta*, no. 32 (August 8, 1990): 7. "Gor'kii" means "bitter," and "bednyi" means "poor."

⁵ Fanger, "Conflicting Imperatives," 111–24.

only with a voice, an ideological position, and an emotional attachment to that position, then Terts's voice in "What Is Socialist Realism?" is the epitome of this technique.

The protagonist in the dystopian novel believes that he is living in the best of all possible societies. He believes in the benevolence of power and its legitimizing ideology. In contrast, the meta-utopian protagonist has already become suspicious of the reigning ideology and finds himself caught in the middle of an ideological stalemate, as it were. Here the argumentative voice in "What Is Socialist Realism?" is exemplary. This is clearly the voice of a former believer who is drawn to the utopian ideal in its romantic abstraction, but is now disillusioned and ironic about the realized utopian experiment. Terts gives a good example of this ambivalence when he discusses the images of genuine heroism and grandeur that he still associates with the phrase "Soviet power [sovetskaia vlast']":

> All I have to do is pronounce the words "Soviet power" for me to imagine to myself the Revolution—the conquest of the Winter Palace, the rat-a-tat-tat of the machine guns, the chunk of bread, the defense of red Piter [the popular name for St. Petersburg]—and I am disgusted at the thought of speaking of it irreverently. Reasoning logically, "Soviet power" and "socialist state" are one and the same. But emotionally they are completely different things. If I have something against the socialist state (mere nonsense!), then I bear absolutely no grudge against Soviet power. Is that strange? Maybe. But that's romanticism.[6] (SR, 204)

Terts specifically blames the failure of utopian faith on the incongruous or, as he puts it, "eclectic" literary style of Soviet Socialist Realism, which is fraught with contradictory goals and values and combines classical hyperbole, a naturalist taste for ugly detail, and romantic élan. Through its conflicting descriptive styles and narrative techniques it has gone far to undermine the monumental sweep of the Soviet social experiment. Terts points to the forced marriage between realism and Stalinist "classicism" in Socialist Realist art, between the close attention to social and psychological detail, for example, in the *bytopisanie* of Chekhov and the monumental, posterlike hyperbolic idiom of Maiakovsky. What results is necessarily self-parody: "It is impossible, without falling into parody, to produce a posi-

---

[6] For more on Terts's sentiments about language during the revolution, see "The Literary Process in Russia," 101–2.

tive hero in the style of full Socialist Realism and yet make him into a psychological portrait" (SR, 213–24). Either one must dispense with verisimilitude or one must abandon the epic style and posturing. Terts proposes to get rid of both styles and their concomitant kinds of thinking, putting in their place a worldview of humorous relativity, making broad use of the grotesque, a complex, ambiguous technique that mixes horror with absurd humor.

Terts is not just attacking the failed Soviet ideology or attempting to replace it with some other system. He is trying to go beyond any system that perpetrates one absolute set of values and refuses to enter a dialogue, to negotiate with other competing systems. Thus, interspersed in his attacks on Socialist Realist culture are barbs against the assumed "enemy," the chief traditional competitor of the Stalinist utopia: Western individualism, with its belief in the "free personality of the superman" (SR, 163). In this attack on "individualism" he exhibits a mentality fed and encouraged by Soviet ideology but with deep Russian roots. Obviously Terts's rejection of one ideological alternative does not imply his adoption of an opposing one. He insists on standing in the ideological middle ground, as is essential for the meta-utopian protagonist. He wants a choice, the right to stand beyond all maximalist ideologies and to conceive more complex, dialogical alternatives.

Finally, if the dystopian protagonist openly embraces the utopian ideal of human nature while unconsciously sabotaging it, the meta-utopian protagonist consciously resists and, albeit with some degree of moral pain, enters into combat with it. Zamiatin's D-503 intellectually accepts the idea of a society built on a rational hierarchy of power, where all alternate sources of power are destroyed, where people become thoroughly transparent and controllable. He feels consciously satisfied by his adulation of the semidivine figure of the Benefactor. Moreover, he is intellectually embarrassed by his "atavistic" qualities, his hairy hands and his erotic yearnings, his imagination; at the end, he is relieved to have the "splinter" of fantasy removed from his brain. Nonetheless, semiconsciously he is continually probing around the edges of the utopian order he consciously accepts. He is interested in irrational numbers. He realizes that if the world ruled by the Benefactor is finite, if it has limits, then there is something beyond those limits. And, of course, he is drawn to the rebellious I-330 by forces of passion that fascinate him but that he cannot control.

In contrast, Terts's voice in "What Is Socialist Realism?" is full of conscious and deliberate irony, pointing out all the illogic of the utopian ideology in which he had earlier believed so fervently. He displays all the complex emotionalism, the anger, sarcasm, and irony, that was to disappear in utopia, harmonized in the quasi-religious utopian mentality in a collective feeling of "enthusiasm," a word used by Terts that has its roots in the Godbuilding utopianism of the revolutionary romantics, Lunacharsky and Gorky.[7] In his discussion, Terts exposes all the illogic of the supposedly scientific Soviet way of thinking. Following Zamiatin and Berdiaev, he points out the religious mentality transposed to political faith in the form of Russian communism and points out that its teleological and deterministic underpinnings are the opposite of the "scientific" ideology with which it legitimizes itself.[8]

In addition, Terts emphasizes the paradoxical relationship of communism's goals and its methods of achieving them. Using all the hyperbole of utopian rhetoric toward his subversive ends, he proclaims, most famously: "So that prisons should vanish forever, we built new prisons. So that all frontiers should fall, we surrounded ourselves with a Chinese wall. So that work should become a rest and a pleasure, we introduced forced labor. So that not one drop of blood be shed anymore, we killed and killed and killed" (SR, 162). Unlike Dostoevsky's anti-utopian underground man, this voice is not one petulantly insisting on its right to "irrationality," for example, to self-contradiction, paradox, willfulness, and so forth. It is a rather more angry, disillusioned version of D-503's voice in its love of rigorous analysis and its fascination with the incongruities it has uncovered. But while D-503 delights in irrational numbers and the like and on some semiconscious level knows that the social values and rituals of utopia are also paradoxical, he stops short of drawing deliberate conclusions. Terts goes further in this regard. Being of "scientific" mind, it is not surprising that at the close of his essay he couches his proposal for an alternative to Socialist Realism in a scientific vocabulary, with all its overtones of irreverence toward received or enforced values. He proposes an art based on "hypotheses" rather than articles of faith—that is, an art that continually tests its own ideological bases.

[7] Sesterhenn, *Das Bogostroitel'stvo bei Gor'kij*, 60–69.

[8] See, for example, Nicolas Berdyaev, *The Russian Revolution* (1931; Ann Arbor: The University of Michigan Press, 1966).

Meta-utopian protagonists, in contrast to dystopian authors, do not merely reject utopia, but debate the pros and cons of utopia as well as of other ideological systems. To be sure, Terts and nearly every protagonist in meta-utopian fiction resemble the anti-utopian thinkers Dostoevsky and Berdiaev and dystopian novelists Zamiatin, Orwell, and Huxley, in that they confront the ultimate paradox of utopia: they admire aspects of the utopian impulse in the abstract, but are horrified at what it becomes when it is acted out in history. But Terts, for example, has a more complex view of the ideology of individualism. He discounts what he sees as the Western faith in the "free personality of the superman," but implicitly defends the rights of the individual when they are placed in jeopardy by an authoritarian system. For example, he treats ironically a comment of Khrushchev's about the Jews, that Jews are "all individuals and all intellectuals. They want to talk about everything, they want to discuss everything, they want to debate everything—and they come to totally different conclusions!" (SR, 176n.1).[9]

How is the process of writing about oneself conducive to the emergence of a meta-utopian consciousness? Perhaps the process is clearest in the earliest example of meta-utopian fiction, Iuly Daniel's *Moscow Speaking* (1961). Here the narrator and protagonist is Tolia Kartsev, a loyal citizen who is writing for himself for the first time. He shares with the general type of the meta-utopian hero a lack of physical attributes, an idiosyncratic diction, and a focus on a complex dialogue with various ideological options. In a real sense, Kartsev must challenge utopian rules of the game in order to make the decision to write about Open Murder Day. Already he has made himself "other" to the existing ideology in his own mind. The experience of Open Murder Day has made him feel that he understands neither himself nor his society, and he feels the need to confront himself. He is fully aware of the danger and illegality of his act, and he faces a dilemma in deciding for whom he is writing and where his work can come out. Like a dystopian protagonist, he still adheres to utopian thinking in that he decides that "really, it's not very nice, publishing in anti-Soviet publications" (MS, 17). He cannot bring himself to cross the defining border between utopia and nonutopia to achieve his goal. He settles for writing for himself alone, believing that without readers he will really tell the truth about himself.

---

[9] It is worth remarking that this footnote is included in neither Russian edition of Terts's essay. See *Fantasticheskii mir Abrama Tertsa* and *Tsena metafory*.

Tolia responds with irony to the utopian rhetoric in which the public announcements of Open Murder Day are couched. Here is the first sign that official ideology is not to be taken seriously. In his report of these announcements, he conveys only the most basic clichés, revealing them for what they are. The radio broadcast is reduced to a few key formulas: "In connection with the growing state of well-being ... in accordance with the wishes of the broad masses of workers ... to name August 10, 1960 ... Open Murder Day" (MS, 14). And the article in *Izvestiia*, entitled "Toward Open Murder Day," is summarized thus: "Growing well-being—with seven-league boots—genuine democratism—only in our country all intentions—the first in history—visible traits—bourgeois press" (MS, 19).

Tolia further unmasks the utopian mentality as he talks to friends and neighbors about the upcoming day. He senses a kind of Orwellian "doublethink," particularly among those whose careers directly involve upholding and defending the utopian dream. For example, his acquaintance Igor, who is a party member and works in the academy (Tolia does not specify what sort of work), insists that "August 10 [Open Murder Day] is the result of the wise policies of our party, ... the decree is testimony once again of the creative initiatives of the masses of the people" (MS, 21). This kind of thinking is paradoxical to the point of absurdity: much as in *1984*, destruction is creation, absurdity is wisdom, and death is life.

A conversation with Tolia's neighbor, a lawyer, reveals another psychological reality belying utopian claims to social harmony and unity: the fear and distrust of the mob on the part of the educated intelligentsia. The lawyer tries to justify the upcoming day in this way: "Consciousness certainly has grown! Ergo: the state has the right to put into play a broad experiment, it has the right to put separate functions into the hands of the people!" (MS, 24). He continues: "The present decree is nothing more than the logical continuation of a process already begun—the process of democratization. The democratization of what? The democratization of the organs of governance. The ideal—you must understand me correctly—is the gradual dissolution of executive power among the broad masses of the people, among, so to speak, the rabble [nizy] themselves. That is, not among the rabble..." (MS, 24–25). Here the lawyer stumbles, realizing his ideological slip. While he overtly justifies this event as the march of Soviet society toward communism, with the ultimate withering away of the state as the implied goal, secretly he discloses an elitism mixed with a distrust and fear of the masses. Everyone with whom Tolia speaks reveals some darker feeling, hostile to the utopian notion of human nature: one expects a pogrom, another wants to murder her husband, yet another sees a repetition of the Terror of 1937. All these responses reemphasize what is already clear: that ultimately there is no such thing as a harmonious collective or even the consciousness of a collective interest. In his conversations with friends Tolia certainly is confronted more than once with his own conflicting feelings about the Soviet utopian project: his own very deep respect for basic utopian principles, embodied, as he believes, in the "genuine" communists of the 1930s, as well as the deep failure of those principles in the real minds and hearts of his fellow citizens.

Finally, Tolia gains new insight into the assumptions behind Socialist Realism. Here epistemological axioms are challenged. Although Tolia does not give credence to official ideology, he still believes that real events have a certain logic of cause and effect. He believes that through writing about them he can make "sense" of an incident that to him, as well as to the reader, is manifestly absurd. Finally, he merely survives Open Murder Day and rejects its divisive and violent social implications, without ever really "understanding" it. Its inexplicability becomes clear in Tolia's comparison of a "real" occurrence on the street on that day to "art," in the form of a political poster designed by his artist friend Sasha Chuprov. Chuprov is another of Tolia's generation who cynically dishes out what the authorities require in order to support himself and his own private artistic experiments. But for the coming Open Murder Day he draws a poster that, much to his astonishment, is rejected by the authorities: "A stereotypical teenage boy and girl were standing against the background of a huge sun either rising or setting; the sun beat down on their backs, and the red shadows of their figures lay diagonally across the poster; at the bottom to the left the shadows merged with a red-black puddle, lying against the corner of a stereotypical house; in the lower right corner lay a corpse with knees hitched up and arms thrown wide apart" (MS, 34). The one corpse he sees as he wanders the streets on the appointed day looks exactly like the one in Chuprov's poster. He is stunned to realize the ultimate failure of social reality to be more real than the product of an artist's imagination. Art, is seems, is not modeled on social actuality, as is assumed in Socialist Realist art. In fact, just the opposite holds: actual events take on an appearance prefigured in works of art.

Tolia finally explains not the event itself but people's reaction to it in fairly general terms as fear—for one person, of the unknown, for another, of past precedent, for a third, of lost social status. He starts to realize that there are options, other possible reactions, as he finds out how people in other parts of the Soviet Union have treated Open Murder Day. While the Azeris and Armenians in Nargorno-Karabakh predictably try to kill as many of each other as possible, people in the Baltic republics ignore the announcement altogether and go about their business as on any other day. Tolia ends by rejecting the officially perpetrated image of his society as a developing communist utopia, as the best of all possible worlds. He consciously chooses to redefine his world according to his own personal taste as a kind of urban idyll. "Moscow speaking," he decides, means lovers whispering to each other in the parks, not some alienating, authoritative voice speaking absurdities over the radio. Here is certainly an example of what one of Zinoviev's protagonists, The Slanderer, says should happen when one has thought through the implications of utopian society or, more broadly, of any reigning ideology: by penetrating the authoritative façade of the ideologically conditioned picture of reality, Tolia regains confidence in his own taste and powers of judgment (MS, 157). Like Terts, in "What is Socialist Realism?", he learns to create a choice for himself.

Another example of meta-utopian consciousness worth considering is Voinovich's protagonist Vitaly Kartsev (intentionally given the same surname as Daniel's character?). Kartsev is a kind of "everyman" or "little man," a type with a long heritage in Russian satirical writing. He is able to talk to anyone on any level, and he is without ideological axes to grind. As a meta-utopian protagonist, Kartsev certainly does not fit the model of the bold questioner of ideologies, Abram Terts, nor is he the bewildered citizen, Tolia Kartsev, trying to hold onto his sanity in an insane society. His position on the border between ideological constructs is purely involuntary, and, as such, provides the basis for the humor in this most humorous of meta-utopian works. For example, he himself has no objection to, and even admires, the original Soviet utopian principles: "freedom, equality, brotherhood, dissolution of borders, withering away of the state, from each according to his ability, to each according to his needs" (M, 34). His only political sentiment is an intense dislike for the Communist party, which he would gladly throw out if given the chance, although he has no idea what kind of governance he would replace it with. His one strong sentiment is that he would simply like to live and let live. It is as a *malen'kii chelovek*, the disempowered, ideologically unaligned "little man," that Kartsev undermines the ideologically committed, influential personalities of Gorky and Solzhenitsyn—one the "father" of Socialist Realism and the other a critical realist and a cultural leader who was not afraid to confront the Soviet leaders openly.

In his Moscow adventures, Kartsev, the apolitical writer, is incongruously put into the position of perhaps the chief Russian model of the politically engaged writer Maksim Gorky. Like Gorky, who returned to Stalin's Russia in 1927 and was much feted and glorified, Kartsev finds himself in the Moscow of the future the center of a new cult, with his books newly republished and streets renamed after him. He is even given a pseudonym appropriate to his standing, Klassik Klassikovich, showing that he has become the center of the new post-Soviet literary canon. In return for his "superstar" status, he must edit his books, and in particular, the book we are presently reading, *Moscow 2042*.

Voinovich shows a strong sense of irony in the implicit comparison of his protagonist with the original supporter of the Stalinist totalitarian experiment, Gorky. Here is Kartsev's test as a meta-utopian character: Will he give into ideological and other coercion, as Gorky did, or will he stay true to himself and remain in that politically dangerous but morally honest limbo between ideologies? Somewhat like Gorky, who from 1927 until the early 1930s was willing to believe that he really was experiencing the "future" of which he had only dreamed, the transfiguration of humanity from savagery to creative self-realization, so Kartsev finds himself willing to suspend belief—if not for four or five years, then at least overnight. His first night he dreams that he has arrived in the land of plenty. Soon he finds himself involuntarily adopting the new rituals, for example, saying "Oh, Gena!" (short for "Genialissimus") instead of "Oh, God!" However, tempted as he is, he finally refuses to alter his chronicle of this trip. He is thrown to the bedbugs in the outer darkness, beyond what is known as the first circle of Moscow, the area within the Boulevard Ring. Here the comparison with Gorky ends. He is so physically uncomfortable in his exile that he decides consciously to compromise himself.

Karnavalov (whose name points incongruously to the character's absent sense of humor) is the twentieth-century, secularized version of hermit–as–social prophet. He is heralded as the "new Tolstoi"

(M, 45). His "realism" consists of a position of aloofness toward flesh-and-blood experience and a concomitant claim to have mirrored perfectly and objectively the Russian social experience. His notion of language embraces the whole of the Russian tongue, tailoring it to express his own oppressive social views. It is certainly significant that he has named his white steed "Glagol," or "The Word," in that he "rides" language in much the same way, using it to enforce a new "Divine Law." Toward the end of gaining total mastery over language, he, like his model Solzhenitsyn, spends time every day studying and memorizing the classic Russian dictionary of Vladimir Dal. His life-work is epic in scope, a many-tomed opus covering every aspect of Russian life.

Kartsev, the unwitting nonideologue who admires and envies Karnavalov his popularity, inadvertently reveals the very nonliberal, inhumane values that underlie Karnavalov's realism. The guiding metaphor in all his works is "prison": all life, from its inception in the womb to its bitter end in the grave, is spent in incarceration. His concept of personality reflects the Godbuilding-Stalinist notion of a cult built around one monumental personality and supported by millions of faceless followers. Karnavalov is deadly serious when he says in the first volume of his intended sixty-volume opus, *The Cell for Preliminary Incarceration* (*Kamera predvaritel'nogo zakliucheniia*), that the development of self starts before conception in the womb when a crowd of 200 million sperm (close enough to the population of the Soviet Union!) all struggle against one another until one of them penetrates the egg and develops into a human person (M, 54). This juxtaposition of the one personality and the faceless crowd pervades Karnavalov's work, appearing even as the title of one of his chapters, "The Leader and the Herd" ("Vozhak i stado"). Clearly Karnavalov's realism is informed by a firm belief in society as *Gemeinschaft*, not by the notion of a civil society or *Gesellschaft* based on a network of individual citizens responsible for making the system work.

Buttressing this general image of the world is a virulent scorn for everything "democratic." The term in Karnavalov's usage becomes *der'mokratiia*, or the rule of excrement.[10] He hates the term *pliuralizm*, and as a sign of contempt gives it as a name for his fawning

---

[10] It is curious that since the real August putsch of 1991, this same term has gained wide currency as widening contempt for parliamentary procedure takes hold. Once again, art anticipates history. See Liah Greenfeld, "Kitchen Debate: Russia's Nationalist Intelligentsia," *The New Republic* (Sept. 21, 1992), 22–25, esp. p. 23.

German shepherd, "Pliushka" for short.[11] Karnavalov lives his life in exile as a self-styled Nicholas I on his estate that ironically bears the same name, "Otradnoe" ("pleasing"), as the estate of the mellow Count Rostov in *War and Peace*. His servants are treated as serfs and are regularly whipped. His wife wears floor-length dresses, stays mostly in her "terem," and vociferously assumes a subservient position to her husband. Upon his return to Moscow in 2042 Karnavalov returns the Russian state to its condition under the Muscovite princes. He sets up thirteen laws of civil behavior that sound suspiciously like Ivan the Terrible's patriarchal book of family etiquette, *Domostroi*.

It is interesting to note parenthetically that Kartsev, as "little man," also disputes the populism in *1984* that motivates Winston Smith's exploration of prole neighborhoods. He certainly does not agree with Winston's thought that "if there is hope, it lies in the proles."[12] As Orwell does in *1984*, Voinovich shows the drab poverty of the Moscow of the future, but in a comic way. Here everyone is desensitized to their surroundings; no one suffers from the inferior food and the general squalor. It does not matter that the Moscow equivalent of the proles have no memory or are trivial and stupid. If in Orwell's version suffering has presumably made them that way, in Voinovich's work they were always that way. What is more, they are still capable of revolt if necessary. What they lack is a sense of judgment: what they revolt for, that is, for Karnavalov's dream, is no better and possibly even more repressive than the current regime.

Both Gorky's and Karnavalov-Solzhenitsyn's visions of the good society, opposite as they may seem to be, are steeped in the same general authoritarian psychology colored by paranoia, suspicion, and coerciveness. Each ideology responds to the other only as opposites on one ideological plane, without understanding that they both share a deeper maximalist social-political mentality. Kartsev gains meta-utopian insight only when he realizes that the claims that each side makes on him result in the same coercive behavior. He would be equally badly off under both systems. From a position of aesthetic

---

[11] In this connection it is interesting to note Siniavsky-Terts's comments on Solzhenitsyn's disparaging use of the term *pluralist* to refer to any Russian dissident writer who does not agree with him. See his "Solzhenitsyn kak ustroitel' novogo edinomysliia," 16. Siniavsky is responding to Solzhenitsyn's book *Ocherki literaturnoi zhizni*, vol. 2.

[12] George Orwell, *1984* (Harmondsworth, Engl.: Penguin, 1979), 59.

integrity he learns to resist both of them: it is the fate of his books, the possibility that they might lose all their character through composition by committee, that makes him realize that he must take a stand. Kartsev establishes a position as a writer somewhere between realism and experimental play. He is aware of the attractions of thinking that one is actually having an impact on political leaders. All his unpleasant experiences notwithstanding, he remains something of a "realist" in the Russian tradition: he still entertains the hope that his tale will be read as a warning or prophecy by the authorities, who, worried by its unpromising picture of Moscow's future, might take it upon themselves to correct neither the author nor the author's fantasy but the quality of life itself. But, in contradiction to this view, Kartsev *also* looks forward to the time when his novel might be published and received as the "fruit of an empty and harmless fantasy" (M, 339). In parting, he takes a final dig at the overused concept of realism. If indeed his work were to be interpreted merely as a figment of his imagination, he realizes, "my reputation as an exceptionally honest person would be fairly dampened, but I am ready to make my peace with such an eventuality." He expresses a simple wish: "The heck with reputations. If only living might become easier. That's what it's all about, gentlemen" (M, 339).

Additional consideration ought to be given to the nature of meta-utopian consciousness in *Liubimov*, because that work has struck other critics as dystopian.[13] I would suggest that *Liubimov* is meta-utopian, in large part because of the emphasis on the variety of consciousnesses and points of view that meditate on the social "thing-in-itself": in fact, Liubimov is nothing but a muddy, sleepy village in the middle of a swamp with a few peasants in it. Unlike Zamiatin's One State, the real existence of which is never called into question, the social-political order in the village of Liubimov becomes whatever those who think about it and act upon it want it to be. As its name suggests, it is the "beloved," that is, a passive object of various characters' desires.

A second quality of meta-utopian consciousness in *Liubimov* is its parody of all valences of the utopian impulse. Not only are positive utopian experiences parodied, but dystopian ones as well. Lënia parodies that Stalinist travesty of selfhood known as the cult of personality. While the mockery of positive utopian discourse is clear, it may

---

[13] See Morson, *The Boundaries of Genre*, 140.

come as a surprise that dystopian discourse is parodied as well. Savely Kuzmich seems to represent a genuine dystopian attitude. For example, he shares with D-503 a willingness to brainwash himself into believing that Lënia's Liubimov is the best of all possible worlds. He also acts from a dystopian consciousness when he refuses to be Lënia's chronicler and "escapes to nature" to Tishchenko, the former mayor of Liubimov, who is out fishing. But here, as in other meta-utopias, "nature" is not a solution to utopian "society," and Tishchenko is clearly very far from being a "man of nature." He is one more petty functionary who had bought into the Stalinist cult of personality. Indeed, the escape offered in dystopias is shown to be merely a reversion to yet another, older variant of coercive monologism.

A third aspect of Terts's narrative that makes it much more of a meditation about all kinds of expression of the utopian impulse than a straight dystopian depiction of a "bad place" from which one wants to escape is its extreme self-consciousness as a narrative artifact. Strongly metafictional in nature, *Liubimov* exposes as the goal of its narrative the very logic, or illogic, underlying utopian narratives. The work brings out the communicative framework in which various parties participate in generating, conveying, receiving, and regenerating "meaning," which then claims some legitimacy as reality. The town of Liubimov is a text generated and apprehended by various "speaking persons." And each speaking person doubles as a player—whether author, narrator, protagonist, or reader—in a metafictional act of communication.

Savely Kuzmich is the "author" of Liubimov-as-utopia, who, as Michel Aucouturier has pointed out, abrogates his responsibility as author and lowers himself to the level of narrator, where he can "just do his job" without taking responsibility for his creation.[14] Semiconsciously he wills into existence Samson Samsonovich Proferansov, on whom he bestows the role of "author" and creator. Nonetheless, it should be noted that Savely Kuzmich is a key perpetrator of a utopian idea, as is half-admitted in the end when he begs Samson Samsonovich to come back and return that "energy, or whatever you call it" to Lënia so that they can build communism "in a jiffy" (L, 424). Still, the most responsibility that he is willing to claim for this utopian yearning is as "co-author" with Samson Samsonovich. It should be

---

[14] Aucouturier, "Writer and Text in the Works of Abram Terc," 1–10.

reiterated that Samson Samsonovich's and Savely Kuzmich's notions of the ideal social order differ substantially. While Samson Samsonovich dreams of some vague union of love (Liubimov) incongruously achieved by rebellion, violence, and abuse, Savely Kuzmich spouts generalities about realizing Liubimov's historical potential and about building communism.

In the narrative that emerges between the split authorial personality of Savely Kuzmich, the realist and chronicler, and Samson Samsonovich, the utopian and dreamer, a small-time tinkerer, Lënia Tikhomirov, is forced into the unlikely role of "hero." He becomes the somewhat unwilling builder of Savely/Samson's utopia who then finds power very much to his liking and is glad to be the center of a new cult of personality. He has the greatest actual power to enforce utopian designs but, like the others, takes no responsibility for his actions. Lënia's utopian consciousness differs more sharply from Samson Samsonovich's and Savely Kuzmich's than theirs do from each other. Samson Samsonovich wants Lënia to enact his dream of love and is shocked to find his authorial intention practiced as authoritarianism, abused in Lënia's coercive exploitation of his subjects.

Finally, the communicative process is completed with the spy Vitaly Kochetov, who, as an outsider and voyeur, acts as a reader and interpreter of the utopian charade. He, of course, belongs to another "utopia," that of Stalinism. He participates in the communicative chain first as "censor" in that he is actually enforcing the exclusivist claims of one utopian vision to truth and ideality in the face of a new challenger. As such, he perceives only a swampy area without any town at all. Once he penetrates Liubimov's magnetic shield, he becomes a rather uncritical reader of and believer in the new text. He is so enthralled by it, particularly by Lënia's powers of mind control, that instead of censoring the text, he proposes to have it become a handbook for Soviet governance.

The whole communicative process, such as it is, is destroyed eventually by physical coercion. Tanks and airplanes invade Liubimov, and nothing is left but Savely Kuzmich, who is scrambling for cover. This ending is the appropriate one for utopia, in which communication amounts at most to imposition of one's own will onto another, and reception and interpretation amount to semiconscious appropriation of another person's word to suit one's own needs. First, despite his allegiance to "facts," Savely Kuzmich wishes to rewrite the history of Liubimov according to his own predilections. Then Samson Samsonovich tries to impose his will on Savely Kuzmich and Lënia. Lënia dictates his wishes to Savely Kuzmich. Finally, Kochetov brazenly appropriates the whole hoax of Liubimov-as-utopia for the benefit of another coercive (Stalinist) order to which he subscribes. Underlying all of these modes of utopian and dystopian consciousness is a strong taste for tyranny—either to be the tyrannized or to be the tyrant. Thus, only from the meta-utopian perspective that *Liubimov* offers can we appreciate the symbiosis that inheres in the relationship between utopian and dystopian consciousness.

As something of a special case, it should be said that *Moscow-Petushki* is closer to a dystopian consciousness than to a meta-utopian one. This work does not show the dispute between utopian positions and the mirror relationships that obtain between utopias of various valences. In Venichka's carnivalesque, Bacchic celebration of drunkenness and sex is, indeed, a reaffirmation of the basic impulses in human nature. *Moscow-Petushki* also shares with dystopian narrative the rejection of social will. All the human-made situations in which Venichka participates—the communal living with his four roommates, his efforts as foreman to cultivate his workers' social consciousness, the revolution that he and his friend Vadim Tikhonov start in the Petushki region—end in ruin. Venichka's tendency to model his own experience on Christ's martyrdom and resurrection, his appeal to God and the angels for their guidance and good will, and his rejection of all human-made social orders in favor of a God-given paradise suggest a more general rejection of the notion of a beneficent human will. Like Dostoevsky's underground man, Venichka focuses on personal, spiritual renewal.

Nonetheless, we have pointed to some meta-utopian aspects of *Moscow-Petushki*. One is the playful juxtaposition of a number of discrete ideologies and the conclusion that all these ideologies are ultimately fictions, without direct referentiality. We have seen how Erofeev plays with notions of progressiveness and perfectibility as they relate to plot construction. And finally, we can point to Venichka's own type of self-consciousness. Venichka is a worker in the alleged workers' paradise, but, unlike the dystopian protagonists, he does not openly embrace this paradise only to sabotage it covertly. He is much more strongly disillusioned and sarcastic, and in his own way, much more sophisticated and cultivated, than his dystopian counterparts. He is determined to topple the ideological pillars of this hell—Lenin, Gorky, Michurin, and Ostrovsky, among others.

What, finally, is a meta-utopian concept of selfhood? It is clear that meta-utopian writing unmasks human nature, stripping it of its various layers of consciousness and reducing it to its lowest common denominator. The best generalization of this tendency is given in Zinoviev's *The Yawning Heights*, in which the twin ideologies of Marxism-Leninism and liberal progressivism, with their high valuations, respectively, of the harmonious collective and individual personality, are debunked. The notion of the rational and harmonious collective is shaped in reality by what Zinoviev calls "social laws," that is, the inherent drive for self-protection and survival. The Schizophrenic, who is writing a tract on social laws throughout the first part of *The Yawning Heights*, argues that lying, duplicity, greed, nastiness to any competitor or inferior are all part of the game of maintaining and improving one's own security: "The impudence and arbitrariness of petty and high officials, the rudeness of salespeople, the arbitrariness of the police, the open corruption in the service sector, in educational institutions, the endless stream of red tape, and so forth—all these are not small shortcomings but the heart of the matter" (YH, 102). The utopian plan known in Zinoviev's book as "ism" has, in fact, created a bureaucratic apparatus that reinforces ugly social instincts, and does not, as had been hoped, build to some higher level of equality, fairness, and love. Zinoviev, as well as other meta-utopian writers—for example, Tendriakov in *A Potshot at Mirages*—argues that people naturally will strive to be unequal, to gain greater comfort, privilege, and influence for themselves with the least possible effort. Thus, Lenin's utopian ideal, "From each according to ability, to each according to need," ends up meaning something quite different: "To each according to position" (YH, 100).

The notion of an independent moral personality that has a beneficial impact on the quality of social life, a favorite value of nineteenth-century realism, is likewise undermined by the mass social experiment, with its goal of equality. In *The Yawning Heights*, equality means bringing the best exemplars of humanity down to the level of mass mediocrity. On this level, most people try to hinder the upward movement of a few. Here both Zinoviev and Voinovich use carnival humor to great benefit, mixing sacred social ideals with profane images of excrement. In this regard, as in so many others, the word *der'mo*, or "excrement," is a frequently used term implying the essential human characteristic. For example, The Spouse (the wife of the well-established Sociologist) in *The Yawning Heights* tries to bring The Schizophrenic down after he claims to have understood the inner workings of Ibansk society and the experiment of "ism." Her only comment is, "You're the same shit as we [all] are" (YH, 118; see also 377, 498). The implication is that The Schizophrenic is perceived to be posturing as a genius. This attitude provides a rationale for discounting all his efforts as mere pretention and posing and for depriving them of the serious consideration that they really deserve. The functional "social rule" here, the one that most undermines the notion of moral personality, is the pressure to "be like everyone else," to conform at a low level (YH, 101). On the other hand, The Schizophrenic cautions that the opposing "principle of the individual" in society also goes against the notion of moral personality. This principle says that an ambitious person will break all rules necessary to put himself in the best light and to gain the greatest independence from others (YH, 102). The general rule of thumb is to delegate unpleasant tasks to someone else and accept credit for other people's good work. Like the "social laws" pressuring the citizen to conform, this rule works to reinforce hierarchy and to oppress.

If meta-utopian writing reduces human nature to its lowest common denominator, it also expresses its own concept of the conscious, moral personality. Predictably, the best human being is the one who becomes conscious of the real effects of utopian, dystopian, and counterutopian schemes as they become fixed as ideology and shape the perceptions and behavior of real people in society. This person is able to negotiate the line between ideologies imposed from outside, to penetrate the mentality underlying these systems, and to make his own independent choices. As Zinoviev's protagonist The Big Mouth puts it, the "moral" person comes to understand the meshing of social laws and social ideals in his own life and chooses to say no, not to be driven by the rat race for power and influence, and to live according to his own conscience. History, he says, is made by people who resist the pressure to conform and the impulse toward crass self-protection that is at the heart of human social instinct. Skepticism about any single ideology or any call to faith; a renewed reliance on one's own critical judgment, personal memory, personal integrity; an ongoing insistence on the possibility of a beneficial social imagination—these are the key elements of meta-utopian consciousness.

PART THREE

THE READER IN THE TEXT:

POPULARIZING THE META-UTOPIAN

MENTALITY

* CHAPTER SEVEN *

Making Meta-utopia Accessible

ZINOVIEV'S *THE RADIANT FUTURE*

CAN NARRATIVE innovation, ideological challenge, and popular appeal coexist in one work of art? According to Irving Howe, one of the major historians of Western modernism, the answer is—no. Literature can no longer be avant-garde if it has become popular.[1] Once it gains broad appeal and is frequently imitated, it loses its "otherness" and becomes simply a marker of the existing ideology. It is by definition no longer new. But according to more recent critics, the Russian apologist for literary experiment V. O. Ksepma or the Canadian theorist of postmodernism Linda Hutcheon, the answer is—yes. Innovative, ludic art can certainly, and in Ksepma's view *should*, challenge but also tease the general reader toward greater ideological sophistication and aesthetic competence. As Hutcheon aptly conceives it, fiction of the last two decades—for example, Christa Wolf's *Kindheitsmuster* or John Fowles's *Magus*—plays with popular forms, bridging the gap between elite and mass art.[2] She calls this art "didactic" in the sense that it undertakes to teach the receptive reader about cultural and ideological countercurrents. It inculcates in this reader a skeptical, questioning attitude toward what Hutcheon calls "inspired vision," that is, a singular, exclusivist concept of the world that acknowledges no alternatives to itself.[3]

Even the most playful and seemingly undidactic of meta-utopian writers are centrally concerned with the general reader. As recently as August 1990, in an interview with *Literaturnaia gazeta*, Siniavsky (Terts) complained of Russian readers' continuing lack of interpretive skill. Typically, the Russian audience takes all statements at face value.[4] As Terts' would-be author and erstwhile reader Savely

---

[1] Howe, "The Culture of Modernism," in *The Decline of the New*, 3.
[2] Ksepma, "'Po tu storonu lobnoi stenki,'" 24–27; Hutcheon, *A Poetics of Postmodernism*, 20.
[3] Hutcheon, *A Poetics of Postmodernism*, 42.
[4] Putrenko, "Pushkin—nash smeiushchiisia genii," 7.

Kuzmich Proferansov suggests, the general Russian reader expects there to be no difference between fantasy and reality. All fiction should be a simple reflection of facts and life experience. Most meta-utopian writers address this reader in some way or other—almost always with the goal of intriguing and making fun of him and thereby goading him to a greater interpretive sophistication.

Popularized experimentation is certainly a central component of meta-utopian fiction. It should be said that the most broadly accessible of these works—for example, Zinoviev's *The Radiant Future*, the Strugatsky brothers' *The Ugly Swans*, Tendriakov's *A Potshot at Mirages*, or Aksënov's *The Island of Crimea*—seem at first glance to miss the connection between literary experimentation and ideological challenge that has been the center of our discussion so far. They appear to encourage ideological skepticism in implied readers without making broad use of the innovative narrative and stylistic devices that Ksepma sees as being so important for winning widespread acceptance for the notions of aesthetic play and cultural competence. All four of these authors use recognizably "realist" techniques of characterization, setting, and plot construction. Instead, literary style and its challenge to ingrained ideology are frequently raised as points of argument between characters in the works. For example, in *The Ugly Swans* a group of teenagers reject the writer Viktor Banev's critical realist idiom and the philosophy of social tolerance that goes with it. Or the newspaper publisher Andrei Luchnikov in *The Island of Crimea* publishes an article, "On Decadence," which is reproduced in the text of Aksënov's novel.

While it is certainly true that the popularized meta-utopias neither flaunt stylistic and narrative play nor manipulate the boundaries between fictionality and reality in the sometimes baffling ways that *The Yawning Heights* and *Liubimov* do, it can be shown that they do indeed make use of the same techniques of defamiliarization to break down monological thinking, though often within more circumscribed bounds, specifically of a critique of Marxism-Leninism. They do it in the context of play with realist convention that makes it easier for a reader used to realist literature to extend himself. The central issue in meta-utopian literature, the relationship between aesthetic experiment and entrenched ideology, is certainly alive and well in these more accessible works. For example, we have seen how Voinovich, whose novel occupies the space between the most radical experiments and more conventional narrative, consistently parodies what Orwell would call "newspeak," the utopian pretention that neologism means new consciousness and greater ideological adequacy. Yet he puts his wordplay partly in the context of political and social acronyms, a convention with which any Soviet is familiar. Zinoviev in *The Radiant Future* plays with well-known political slogans and billboards.

An issue deeply familiar to those who tread the boundary lines of the permissible in Soviet culture is the problem of Aesopian language. Many writers and readers have used it as the one broadly accessible medium for language play and ideological protest. We have discussed how in intellectual debate of the late 1980s Aesopian language was spurned as a weak form of dissent.[5] Works such as *Rabbits and Boa Constrictors* and *The Radiant Future* will focus on the deeper, psycholinguistic import of Aesopian language as a duplicitous mode of expression that divides and weakens individual consciousness, making a citizen incapable of effective challenge to the existing state of things.

The goal of our discussion of popularized meta-utopian fiction, then, is to examine how the "implied reader" is delineated in the text and how the reader's "horizon of expectation" is established and manipulated.[6] Thus, one can assess the extent to which authors try to reach nonelite readers and to teach them to seek in literary play a serious challenge to constraining ideological structure.

Our first example, Zinoviev's *The Radiant Future*, perhaps best highlights issues involved with addressing and educating a general reader because it was written directly after and can be seen as a popularizing shadow for the much more abstruse work, *The Yawning Heights*.[7] It should be noted first that Zinoviev is directly, if very ambivalently, concerned with the problem of the reader even in *The Yawning Heights*. While in the early sections of the book Zinoviev clearly sets out to undo "utopian" ways of reading—that is, to

---

[5] See Chapter 2 and Arapov, "Iazyk utopii."

[6] I use this term as it is defined in Hans Robert Jauss, "Literaturgeschichte als Provokation der Literaturwissenschaft," in *Literaturgeschichte als Provokation* (Frankfurt: Suhrkamp, 1970), 175.

[7] Arnold McMillin, "Zinoviev's Fiction in the Context of Unofficial Russian Prose of the 1970s," in *Alexander Zinoviev as Writer and Thinker: An Assessment*, ed. P. Hanson and M. Kirkwood (New York: St. Martin's Press, 1988), 61–70. McMillan points out the parallels between the two works, emphasizing the conventional character of *The Radiant Future*.

confound the reader's expectation of a singular message, the promise of a better future, a clear-cut evaluation of society and its good guys and bad guys—he also undoes all kinds of narrative logic by exposing devices for structuring plot. He leaves the reader wondering what exactly the principle of signification, or, to use Jakobson's term, the "dominant," will be in his book. It does eventually become clear, as we know, that the activity of reading and responding to the various fragments of manuscript written by Zinoviev's three protagonists is the main "event" of the book. Thus, the reader and his process of interpretation and meditation on himself and his social condition is, indeed, at the very heart of Zinoviev's experiment (YH, 236). It is significant that the ultimate act of despair in *The Yawning Heights* is not The Big Mouth's suicide but his decision to destroy some of the manuscripts in his personal archive, that is, to deny these works an eventual readership. Openly challenging Bulgakov's optimistic dictum, "Manuscripts don't burn!"—that is, that they sooner or later find readers who will reinvigorate them with new interpretation and even creative transformation—The Big Mouth maintains that in fact they are made to disappear by powerful people who feel threatened by them. Or, as in the case of The Big Mouth, some works are the victims of self-censorship and never "get born" at all (YH, 212).

If the response of the intelligent, contemplative reading individual is the key to what narrative dynamism does exist in *The Yawning Heights*, the general reader is treated with much greater ambivalence, even bordering on contempt. This reader has at best very limited intellectual ability and is easy prey for unscrupulous scientists and politicians. In his writings on science and ideology The Slanderer attacks the political and intellectual leaders who use popularization to perpetrate false claims and implicitly reinforce oppression. He argues that the popularization of scientific theories by those in power assigns too much significance to certain discoveries as watersheds in the evolution of human consciousness. The Slanderer argues that such an emphasis has the real effect of making the popular reader doubt her own senses. Because she does not have the tools to understand scientific advances and put them into proper perspective, she is left wondering whether, indeed, she has achieved a sufficiently high level of consciousness to be competent to judge the ideological claims made by the ruling elite (YH, 157). By thus disarming potential opponents, an oppressive ideology can arrogate for itself still greater legitimacy and influence.

In contrast, both The Big Mouth and The Dauber wonder about the abilities of a mass audience to perceive aesthetic experiment and benefit from the ideological challenge embedded in it. Although The Big Mouth insists in his discussion of The Dauber's art that all great art must be mass-oriented, toward the end of *The Yawning Heights* he wonders whether art can really alter popular taste or whether it ends up merely catering to it (YH, 276). As he and The Dauber contemplate the opposing alternatives offered by the highly original but difficult writings of The Double Dealer (Siniavsky-Terts) and the easily read novels of The Truthteller (Solzhenitsyn), he decides that The Double Dealer's more profound insight will never win the attention of the broad reading public. The Dauber observes: "The wrong and superficial ideas of The Truthteller enjoy sensational success and have an enormous influence. The accurate and profound ideas of such people as The Schizophrenic, The Slanderer, and even The Double Dealer have neither serious success nor influence" (YH, 441). To which The Big Mouth replies: "Accurate and profound ideas are oriented toward individuals, false and superficial ones are mass-oriented. People as a whole lean toward delusions and sensations" (YH, 441). And yet, despite his misgivings about the interpretive skills of most readers, The Big Mouth still holds to a social order that has to rely on the responsible participation of an informed and discerning citizenry. Well before Gorbachev's time, he asserts the need for glasnost, for informed, openly expressed public opinion and its legal guarantee, as the basis for a moral society (YH, 556). By implication, the mass reader-turned-citizen is capable of greater sophistication given more open social conditions.

If *The Yawning Heights* conveys at best an ambivalent view of the popular reader, Zinoviev's second fictional experiment is motivated by the hope for a more sophisticated, ironic, and self-aware general reader. *The Radiant Future* takes as its point of departure the reader's "realist" preferences. It has individualized characters with real names, past histories, personal development, positions in family and society. The characters' ideological values are much clearer and simpler than in Zinoviev's first experiment. The novel's events take place in familiar Muscovite settings in the environs of Cosmonaut Square.

Disguised by the familiar setting and the recognizable character types, Zinoviev's narrative here is built on much the same principles as in his earlier work. Although the novel's plot has much more drama than the antiplot of *The Yawning Heights*, it still makes use of a modified "Chekhovian" narrative technique in which the real drama of the novel, the emergence of consciousness, goes on in the background concealed by a nonevent. At first glance, the central event would seem to be the narrator's efforts to be elected to the Academy of Sciences, but it gradually becomes clear that the real focus of the novel is the emerging truth about the narrator's past and present relations with the dissident and former *zek*, Anton Zimin. Related to this process and of still greater importance is the ideological coming-of-age of the narrator's daughter, Lenka, a student who is quickly learning the adults' "utopian" linguistic game of doublethink and doublespeak. In both of Zinoviev's works the plot, such as it is, builds on the same two main events, the nonevent of an upcoming election in the academic world and the dialogue and change in consciousness engendered by reading and responding to unpublished manuscripts. In *The Radiant Future* the manuscripts are Anton's study of Soviet society, "Communism: Ideology and Reality," and a series of satirical poems that Lenka brings home from the institute to show her father. Given the emphasis on writing and reading as chief modes of achieving self-consciousness, the protagonists thus turn out to be not the narrator, an established "liberal" sociologist, but Anton and Lenka, two relative outsiders.

The Radiant Future hews close to the realist tradition also in terms of its characters' preferences in reading matter. It is true that Zamiatin and Orwell are mentioned several times along with Solzhenitsyn as important saboteurs of Soviet ideology. Anton defends "modernism" (understood as experimental or avant-garde art, in general) against official accusations of being the tool of "enemies of the people" (RF, 133), and the narrator admits to enjoying contemporary experimental prose in the "modern" style (RF, 211). Nonetheless, both give much more moral weight to realist prose. In his manuscript Anton consciously and decisively departs from the modernist dystopian tradition of Zamiatin and Orwell. He does admire and agree with the "true observations" that they make about Soviet society and with their general thrust that realized utopia is a nightmarish disaster. But in contrast to them, he is possessed of a strongly historicist mentality. He believes that an author must strive to lay out the historical facts accurately and clearly before all else, and that one must stay with the effort to describe in detail and change the social environment in which one lives. Quite in contrast to the central characters in *The Yawning Heights*, Anton argues that the realist exposure of the facts of the Stalinist era, particularly by Solzhenitsyn, dealt the final blow to Marxist claims to ultimate truth and opened the way for other social options:

> Ideology can be defeated by the facts of the reality which it claims to illuminate. In the given case, that means the facts of that social reality which it claims to recognize, foresee, and theorize about. The facts drive Marxism into its own trap. That is why Nikita's speech and Solzhenitsyn's books dealt a much heavier blow to Marxism than all the critics of Marxism.... That is the path of any real criticism of Marxism—an uncompromising analysis of our society, and the publication of the facts of its existence. And it is the only path ... by which it is possible to develop an ideology more appropriate than Marxism is to man in modern society (RF, 102).

Anton's ideological profile is ambiguous, at once critical of ideological constructs and yet seduced by the possibility of an ideology that might be "adequate" for whole epochs. As an ideological type, Anton bears an important relation to protagonists in the dystopian novel. He acts much like D-503 or Winston Smith, seeming at first to take the reigning ideology as gospel truth. And yet, true to meta-utopia, it soon becomes clear that Anton is using this position to play devil's advocate. He claims that Soviet society is the classic model of communism, the only true realization of Marxism. Then later he argues from a classically anti-utopian position, paraphrasing Berdiaev: "I believe that the brightest dreams and ideals of humanity, when they are realized in concrete form, produce the most disastrous consequences" (RF, 185). All this posturing is used ultimately to arrive at the options open to a thinking person living in a realized utopia. Reforms have been shown to be out of the question. Innovation and adaptation will be quelled by neo-Stalinists who hold key positions of power. One can either remain with Marxism-Leninism or reject it altogether. In rejecting it, one must find a wholly different framework within which to function, while still trying to fight and disprove Marxism, for example, as Anton suggests, by putting it in the context of other religious systems.

Ultimately, however, Anton is not truly "meta-utopian" in his outlook: realizing that Marxism is a fiction, he nevertheless steps away in his own thinking from the border between ideological constructs that the meta-utopian protagonist straddles. Like the writer he admires most, Solzhenitsyn, he feels an implicit affinity for Christianity, with its appeal to the integrity of the human soul. In this, too, he is closer to Russian realist predecessors Tolstoi and Solzhenitsyn than to the more playful protagonists of other meta-utopian works (RF, 102–3). It will be Lenka who emerges as the real meta-utopian voice. She recognizes the myth of the radiant future as a "deception and a self-deception," but is also tragically torn apart by her refusal to play at doublethink even within the private world of her family (RF, 52). She is likewise unable to find a moral position beyond existing ideological constructs.

The central goals of both of Zinoviev's works are the same: to discredit Marxism's claim to be "science" by applying a scientific form of reasoning to it and to chart the way out of the linguistic prison house created by Soviet (utopian) rhetoric. If in *The Yawning Heights* the language problem is illustrated in puns and paralogisms, in *The Radiant Future* it is anchored in one linguistic leitmotif that runs throughout the novel, from the title to the very end. This is the image of the political sign on Cosmonaut Square, "Long Live Communism, the Radiant Future of All Humanity." Expressing much the same idea as The Schizophrenic does, Anton says that the chief problem confronting Russians is to free themselves from the oppression of the future, with its firm promise of an ideal society and its permissiveness toward any and all means of achieving that society. The problem is to open the future to the question, "Where are we going?" This general moral issue is made concrete in the fate of the sign on Cosmonaut Square.

The actual sign becomes emblematic of the reasons why the Marxist-Leninist orientation toward the future is perceived to be a lie. The sign occupies a dominant position, symbolizing the promise of Khrushchev to build communism "within the lifetime of the present generation" (RF, 14). Now under Brezhnev the sign grows gradually shabbier along with the social conditions that it symbolizes. From time to time workers spruce it up for some official occasion or other. The rest of the time people use its enormous tin letters for shelter. By the end, several of the letters have disappeared, stolen for personal use, for example, to put a new roof on a dacha. Toward the end the narrator walks through Cosmonaut Square and notices that the huge neon Lenin that hangs over the square has lost an eye and now wears on his face an expression of "sheer ill temper" (RF, 224). The letters of the slogan have been lost, stolen, or desecrated by resident pigeons, and now spell the absurd "——ong ——ve com——nism

[Da ravst uet kom nizm]" (RF, 182). Here is the concrete deconstruction of the Marxist-Leninist claim to legitimacy. The firm promise of a brilliant future is obviously a sham. Devoid of actual meaning, the letters belie blind faith and invite disillusioned laughter, thus opening the way to the imagination of other social alternatives.

Perhaps the most familiar and concrete language problem known to any Soviet reader is the problem of Aesopian language. In his excellent study of Aesopian language Lev Loseff points out the weakness of this sort of protest.[8] The Aesopian text is designed only to confirm what is already known or felt by a relatively circumscribed circle of receivers.[9] Because of what Loseff calls its "ambivalence," Aesopian language is powerless to convey new information or a new perspective.[10] That is, it must mold itself in such a way that its message escapes vigilant censors, and thus it cannot openly challenge stylistic and ideological stereotype.

Although they make broad use of such Aesopian techniques as allegory and ellipsis, both *The Yawning Heights* and *The Radiant Future* go beyond the bounds of the Aesopian. Zinoviev shows repeatedly that a typical Aesopian reading is not a productive one. For example, in *The Yawning Heights* The Sociologist and other official personages read The Schizophrenic's first, fairly open attempt at analysis of "social laws" as a secret statement that he does not "like" "ism" and thus must be an enemy and a "deviant" (YH, 116). After The Schizophrenic has been incarcerated in a mental hospital, The Big Mouth finds that his work has turned up in bookstores disguised as a book on the behavior of rats. Whatever challenge it may have had in an earlier version it has now lost. What had been designed as a constructive analysis of the Ibansk experiment is now little more than a secret satire. It is in the dialogues and manuscripts of The Big Mouth and The Slanderer that his work finds a more constructive response. The reader, of course, is privy to even more information. She is allowed to see both versions of the work, as well as the unpublished studies of other underground characters, and is urged to

---

[8] Lev Loseff, *On the Beneficence of Censorship: Aesopian Language in Modern Russian Literature* (Munich: Sagner, 1984), 219.

[9] For other examples of the function of Aesopian language in the post-Stalinist era, see my article "Kafka and the Modernism-Realism Debate in Literary Criticism of the Thaw," in *The European Foundations of Russian Modernism*, ed. P. Barta in collaboration with U. Goebel (Lewiston, Maine: The Edwin Mellen Press, 1991), 295–325.

[10] Loseff, *On the Beneficence of Censorship*, 34.

understand the Aesopian protest as it really is: a truncated, inconsequential statement leading at most to cynicism and despair of real change.

Aesopian language is treated only by implication in *The Radiant Future*. Both authors in this work, Anton and Lenka, are striving to find their own idiom free of the techniques of verbal concealment and half-spoken protests forced by the censorship. Both bypass censorship, Anton by publishing his study abroad and Lenka by limiting herself to the realms of oral art and unpublishable writing "for the drawer." It should be said that Lenka does submit to constraints imposed by official culture to the extent that she hides the fact that she is the author of all the satirical verse she brings home. She claims that a boy at the institute has written the poems and that there is a whole crowd of students who share this material. Toward the end, her father figures out that she is in fact the sole author.

The duplicity of contemporary language use, doublethink and doublespeak, is another problem related to Aesopian language. It is particularly poignant in the experience of Lenka, who is growing up in Soviet society. By nature she is very frank, incisive, and, indeed, cutting in her observations about the people around her. In time she learns to play the most damaging word game of all, which every Soviet eventually learns, to think and say one thing in private and its opposite in public. At the novel's outset, she appears to say what she thinks both at home and at school. Then she starts to lie, inventing a support group to legitimize her outspoken views and hinting that she runs with a crowd of relative freethinkers who are not afraid to write what they believe. With time, of course, it becomes clear that there is no such crowd of fellow satirists. Finally, Lenka perfects her hold on doublespeak when she announces that she is playing the prominent role of the partisan in her school's production of the fairy tale "The Crimson Flower" (RF, 196). She has learned to do the right things, to make the right impression, in order to achieve eventual goals, for example, a good academic record or a good job. It is when she is forced to play the game of doublespeak at home in front of her intolerant, Stalinist mother and relatively lenient but cowardly father that she is finally undone. There is no arena in which a young person can develop moral integrity.

Yet it is Lenka, even more than Anton, who comes up with an alternative to the constraints of utopian language and consciousness. The wordplay in her poetry starts with the juxtaposition of utopian hyperbole with wooden, bureaucratic language and a crude, subliterary idiom. She arrives at a formulation of her own *parole*, a clear and unambiguous judgment of the linguistic absurdity of the Soviet *langue* and the immorality of its users. The most significant poem in her repertoire acts as both a thematic and a chronological frame for the rest: she recites the first part of the poem in her first private performance for her father and finishes the recitation near the end of the book, as one of her last performances—after her father has figured out that she is the author of the piece.

The poem is cited in its entirety below. Breaks in the poem preceded by a number indicate the way it is broken up in the text of *The Radiant Future* and the number of the page in the Russian edition on which the given fragment falls. My own prose translation is provided on the right:

Прекратим на мгновенье спор тот пустой.	Let us stop this empty argument for a moment.
Пусть реальностью станет, во что мы не верим,	Let what we do not believe in become reality,
Пусть воздвигнется Светлое Здание то,	Let the Radiant Edifice be erected,
И широко раскроются Райские двери. (28)	And let the gates of Paradise be thrown wide open.
Пусть к живущим могучие трубы взовут	Let the mighty trumpets call to the living
В учрежденные свыше законные сроки.	At the legal time, appointed on high.
И счастливцы, обнявшись, в те двери войдут,	And, embracing, those happy ones will enter the gates,
Отряхнут у порога былые пороки. (28)	Will shake off past vices at the threshold.
И в чаду справедливости и доброты,	And in the ravings of justice and kindness,
Воплотившем прогнозы марксистского знания,	That fulfilled the prognoses of Marxist knowledge,
Меня ласково спросят вожди: ну, а ты?	The leaders will affectionately ask me: and what about you?
Или наши не слышишь, стервец, приказанья?!	Don't you hear our orders, you shithead?!
Что стоишь, словно пень, не подымешь ноги?!	What are you standing there like a stump for, move on?!

Коли в чем провинился— прощаем. Заходи в коммунизм. И кусай пироги. Запивай их с конфетами чаем. (29)	If you're guilty of something, we forgive. Come on into communism. And have some bites of pie. Drink them down with tea and candy.
Я отвечу: когда-то меж бывших живых Шевелились кошмарные слухи, Будто много зазря уничтожили вы В той открывшей наш век заварухе. Будто много зазря потесали углов Ради этого самого рая. И без счету снесли неповинных голов В гуманизм и заботу играя.	I will answer: at some time among the former living Nightmarish rumors were afoot, That you wasted many in vain In that commotion that opened our century. That you cut a lot of corners in vain For the sake of—uh—paradise. And you cut off innumerable innocent heads While playing at humanism and concern.
Да, мне скажут они, нету смысла скрывать. Победителей вроде не судят. Мы затем и ломали когда-то дрова, Что Грядущее, верили, будет.	Well, they'll say, there's no point in hiding it. They don't really punish the victors anyway. We cut wood at one time because We believed that the Future would come to pass.
Заходи, как и все, и мозги не мути. По потребности ешь. По способности делай. А про жертвы забудь. То издержки пути. Даже память о жертвах потлела. Значит были, скажу я, тогда палачи. Значит были и те, кто страдали. Значит будем теперь пожирать калачи,	Come on in, like everyone else, and don't muddle your head. Eat what you need. Do what you can. And forget about victims. Those are just travel expenses. Even the memory of victims has rotted. So you were, I will say, the executioners then. So there were those who suffered. So we're now to gobble down the white loaves,

Что в дороге другим
    недодали.
Не войду, я скажу, в ваш
    Сияющий Дом.
Лучше тут упаду, у порога.
 	
Если все мы в него, как
    бараны войдем,
Повторится все та же
    дорога. (RF, 160–161)
	That you withheld from the
	    others on the way.
	I won't come, I'll say, into
	    your Radiant House.
	I'd be better off falling dead
	    here at the threshold.
	
	If we all enter in like sheep,
	
	The same road will just be
	    retraced.

The poem begins and ends with utopian-apocalyptic hyperbole, images such as the "Radiant House," "gates of Paradise," "mighty trumpets." The Russian, high-style word for "future" that is used here, "Griadushchee," bears heightened, even apocalyptic overtones. Forms of the verb such as the third-person imperative and the future perfect convey the will to turn the fabulous dream into reality and the confidence that it will happen. In the second part of the poem the poet undermines this imagery by mimicking it in incredulous tones.

Gradually a dialogue between the gatekeeper-leaders and the doubting poet develops. In the course of their interchange the leaders' miasma, their inability to perceive reality, their arrogance, and their contemptuous, patronizing attitude toward their prospective subjects all become obvious. The grand apocalyptic images give way to a wooden bureaucratese. For example, communism will come to pass by "legally appointed deadlines." The "ravings of goodness and justice" will "embody the prognoses of Marxist knowledge." The leaders show their lack of moral consciousness by couching what was really genocide in harmless-sounding euphemisms, such as "cutting wood" and "travel expenses." The worst aspect of the leaders' language is the condescension that is evident in the way these leaders treat the citizenry, almost as a herd of animals. Those who doubt, who do not buy into their hyperbole and who show the glimmerings of an independent consciousness, are addressed with rude expletives, which reinforces the impression that the Stalinist dream is completely without moral substance. In addition, it becomes clear that the leaders assume, as did Dostoevsky's Grand Inquisitor, that all that people need for happiness is minimal material welfare. The leaders advise the poet not to "muddle her head" and to come fill herself with pies, candy, and tea. Lenin's utopian dictum, "From each according to ability, to each according to need," is flippantly cited only to support this cynical view. Thus, the leaders' use of language is that hypothesized by Nietzsche: language in its social function enforces social conformity, the "average," the mentality of the herd animal, and language in its social function suppresses what is original and unique.

The poet, by contrast, begins her questioning of the blind faith expected by the leaders by referring to past experience, to historical memory, something that the leaders would like to obliterate. Her past tense challenges their future perfect. Out of habit, she starts by speaking in euphemistic metaphors, such as "commotion" and "cutting corners." But she soon comes into her own, calling past acts by their correct names. Then she draws the leaders into her own clear, direct language—they admit the existence of "victims," although their concern here is to encourage the living to forget them. The poet comes to the unambiguous conclusion that the leaders were "executioners," that there were indeed "those who suffered," and that the living were being asked to eat loaves of white bread withheld from those who died. Personal language prevails: the poet refuses to enter paradise, to forget the past, knowing that the same nightmare will repeat itself if she does.

Lenka's final poem is about Brezhnev. It serves as a kind of coda, reemphasizing the link between language and social consciousness:

Что ни жест—историческое событие.	His every gesture is a historic event.
Что ни шаг—эпохальное свержение.	His every step is an epoch-making upheaval.
Теоретик,—не сделавши открытия,	A theorist without ever making a discovery,
Полководец,—не выигравши сражения.	A commander without ever winning a battle.
Что ни слово—озарение гения,	His every word is the illumination of genius,
Проникновение в глубины мироздания,	A penetration into the depths of the universe,
Вклад в развитие передового учения,	A contribution to the cutting edge of science,
Всему человечеству мудрейшие указания.	For all humanity the wisest instructions.
И за годом год этот бред все тянется,	And year after year this gibberish drags on,

И никто открыто сказать не может: Это ж косноязычный маразматик и пьяница На арене истории корчит вам рожи!! (199)	And no one can say openly: This is an inarticulate senile old drunkard Making faces at you from the stage of history!!

Lenka exposes all the hyperbole of the Soviet lingo for what it is, "gibberish." The "word" of the leader, the language standard that he perpetrates, comes in for much more sarcastic treatment than other aspects of his public image, for it is language that creates the basis for social consciousness. Brezhnev's linguistic medium is none of the grand, truthful things it pretends to be, and certainly is far from providing a standard for public discourse. Rather, it is the inarticulate clowning and mimicry of an old fool.

Lenka's poem is read in a dramatic context that pits her search for a language of moral clarity against the forces of social conformity. When she has recited her poem, her mother, Tamara, a straight-laced Stalinist, slaps her in the face, rips the paper out of her hand, tears it up, and proclaims that Lenka will be disowned if she continues in this vein. The narrator, who fits the typical Russian stereotype of a liberal, a spineless coward, does not defend Lenka but retreats to his study. Thus, the game of doublethink and doublespeak of the outside world forces its way into the inner sanctum of the family. There is no haven for those in search of a private language of integrity and clarity. The split in mood, thought, and language is clearly too much for Lenka and very likely lays the foundation for her eventual suicide. The discovery that her father sided with the political enforcers is the last straw.

If more radical meta-utopias posit in the abstract a moral-linguistic stance on the boundaries between ideological systems, popularized meta-utopian fiction, such as *The Radiant Future*, show what such a stance might mean in "real" life. Anton manages to define a kind of moral integrity on the margins of Soviet society. In contrast, Lenka has her future before her and is not content simply to meditate on the insufficiencies of Soviet ideology. She finds a space for herself neither inside nor outside of society. Her private language, without a community of like-minded people, cannot survive or sustain her. Although it may contain the seeds of a new kind of social sensibility based on the dialogue between private modes of diction, the makings of such a society are nowhere apparent in *The Radiant Future*. Lenka ends up both a victim and a potential forerunner.

Beyond the critique of the Soviet myth of the future and the rhetoric in which it is couched, Zinoviev delivers a blow to the utopian notion of a rational, harmonious, communal human type, the Marxist-Leninist ideal of a "new man," that is familiar to any Russian reader. If *The Yawning Heights* again lays out the problem in an abstract, somewhat fragmentary form, debate in *The Radiant Future* provides a much more familiar picture of a person who is two-faced—nice in private and nasty in public—bored and boring and mentally blank from years of fruitless waiting, and unhappy with whatever position he or she occupies in the social hierarchy. Just as The Schizophrenic points out in his writings, the chief traits of this type are malice, gloating at others' failures, and status-consciousness. The narrator's drinking buddy, Edik, points out that the "new human type," far from being ideal, combines into one loathsome whole the "most repugnant qualities of human nature" (RF, 85). Anton remarks somewhat later on the far-reaching implications of this social experiment on human nature. Marxism has produced the "quintessence of mediocrity" (RF, 125). This mentality has become the bedrock for future generations and will certainly be the basis for whatever the "radiant future" will bring.

This popularized parallel text to *The Yawning Heights* leads to some firm conclusions while retaining its essentially meta-utopian quality of continual questing and questioning about the nature of ideology. As everywhere in post-Stalinist meta-utopian writing, Marxism is shown here to be a fiction among other fictions. It has no basis for claiming absolute truth. "Real" ideology is a provisional thing, as Anton points out, a rhetorical defense against the worst conditions in which one might live (RF, 248).

Without spelling out any alternative, which would contradict the spirit of meta-utopian thinking, various characters in the novel, particularly Edik and Anton, counter Marxist mediocrity and the morality of malice, each with his own "protestant" morality of the "significant personality" who decides to resist the utopian experiment. During Stalinist rule, this type has been destroyed, or his criticism deflected toward trivial objects. Anton says that now there exists no morality of "disinterested acts," by which he means "actions performed by one person toward others without being obliged to [perform them] by law or custom, which are of no benefit to the person who performs them ... but which will be of benefit to the people toward whom they are directed" (RF, 96).

Other suggestions and warnings are made toward the end of the novel. Anton warns that Russian nationalism could easily degenerate into anti-Semitism (RF, 260). He cautions that Russians must confront the deeper, historical problem in themselves of collective mediocrity. While Russians taken individually are often smart and even ingenious, collectively they are muddled. Finally, following Anton's general line of thinking, the narrator's son, Dima, suggests that no reforms of the system will work, in industry, agriculture, or any other area. He feels that public demonstrations and strikes will be necessary to change things (RF, 268).

The effect of such statements and suggestions is to satisfy the general reader's need to "learn a lesson," to be provided with a moral to the story, even though a concrete one is not forthcoming. By stating that there is no such moral, Anton implies that there ought to be one. Catering thus to the tastes and needs of the popular reader, Zinoviev, along with the Strugatskys, Tendriakov, and Aksënov, pursues a more moderate strategy than either Iskander or Voinovich will. Iskander and Voinovich will emerge as the boldest of the "popularizers" and ultimately offer the most radical challenge to the general reader's interpretive skills and moral values. While Iskander will confront the reader and her conventional reading habits and Voinovich will question the very possibility of a popular reader in an authoritarian society, Zinoviev urges a greater degree of critical thought, but without separating the reader altogether from old habits of didactic thinking and literalist interpretation.

* CHAPTER EIGHT *

Utopia, Imagination, and Memory

THE STRUGATSKY BROTHERS'

THE UGLY SWANS,

TENDRIAKOV'S *A POTSHOT AT MIRAGES,*

AND AKSËNOV'S *THE ISLAND OF*

CRIMEA

During a roundtable discussion on fresh departures in literary theory held in 1987, the Soviet critic Mikhail Epstein had the following to say about how utopian thinking can curtail creative imagination: "Imagination is the chief among liberating forces that move humanity forward; but when such archaic instincts as the will to power or [the desire for] universal leveling are attached onto the imagination like cars onto a locomotive, then imagination turns into utopia, sets limits for itself, stopping at some one, unshakable, and absolutely 'correct' vision of the future. Utopia is the suicide of the imagination: convening the masses of people for the reshaping of the world, it transforms them into the gravediggers of their future."[1] While Epstein overgeneralizes the repressive effect of utopian thinking on the creative imagination, extending it to all utopias, he is certainly right if he is referring to Plato's *Republic* and certain of its authoritarian descendants. In the ideal republic all moral-ideological probing is disallowed, and Socrates systematically turns his precursor/rivalHomer into the author of little more than a book on personal hygiene. Even More's more mild and ambiguous *Utopia*, which does not openly concern itself with circumscribing the imagination, does imply a certain limitation of imagination. The Utopians are not familiar with philosophy or literature. Although they read a great deal, they typically read books that are useful to their trade or craft or they read for entertainment and pleasure.

[1] "'Kruglyi stol,'" 25.

Epstein's observation could be applied to historical memory as well, which can be severely deformed and restricted in utopian writing and certainly in realized utopias: either past experience is considered to be irrelevant to utopian experience, which perceives itself to be on the other side of a temporal abyss from "history"; or history is conceived as a predetermined series leading to its own negation, that is, a final state of perfection that would implicitly obviate history as a category of human thought. As the Stalinist *Concise Philosophical Dictionary* of 1952 puts it: "Communist society represents a structure that is fundamentally different from any previous socioeconomic formations. It is not just another social form in the course of humanity's development, but the greatest turning point in the history of society, a turning point that will bring about a completely new era in the life of people."[2]

Three popular meta-utopian works, *The Ugly Swans*, *A Potshot at Mirages*, and *The Island of Crimea*, focus on the restrictions imposed on imagination and memory in a utopian context. These faculties are then unharnessed to give needed perspective on the experiment that they inhabit. In *The Ugly Swans* the novelist, Viktor Banev, who lives in a kind of twentieth-century welfare utopia gone bad, has to confront his own fantasy when it is taken to be "history" by the younger generation. The physicist, Georgy Petrovich Grebin, in *A Potshot at Mirages* is deep down a frustrated historian worried about humanity's future. He challenges progressivist and utopian assumptions about history by creating a series of historical fantasies that then can be brought to bear on the current dilemmas facing Soviet society. And Aksënov in *The Island of Crimea* posits a different historical outcome to the Bolshevik Revolution. Here the familiar peninsula of Crimea is remapped as an island the Whites defended against the Reds and which to the present day stands as an ideological challenge to the Soviet experiment, as a self-proclaimed "showcase for democracy" (IC, 5). All of these works question the conformity enforced by Marxist-Leninist historical determinism and Socialist Realist literalism.

A great deal has already been said here about treatment of memory and imagination in meta-utopian fiction, and particularly in Voinovich's novel, *Moscow 2042*. In contrast to Voinovich, who uses brain-teasing time imagery and intertwines contradictory notions of fiction as fantasy and historical documentation into a mutually

---

[2] *Kratkii filosofskii slovar'* (Moscow: Gosudarstvennoe izdatel'stvo politicheskoi literatury, 1952), 473.

compromising relationship, these works are more firmly rooted in the Russian realist tradition of the novel of ideas, that is, fiction as debate of current moral issues. Instead of challenging the credibility of the text and its status as a product of memory, as Voinovich does, they pose the problem at a greater distance, in terms of framed narratives within the larger text and in terms of characters' debates about issues of memory and imagination, all in the context of the credible, fictive world established within the text.

The implied reader in *The Ugly Swans* and *A Potshot at Mirages* is easy to identify and is characterized by a simple, literalist way of interpreting narrative. The situation in *The Island of Crimea* is somewhat more subtle. In *The Ugly Swans* one clear way in which the Strugatskys establish an implied reader is through characters' literary taste and interpretive habits. The main readers are the students with whom the writer Viktor Banev conducts a discussion about the purposes of fiction. These adolescents and pre-adolescents represent a naive "Socialist Realist" approach to reading: they expect from fiction an unequivocal ethic of devotion to a utopian social cause and a clearly drawn plan for social action. They do not perceive the use of imagination and memory to be issues, but rather assume that both serve the single purpose of creating the "good" society.

In Tendriakov's novel, the narrator Georgy Petrovich addresses the potential reader directly through his own query about the nature of time and the possibility of historical progress. However, as the novel advances, it becomes clear that Grebin is more than a narrator who is using a combination of history and fantasy to explore the relationship between social-technological progress and moral consciousness. As he interprets the historical fantasies that he and his assistants create, we see that he embodies the very practice of reading that he challenges, that is, a Marxist-Leninist belief that "history," the continuing development of social consciousness, is the result not of human will or conscious choice but of impersonal—social, economic, and technological—determinants.

In a preface written in 1983, two years after the appearance of the Russian edition of *The Island of Crimea*, Aksënov reveals the reason for his appeal to an educated, youthful, and quietly rebellious reader: "Every Russian schoolboy knows that Crimea is connected to mainland Russia by an isthmus, but not every adult knows how flimsy an isthmus it is. When a Russian rides along it for the first time and sees it for its narrow, swampy self, he can't quite suppress a seditious 'what if'" (IC, n.p.). Geography and history are reinvented at the authorial level, and the reader is expected to follow suit. Aksënov's narrative functions very much as a wish-fulfillment dream for a chic, young, educated Soviet. Here is a refantasized and rehistoricized version of the gray town of Simfiropol, now the jet-set capital of Crimea, a center of international finance, full of expensive cars and wondrous architecture. Characters read prerevolutionary philosophy and fiction (IC, 50)—thus fulfilling the nostalgic longing of the 1970s—but they also play and listen to contemporary jazz. They trade and travel at will.

All of these novels deliberately oppose traditional Socialist Realist practice, which makes memory the basis for a simplistic, epic referentiality. Aksënov sees almost everything to do with human relations—history, society, ideology—as the working of imagination. As Luchnikov puts it, "We Russians are known for our imagination.... Those endless pages of propaganda in the Party press are as much the product of our imagination as everything else Russian. Take our all but imaginary island, for example.... Our whole world is built on fantasy, on the free play of the imagination" (IC, 115). All three works question the reliability of an "observed" past and present fixed by "hard" fact. And all challenge the notion of disinterested objectivity and put greater emphasis on functions of critical interpretation and imaginative play than on the facts themselves.

In the Strugatskys' novel, history first arises as an issue when Viktor meets with the students to talk about writing fiction. The students reveal a strongly utopian-apocalyptic view of time. "History" as a way of ordering time and human experience is rejected altogether by the students who believe that "past history has come to an end, there's no need to refer to it" (US, 76). By contrast, it soon becomes apparent that for Viktor the most significant "history" is not the epic "History" of nations and mass movements but personal memory and one's private inquiry into the valuative frameworks into which one was born.

Imagination appears at first to be similarly harnessed to ideological interest. The students and, at first glance, Viktor appear to treat fiction as objective social document, as eyewitness to one's own time. Imagination per se is granted very little importance. At first, even the narrative structure of the novel itself seems to bear out this position. Even though it includes fantastic characters and events, such as the final, apocalyptic awakening of a "brave, new world," *The Ugly Swans* would at first seem to be less about imagining than about compiling a historical collage of intellectual, social, and political trends in the twentieth century. Indeed, Viktor and others would probably agree with the students' opinion that the art of every "well-known author expresses the ideology of his society or of a part of that society" (US, 76). Works of art are worth reading only to discover that ideology. It is implied that writers are not and should not be capable of independent, oppositionist imagination, unless they belong to a part of society that stands in opposition to the whole. Imagination has one use for all of Viktor's readers, students and older people alike: to create a blueprint, a program for the future, whether progressive or regressive, to provide an alternative to an insupportable present existence.

At first Viktor himself seems to be a kind of "critical realist" of a Chekhovian cast, whose heroes are ordinary people trying against all odds to hold onto their humanity (US, 71). In addition, despite having some obvious trademarks of a science-fiction novel, such as the presence of hostile extraterrestrials and the clash of human and alien civilizations, *The Ugly Swans* itself makes a "realist" claim to be a kind of social document, a profile of a town and its inhabitants. The story takes place in what used to be a spa, a "nowhere" out in the middle of the steppe. It has been raining for years, everything is rotting, and the healthful atmosphere has been destroyed. The rain, it turns out, is a scourge brought by some extraterrestrials, known as "slimies," who have settled into a building complex that used to be a leprosarium. They need the precipitation to stay alive. It should be noted that the slimies' presence is perceived by characters not as fantastic or extraordinary but as a rationalizable phenomenon. They are treated as humans with some fatal disease, like leprosy, popularly thought to be contagious. Believing that they will be infected by the slimies, the townspeople rebel against them; there is an increasing incidence of beatings and near-lynchings.

The traditional thematic of realist fiction, public affairs and the tension between public and private life, figures prominently in this novel. Town politics are very conservative. A trademark of the Strugatskys' works from the mid-1960s onward, the Stalinist brand of Marxism is seen to be inseparable from Nazi ideology. Also present in this mix is the postwar notion of the capitalist welfare state that the students see as a façade for the "military-industrial complex" (US, 68). The existing government is headed by a Stalinist dictator-*cum*-president who calls himself the "Father of His People" (US, 11). The town is run by a corrupt mayor and his enforcer, Pavor, who, it turns out, is a fascist with a dream of a "final solution" for society—to get rid of all workers and to create a fully automatized society where everyone lives in leisure.

A first challenge to conventional didactic reading habits—and particularly the conflation of imaginative and mnemotic faculties traditional in Socialist Realism—comes early in the novel. Viktor agrees to meet with the students in the school auditorium and talk to them about his writing. In their interview the students leave aesthetic matters aside and bring up ideological issues. They insist that art provide a strong utopian view of the future, that it present an "affirmative program" (US, 69). Viktor does agree that art first and foremost serves a didactic purpose. The broad purpose of art is to civilize, to "transform people into clean and pleasant types" (US, 69). But he goes on to say, "Literature is not the place for teaching, for proposing specific paths or concrete methodologies" (US, 69). Although he criticizes the classical realist Lev Tolstoi for his preachiness, he does endorse the "realist" view of the writer as "an instrument which indicates the condition of society" (US, 70). The writer, thus, is a tool, not a force of creative will or a consciousness that molds reality, bending events and compelling a fresh way of seeing them.

Viktor does resist the raison d'être for Socialist Realism. Literary imagination, when it is used to invent a single grand social scheme, is ultimately harmful, and the realization of utopia brings disaster. Literature should not raise bright banners promising some radiant future, but should civilize and refine. His view is a tolerant one engendered by despair, what Nietzsche might have called the "anesthesia of the spirit," and what the students call "The end of hope. The end of humanity. A dead end" (US, 73). Social progress, such as it is, involves the tempering of excess, the civilizing of human behavior, the "movement of society toward a state in which people don't kill, trample, and torment one another" (US, 71). The students' aversion to the society to which they were born and their yearning for a fresh start, for some mystic transfiguration, Viktor calls "cruelty out of the best possible motives" (US, 75). He argues that this Bakunin-like urge to destroy the old and create the new

> can't bring anything except fresh grief, fresh tears, and fresh baseness. That's what you have in mind. And don't think you're saying something very new. To destroy the old world and build up a new

one on its bones is a very old idea. And never once has it brought the desired results. The same thing that calls forth the desire for merciless destruction in the old world quickly adapts itself to the process of destruction, to cruelty and mercilessness. It becomes essential to this process and always gets retained. It becomes the master of the new world and, in the final analysis, kills the bold destroyers themselves (US, 75).

Viktor gives a psychological explanation for the failure of all utopian schemes. The destructive impulse cannot be transformed into a creative one. The "leather jackets" who tear down the old order will always remain leather jackets and will poison the new order with their physical coerciveness. The old order must be superseded and incorporated into the new, Viktor implies.

The young suggest that they have no intention of tearing anything down: they just want to build beyond the dead end in which present society finds itself. In this intention they seem to offer yet a new hope, an alternative for the future. Indeed, one of the student leaders, Bol-Kunats, accuses Viktor of being the cruel one. He argues: "[Y]ou can't imagine building the new without destroying the old. And we can imagine this very well. We'll even help your generation to build its heaven, and you can drink liquor to your heart's content. We're building, Mr. Banev, only building. We're not destroying anything, only building" (US, 75–76). All this sounds like a very peaceable answer to the modern paradox of ends and means that has thwarted the actualization of utopian designs. And in the end Bol-Kunats and Viktor's daughter, Irma, reappear as flower children (which is appropriate, since *The Ugly Swans* was written in 1966–1967), beautiful people in a world reborn where the sun is shining and nature has reclaimed its place over the vestiges of the old civilization.

Nonetheless, several aspects of the students' rhetoric and behavior arouse Viktor's suspicions. Toward the end of his first meeting with the students at the school, Viktor's reminder that classically "old worlds have had to be destroyed because they got in the way" is answered with the classically utopian thought that the "present old world . . . will not get in our way. . . . Past history has come to an end, there's no need to refer to it" (US, 76). Utopia traditionally does not tolerate the notion of historical development, being itself a complete social order. Already Bol-Kunats is expressing but not confronting the problem of the border between history and timelessness.

At the novel's end, Viktor decides out of sheer curiosity to stay with the children and find out how the new world will be built. The Strugatskys show not a new order but the moment of triumphant ecstasy, stupendous beauty, and purity that is the real experience sought by the apocalyptic utopian mind. But even into this newborn world comes the hint of vindictiveness. The beautiful, suntanned Irma holds a twig in her hand which she points at Viktor and uses symbolically to shoot him. The last line of the novel is Viktor's reminder to himself that he must "return" to the old world. A writer who insists on freedom of imagination, he must always seek out the borderline between systems of value, neither blindly embracing nor rejecting but balancing and negotiating human possibilities.

The Ugly Swans presents another challenge to a reader used to expecting in fiction a "realist" reflection of human life. The novel sustains a meditation on the concept of realism itself. Viktor muses that there can really be no scientific definition of realism. Realism as a single concept is quite meaningless because there is no such thing as objective reality. As Viktor conceives it, rather simplistically, reality is "the world plus the observer's effect on it" (US, 139). He decides that reality is what each person imagines it to be. Each person perceives reality through his or her own ideological prism. Indeed, we have seen how Bol-Kunats, the student leader, sees the present and the future as completely inimical to one another. Yet the students themselves do not share a common perception of social reality. Even the way in which each separate student treats Viktor shows a wide variance in their opinions and behavior. Some scoff at him, while others seem sympathetic. Still others admire him as a major cultural figure, even asking for his autograph. The same is true of the adults' dreams for the future. For example, Pavor's dream of a "final solution," a golden age in which all workers will be liquidated, is only one of many ways in which characters see things. The doctor Golem looks to the future for a brilliant technocratic society inhabited by intelligent, sensitive people.

Narrative techniques employed in *The Ugly Swans* also work subtly to undermine Viktor's claim to be a realist writer. The novel is told in the third person, but as the plot develops, it becomes clear that, as in a Kafka novel, narrative point of view is essentially that of the protagonist. Everything is told from Viktor's perspective, which turns out to be spatially as well as conceptually very limited. His senses are restricted by physical boundaries—walls, doors, driving rain. And his perceptions are frequently confused by sleep or alcohol. His judgments of the people around him—for example, the doctor at the leprosarium, Yul Golem, Diana, Pavor, or the slimies—are often shaky and unreliable, and they change as events develop. One has the sense that there is a great deal that Viktor does not know about the story in which he plays the central role. The effect is to disorient the reader, to give him a sense of the relativity of all judgment and all ideological frameworks, and, in terms of the plot, to keep him guessing as to what is "happening."

The conventional Soviet reader, raised to be suspicious of "decadent" formalism and aestheticism and of moral relativism, is brought around to a meta-utopian view not by open confrontation but indirectly—by following Banev's responses to real political demands placed on his art and Banev's inner monologue about plot construction and the worldview implied therein. For example, at his meeting with the students early in the novel Viktor asserts a broadly held opinion that "there is nothing particularly interesting in learning how a novel was written" (US, 65). But he persists in playing with conventional plots, such as an "optimistic story" about Christ that would differ from the versions created by the evangelists. He also muses over a science-fiction plot with a war against extraterrestrials (US, 153–54) and an anti-utopian, what he calls "Orwellian," scenario about the fate of the "superman" hero in modern society (US, 197). All of them are ironic, showing the author's awareness of his own ideological-moral claims and the values embedded in previous versions of the plot. All expose the coercive power of ideological constructs to censure imagination and force a specific progression and outcome of the narrative. Viktor always insists that there are other, possibly better variants of a story that do not see the light of day because they do not fit in with the reigning status quo. For example, he muses about the following "optimistic story":

> You could always write about a man whose work consists of loving his neighbor, and who is happy because he loves his neighbor and he loves his work. But that was already done, a couple of thousand years ago, by Messrs. Luke, Matthew, John, and one other—four of them in all. Actually there were a lot more of them, but only those four were ideologically reliable, the others lacking various things, national self-awareness, for example, or mailing privileges. And the man they were writing about was, unfortunately, feebleminded.

> Although it would be interesting to write about Christ coming down to earth today, not like Dostoevsky did it, but like that Luke and company. Christ arrives at staff headquarters and makes his proposals about loving thy neighbor, etc. And naturally they've got some anti-Semite sitting there. (US, 101)

Viktor himself is continually being put under pressure to write denunciations and to support various interests, the state, the students, the slimies. He always refuses, lending his assistance only once to help in the arrest of the fascist Pavor.

Thus, the Strugatskys make use of a fairly typical realist protagonist first to challenge the constraints on memory and imagination imposed by Socialist Realism and then to call into question the very notion of realism itself, its discrediting of fantasy, and its claims to scientific objectivity and historical verisimilitude. Within the limits of a conventional science-fiction plot involving the confrontation of people with aliens, the Strugatskys hint faintly at a notion that is central to the Western *nouveau roman*: that plot is endlessly variable. Viktor's insight that imagination and memory are only relatively "free" when they mark out the boundaries of ideological constructs, the fissures in them between coercion and value, parallels Ricoeur's idea that the utopian imagination points out the gap between citizens' faith in an existing ideology and a ruler's use of that ideology to lend authority (US, 17). Some perspective on the distorting effect of ideology can be attained only in confrontation and dialogue between ideologies. That dialogue goes on in *The Ugly Swans* within the mind of Viktor Banev.

Both Tendriakov and Aksënov approach the interaction of memory and imagination from a perspective quite opposed to that taken in *The Ugly Swans*. To free imagination and memory from the restrictions of an oppressive ideology, the Strugatskys use the interior monologue and dialogical technique inherent in the conventional novel of ideas. In contrast, Tendriakov and Aksënov use what E. L. Doctorow has called "speculative history."[3] Tendriakov's goal is specifically to question the Marxist-Leninist notion of historical determinism. Here he employs a technique, familiar in Bulgakov's *The Master and Margarita* and, as well, in Kingston's *The Woman Warrior*, Eco's *The Name of the Rose*, and Coetzee's *Foe*, of consciously fictionalizing

---

[3] Cited in Hutcheon, *A Poetics of Postmodernism*, 112.

history in order to tease out experiences and ideologies of the disenfranchised.

In his novel, Tendriakov challenges specific aspects of Marxist-Leninist historiography, particularly the secondary role it assigns to human will, the determinist relationship it posits between social environment and the formation of moral character, and its inherent optimism. The narrator, Grebin, is a physicist with a strong interest in how people perceive time. He suspects that technological advance in the twentieth century has moved humanity anywhere but forward, and he is deeply worried about the future. People always scorn their own present time in favor either of some past golden age or of some future order. Technological advancement has not brought moral improvement. People are not any kinder or happier than they used to be. He laughs at the envy that the nineteenth-century forefather of Socialist Realism, Vissarion Belinsky, felt toward people who would be living in 1940, one hundred years after his own time. He was sure that people would be well-off and productive (PM, 69). Grebin's concern is that humanity flourish. The way to make that happen, he feels, is to gain a sober perspective of our place in history, to examine the prejudices with which we view our past, present, and future.

This concern brings Grebin to try a completely fanciful experiment with a computerized model of history that would test the hypothesis that human will is of little importance in the making of historical events. He decides to remove from history one of its key personalities, Jesus Christ, as if Christ and his teaching had never existed. In Proppian terms, Grebin wants to test whether in historical narrative the series of plot-functions determines character. Clearly borrowing a tactic made popular by Bulgakov, Tendriakov weaves five separate historical fantasies set in the ancient world and the Renaissance into the main setting of Moscow in the 1970s. Although plausible, none of them is true. Each treats some aspect of Western moral-religious consciousness, linking it to material, technological progress and political development, but positing its emergence without the influence of the figure of Christ. One of these fantasies takes place before the time of Christ and deals with Diogenes' quarrel with Aristotle about moral education and its effects on social behavior. Others tell about Jesus' premature death at the hands of an irate crowd, the "conversion" of Paul, and religious teaching among slaves in the late Roman Empire. The final one is a dialogue about the failure of realized utopia between the dying Tommaso Campanella and his characters from *The*

City of the Sun. Each of these episodes shows in its own way the insufficiency of technological invention as a determinant of moral character. Perhaps predictably, this series of episodes reconfirms the need for the childlike, ascetic type that Christ may have been as a counterbalance to temporal power.

Grebin feeds into the computer a variety of human personality traits and has the computer "resketch" moral ideals of each period as it would have been without Christ. Each time the computer re-creates the personality of a Christ figure as the highest moral type. In a way, Tendriakov here mimics Dostoevsky's famous remark that, if Christ did not exist, people would have invented him. The vision of history implied here is strongly deterministic in the sense that plot-functions force a kind of moral character type and not the other way around.

Nonetheless, Grebin's experiment does challenge the determinist Marxist-Leninist truism learned by every schoolchild that "the means of production of material life condition the social, political, and spiritual processes of life in general" (PM, 136). What he concludes is that people yearn for some moral force to counter the impulse merely to submit to the existing political and economic order. He finds a consistent if weak "utopian" impulse in human nature to strive for justice and happiness. People want an uplifting idea to sustain them. On the other hand, neither utopian experiment, such as Campanella's, nor technological advancement satisfies that need. It is implied, too, that the grand Soviet utopia has likewise done nothing to make people better or happier. As Grebin's assistant, the history student Tolia, points out, people are now materially better off than they have ever been, but by no means do they behave better morally.

Tendriakov establishes the horizon of expectation of his implied reader in two ways. He suggests to the reader a thoroughly acceptable degree of fantasy and experimentation through the use of inserted historical fictions about Jesus' life. Since the appearance of *The Master and Margarita* this technique has been repeated in other works, for example, in Chingiz Aitmatov's best-seller, *The Executioner's Block* (*Plakha*, 1987). Grebin also conveys his moral concerns through direct address of the reader. He starts the novel with his own musings about time and the relationship between scientific and technological advancement and moral betterment. He expresses concern for the future welfare of humanity and appeals to the reader's sympathy, begging her "not to judge [him] harshly for this triviality" (PM, 70). He also defines his own moral character to the reader, assuring her that he is not a typical messianic utopian: "I am afraid that the impression might be formed: oho, doesn't this guy suffer from some messianic mania? A malaise, it's true, that is not so rare in our rationalistic age" (PM, 70).

One of the questions that Grebin raises at the beginning of *Potshot* is Tolstoi's query as to whether history really should be conceived, as it has been classically, in terms of great personalities and the force of human will. An alternative frame for interpreting historical events is defined in terms of the scientific discoveries that make possible a higher level of human civilization. The first three of his historical fantasies posit a situation in which moral consciousness is achieved through spiritual revelation or moral education. All conclude with the continuation of the same bad old social behavior. After receiving an education from Aristotle, the greatest teacher in the ancient world, Alexander the Great will go off to war and kill thousands of people for his own aggrandizement. After they have heard the gentlest and most self-abnegating of moral "physicians," people will still give into mob suspicion of individual morality and will stone Jesus of Nazareth to death. After a heartrending and guilt-inspiring confrontation with a little girl and the massacre of her family of religious renegades, Paul will cease to serve the Sanhedron but will nonetheless continue to preach submissiveness to temporal authority.

In the second group, each of two fantasies juxtaposes moral teaching and technological advance, for example, farming with a plow instead of with a hoe, in the context of a consciously chosen social experiment. The supposition here is: "If natural human [social] systems are capable of forcing the most humane person to kill, the compassionate to be cruel, the honest to prevaricate, then in theory the opposite should be possible—some kind of social mechanism that compels the hard-hearted to be compassionate, the egoist to perform magnanimous acts" (PM, 128). The first of these social experiments is set in Roman times. Slaves receive a parcel of land to farm and are given greater freedom to work the land as they choose and for their own profit. More efficient forms of farming have become possible, potentially relieving laborers of drudgery. The more radical experiment dramatized here is, of course, Campanella's city of plenty in which perfect social equality reigns.

Both experiments are shown as disastrous failures. The Roman slaves on their freely held land will become not better, harder-working, or kinder, but merely smug and cynical. Grebin decides that neither technological nor social change imposed from the outside can significantly alter one's moral consciousness. Likewise, in its realized form Campanella's egalitarian construct brings out the very worst sentiments of jealousy and greed in people. Paradoxically, equality imposed upon people carries with it its own injustice. It is unfair to reward equally people who are inherently unequal in intelligence, kindness, ability, and industriousness.

These experiments in historical fantasy are woven together with two other subplots taken from "personal history" that are familiar in some form to most Russian readers. The implication here is that the Marxist-Leninist experiment should have created the perfect social conditions for the emergence of an ideal moral consciousness. One such subplot is the narrator's unsuccessful relationship with his rebellious son, Seva. Both Grebin and his wife, Katia, feel that they have done their very best in raising their son, giving him every available opportunity. But as Katia realizes, all they have done is protect him, cover up his mistakes, smooth the way, and make excuses for all his failures. He has never had to work things out for himself and has become a spineless, resentful, and dishonest young man who fails at one job after another and cannot build lasting relationships with other people.

Another contemporary subplot involves Grebin's encounters with his mentor and friend from the army, Golenkov, who, finding himself near death, is reassessing the achievements of the revolution, the Civil War, and World War II. Golenkov particularly regrets his failure to build anything in his life. He questions his enthusiastic participation in the destruction of churches, of the country's spiritual and cultural heritage (PM, 74–75). Now, at the end of his life, he has alienated his children and can find no meaning or satisfaction in his existence. Thus, Golenkov's personal memories of lived experience, like those of Paul in Roman times, serve as the basis for the emergence of moral consciousness. These subplots function as sixth and seventh historical episodes that, seen in the light of the five historical fantasies, lend themselves to deeper, nontraditional interpretations. Here the implications of the fictional constructs are juxtaposed to the very real Soviet experiment, with the result that the monumental myth of Soviet history is undermined. It is clearly no good as a model either for the present or for the future.

The end of *A Potshot at Mirages* is unsatisfying, although unsatisfying in significant ways that spur the reader to pursue the moral implications of Tendriakov's historical game. In his personal life Grebin is unable to confront and examine his failure in his son's upbringing. His wife Katia does seem to break through to some new understanding, but Grebin himself remains in the same distant, passive position that he has always maintained. He has not developed new insight. His historiographical experiment, as flimsy as it may be, does raise intriguing questions about past religious movements and social experimentation. All of his assistants go through some kind of process of rethinking their values. They grow in some way, and yet Grebin clings to his old Marxist-Leninist determinism, the belief in the power of social and technological conditions to shape moral character. In this respect, as well, Grebin has failed to grow. What is obvious here is Grebin's lack of self-reflection, his inability to grow through his creative activity.

One alternative to this moral blindness is offered by Grebin himself. Meditating on Golenkov's misery, Grebin remembers Pushkin's poem "The Sower of Freedom in the Desert" ("Svobody seiatel' pustynnyi"). He agrees with this poem's rather existentialist conclusion that each person is born responsible for his own vices (PM, 149–51). People do not seem capable of being improved by doctrines that are imposed from the outside. Grebin, however, does not apply this idea to his own life and seems incapable of reflecting on his own vices.

With his coupling of fantasy and history, Tendriakov has managed to convey the idea that historiographical convention, far from being set in stone, is founded on problematic ideological assumptions. In this way, imagination and memory can cooperate in uncovering those assumptions and finding more adequate ways of conceptualizing past, present, and future. Fiction and historiography have a vital relationship to each other, fiction perhaps being the more capable of posing vital philosophical and moral questions and historiography having the greater ability to "prove" and convince—in a word, to legitimize. In this testing of historiographical assumption Tendriakov's experiment is somewhat reminiscent of Gore Vidal's historical novels from the 1960s and 1970s, such as *Burr* and *Julian*. Vidal uses fiction to focus on history's antiheroes and their alternative moral views while Tendriakov's narrative probes the links between religious faith and grand social experiments, between spiritual need and temporal power, between technological advance and human perfectibility. Nonetheless, both revive interest in history by speculating about important moral questions linking the present with the past that academic historiography cannot usually address.

A Potshot at Mirages arrives at a position quite in agreement with the concept of history put forward by Ortega y Gasset in *History as System*. Here Ortega claims that history is the only "science" capable of giving human existence meaning. He argues: "History is the systematic science of that radical reality, my life. It is therefore a science of the present in the most rigorous and actual sense of the word.... The opposite—and customary—interpretation is equivalent to making of the past an abstract, unreal something lying lifeless just where it happened in time, whereas the past is in truth the live, active force that sustains our today.... The past is not yonder, at the date when it happened, but here, in me."[4] By deliberately playing historiological games, Tendriakov overcomes utopia's disastrous, apocalyptic rejection of the past as dead and irrelevant. Rather, he succeeds in bringing past events into a relationship with the present that can illuminate the dilemma of the present and make possible a future that will not merely be a continuation of the bad old present. As Ortega notes, while consciousness of the past certainly limits the possibilities open to a person or a society in the future, it is only by becoming conscious of past experience that one can have a future at all.[5]

Of the three novels considered here, Aksënov's draws most successfully on the tension between imagination and memory. Framed in the popular genre of the international thriller combining adventure, romance, and intrigue, *The Island of Crimea* builds on both realist representational technique and world-inventing fantasy. The goal is to revisualize twentieth-century history based on a plausible although, of course, not factually "true" hypothesis, to imagine another outcome to the revolution and what might then follow. This process of reimagining apprehends aspects of moral and political identity in a surprising way.

Unlike nearly all the meta-utopian fiction considered here, which generally moves from various forms of ideological monologism to various kinds of debate and dialogue, *The Island of Crimea* posits a pluralistic cultural and political context that then poignantly reverts to monologism. Cosmopolitan playground, center of world trade and diplomacy, and technological miracle, this hypermodern Crimean

---
[4] José Ortega y Gasset, *History as System* (New York: W. W. Norton, 1961), 223.
[5] Ibid., 208.

meta-utopia is based on a multiplicity, one might even say "cacophony," of ideological voices—monarchists, liberals, radicals, fascists, defendants of ethnic rights—all coexisting in provisional and constantly fluctuating forms of consensus and compromise. The Crimea of Aksënov's fantasy is striking for its proximity to a geographical entity, the Soviet Union, that represents its ideological opposite—monological, ideologically fixed, stagnant, in short, a traditional utopia. In its structure it contains the unresolved oppositions of a utopia: it is isolated, yet claims international influence, drab and egalitarian yet hierarchically regimented, oppressive yet proclaiming liberationist policies.

This novel succeeds in going a step further than much meta-utopian writing: the author creates dramatic poignancy around an image of the meta-utopian "paradise lost." Only when one has imagined, made palpable, and, in a way, realized in novel form the kind of heteroglossic society and civil social discourse that meta-utopias only theorize does one feel its value and urgency most strongly. The flaw is in the novel's middle-aged protagonist, Andrei Luchnikov, a self-proclaimed liberal who enjoys all the benefits of this society won by his monarchist mothers and fathers. The society is now being challenged by a new generation of daughters and sons who wish to achieve a new kind of social justice and equality by winning the right to greater social well-being for the island's ethnic minority, the Yakis. The editor of the influential liberal newspaper, *The Russian Courier*, Luchnikov traverses all borders and has access to all forms of discourse. His failing is typically Russian and even recognizable in contemporary communist diehards who posit anarchy and apocalypse as the only alternative to party control: Luchnikov interprets the ideological multilingualism that is a central trait of meta-utopian pluralism as chaos, and he imagines that Crimean society is on the border of collapse.

Possessed of a nostalgic, semi-Slavophile attachment to an ideal of mythic national unity, Luchnikov dreams of erasing geographical borders between the Soviet Union and Crimea and the ideological boundaries that they symbolize. He and like-minded Crimeans have formed an organization known as the Common Fate League. Its Russian acronym, SOS, which stands for "Soiuz obshchei sud'by," emphasizes its members' consternation at the social "chaos" that surrounds them. Crimea, in their opinion, is in the "backwaters of civilization" and needs to be "rescued." Their nostalgic dream is informed by an age-old sense of Russian messianism.

Luchnikov imagines that reunification will bring needed healing, harmony, and wholeness to Crimea. He uses *The Russian Courier* and, as well, his considerable public charisma to spread and legitimize the central idea of the Common Fate League. Finally, he lays the groundwork for a reconciliation, which, against his naive expectation, ends in the intrusion of Soviet military force. Thus a vibrant and viable meta-utopian "someplace" is consigned to the status of a genuine "no place," a "utopia" that destroys the tension and resistance of continual discursive negotiation and opens up a vacuum in which there will be no discourse and people will merely fall silent.

It is, of course, amusing and ironic that Luchnikov's various associates in Moscow, no matter what their status and ideological penchant, consider him blind and his intentions insane. His friends in avant-garde, countercultural circles despair of his mental health, trying to prove again and again that the real isolation and stagnation of Russian culture has occurred within the Soviet Union itself. As one person says about experimental art, and, by implication, about pluralist society, "There's no degeneration or decay in ... any avant-garde art. The whole point of the avant-garde is to shake things up, put new blood into circulation. If what you want is honest-to-goodness decadence, then try socialist petrified realism" (IC, 140). Highly placed functionaries feel that Luchnikov's designs are fundamentally "sadomasochistic," based on a sense of guilt (IC, 317). And, indeed, they are right: Luchnikov has made it clear from the start that he considers Crimea an "immorally rich country" (IC, 8). Even the KGB's Comrade Sergeev sees the present Crimea as a useful neutral ground for spying and cannot see why it should revert just yet to the Soviet Union.

Aksënov uncovers several aspects of a peculiarly Russian historical mentality that make a meta-utopian society difficult to sustain in the context of the mainstream Russian social and intellectual tradition: a historical unwillingness to approve of material wealth, a sentimental political imagination, and an alarmist, even apocalyptic attitude toward serious open disagreement and debate. More specifically, *The Island of Crimea*, like all other meta-utopian fictions, undermines the twin historical pillars that support Marxist-Leninist claims to legitimacy, its determinism and its promise of a bright future completely divorced from the miseries of the present and the past. Clearly the Soviet Union is described in all its familiar dreariness and backwardness. Its cultural and political elites have long since rejected the idea that the Soviet Union is a progressive society. In an interview titled "On Decadence," published in Luchnikov's newspaper, one defender of the cultural avant-garde argues that the "esthetic of revolutionary societies with its fear of change, all change, everything new, with its periodic orgies of dreary propaganda—listless flags, endless waves of identically dressed athletes, speeches stupefyingly uniform year in and year out, the ceremonious pose of an entire nation—is an esthetic of degeneration" (IC, 140). He goes on to relate cultural degeneration to the nature of revolution itself, which, far from being a leap toward a new and better state, is a step backward to more primitive and violent social behavior. The aesthetic of degeneration "goes back to the roots of revolution in general, because revolution is a twilight phenomenon to begin with, a giant step back to primordial gloom and the glory of bloodlust, because what could be more degenerate than the most ancient form of interpersonal relations, by which I mean violence" (IC, 140). The Soviet Union, in other words, was founded on wholly nonprogressive premises.

The notion of historical determinism resonates throughout *The Island of Crimea* as perhaps its central point of debate. Far from being the cornerstone solely of Marxist-Leninist ideology, it is linked to a nostalgic, Slavophile mode of Russian nationalism. The tired rhetoric of Soviet messianism echoes ironically in the speeches of the rather Slavophilic Common Fate League. As one of this fellowship puts it: "What holds our adherents together is the feeling of a bond with our Historical Homeland, a desire to move beyond insular isolation, for all its euphoria, toward the great spiritual development of mankind in which the country called Russia by us since childhood but in fact called the Union of Soviet Socialist Republics has been assigned a cardinal role" (IC, 291). Implicit in Aksënov's novel is the thought that historical determinism is a mask for an intellectually lazy and politically ruinous nostalgia for some *Gemeinschaft*, some easy social harmony and unity that never has existed and never will exist. In the case of Luchnikov the dream is certainly more appealing than reality; his powers of fantasy are stronger than his powers of observation of actual Soviet reality. After seeing and living the relative intellectual and material desert of Soviet life, he can still tell a foreign journalist that the Soviet authorities will not close the newspapers when they take over Crimea, as they did in 1918. And, predictably, the Soviets' first step at the end of the novel is to silence the television and the newspapers.

Finally, *The Island of Crimea* plays with traditional ideas of aesthetic representation to make plausible a different historical sensibility. Aksënov tries to establish and legitimize a meta-utopian scenario in the context of a new "realism," understood in the Jakobsonian sense of a literary style that appears to represent some dominant aspect of lived actuality more adequately and plausibly than competing standards. Within the frame of a frankly and openly fabricated fictional world Aksënov makes plausible, indeed, fully imaginable, a Russian meta-utopian social scenario and calls forth a concrete response to it in his reader, who has to watch the painful drama of this scenario's (completely unnecessary) collapse.

An additional point becomes apparent in the four popular meta-utopias that we have discussed so far: meta-utopian thinking is not the same as political "liberalism," and least of all in the Russian sense of that word. In *The Radiant Future*, *A Potshot*, and *The Island of Crimea* liberal protagonists are characterized as intellectually lazy, overly lenient, spineless, cowardly, and misguided. And in *The Ugly Swans*, Banev is attacked by the students as being weak. Ultimately, however, Banev is the only one of these four protagonists to tread the difficult middle realm—to be tolerant, perceive a variety of ideologies, and still act with moral integrity, without compromising himself. All the others end up misapprehending their own life situation and passively allowing some extreme vision to take the upper hand. Zinoviev's protagonist is implicated in the arrest of his friend Anton. And then he does not defend his daughter Lenka from the attack of her Stalinist mother. Grebin is sensitive, intellectually inquisitive, and morally concerned, in the abstract, but is ultimately blind to the implications of his intellectual play for his own life. And Luchnikov, the most openly "liberal" of all these characters, panics at the lively political debate in Crimea, mistaking it for unworkable fragmentation. He ends by blindly making a present of wealthy and culturally sophisticated Crimea to the hopelessly stagnant Soviet Union. With the exception of Viktor, these liberals do not define or defend the middle sphere. To do that one must recognize and define the opposing poles on which ideologies classically take shape and then let the various forms of maximalism subvert one another. It is up to the meta-utopian self to define and act in the moral and political middle ground and not give in to one extreme or the other.

Finally, history and fiction find a productive tension in Aksënov's, Tendriakov's, and the Strugatskys' work, one that overcomes the simple and disingenuous conflation of the two in Socialist Realism. History as documentation of experience and fiction as epistemological play interact in a way similar to that defined by E. L. Doctorow when he said that history is "a kind of fiction in which we live and hope to survive" and fiction is a "speculative history."[6] Fiction offers the framework for the continual process of resynthesizing historical experience with present experience, while history offers the perspective from which the reader can define an identity within a specific space-time matrix of her own. Thus, through remembering the past and reimagining its relation to the present, we can ensure that moral survival is possible and even likely.

[6] Cited in Hutcheon, *A Poetics of Postmodernism*, 112.

* CHAPTER NINE *

Parody of Popular Forms in Iskander's *Rabbits and Boa Constrictors* and Voinovich's *Moscow 2042*

THROUGHOUT the Soviet period two popular genres, the fable and the science fiction novel, have been used as vehicles for legitimizing communist ideology.[1] Maksim Gorky before the revolution and Demian Bednyi after were among the most prolific of writers of political fables, and I. A. Efremov and the Strugatsky brothers wrote a kind of science fiction in the late 1950s and early 1960s that conveyed a youthful optimism about the communist future.[2] During the 1960s, of course, both forms changed and became a good deal more ambiguous with relation to the ideology they had earlier supported. Animal figures from fables, particularly the rabbit and the bear, became favorite characters in popular anecdotes. In addition, Western political allegories, such as Orwell's *Animal Farm*, that made their way into the literary underground contributed to the growing irony with which educated readers greeted such forms.[3] Since the mid-1960s science fiction, and particularly the Strugatskys' work, has gained in depth and complexity.

Iskander's fable, *Rabbits and Boa Constrictors*, alludes to the tradition of the revolutionary fable, while more broadly addressing habits of reading and thinking that have been fostered in the Soviet era. We will see how this "antifable" plays on revolutionary themes from fables by Demian Bednyi and Maksim Gorky.[4] Perhaps more impor-

[1] Stites, *Revolutionary Dreams*, 167–89.

[2] Peterson, "Fantasy and Utopia," 81–85.

[3] So far no thorough reception history exists for these popular forms. For more information on *Animal Farm*, see Chapple, "Fazil Iskander's *Rabbits and Boa Constrictors*."

[4] In her unpublished paper "Iskander's Anti-Idyll," read at the national meeting of the American Association for the Advancement of Slavic Studies in Phoenix, Arizona, on November 22, 1992, Laura Beraha refers to Iskander's story as an anti-idyll. I prefer

tantly, it tackles readerly habits such as simplistic allegorical thinking and an unexamined didactic response, that is, an expectation that the text will furnish a simple and concrete moral. The kind of mentality that Iskander's story supports in its implied reader is specifically meta-utopian. It encourages an ability to weigh several kinds of ideology, among them that of the realized utopia, to see ideological structures individually and together in their relationship to sources of political power.

The Aesopian approach to interpretation assumed by Iskander's implied reader seeks out simple, one-to-one correspondences between the characters and their situation in the fable and real people and conditions in Soviet society and politics. Iskander's story deals with the struggle for survival between rabbits and boa constrictors (and, less importantly, the aborigines or natives [*tuzemtsy*]). Here the rabbits eat out of the natives' gardens. In turn, they are stalked by the boas, who swallow them whole after "hypnotizing" them into physical paralysis. The rabbits are the more intellectually sophisticated and more socially "organized," while the boas are physically stronger. Although the story appears to invite the reader to match the figures in the fable to correlatives in Soviet life, the more one examines them, the clearer it becomes that there is no real one-to-one match. In his article on *Animal Farm* and *Rabbits and Boa Constrictors*, Richard Chapple suggests that there is in Iskander's tale an allegorical context for the triangular relationship between rabbits, boas, and humans in the international political relations between East, West, and Third World.[5] This claim seems unconvincing since both boas' and rabbits' states are recognizably Stalinist. The boas have a Spartan, militaristic way of life. They are ruled by a dictator known as the Great Python who forces boas to compete ruthlessly with each other in the hunt and even to destroy divergent fellow boas. By contrast, the rabbits think of their state as a kind of elective monarchy, with the king "democratically" chosen. In fact, the tenor of political life is conditioned by the rather Byzantine court of the Rabbit King, which functions on a system of favors and rewards for service to the throne and increasingly caves into the paranoia of the King and his army of surveillance operatives and informers.

---

the term *antifable* because, in my view, it suggests more fully Iskander's parodic attention to allegorical and didactic strategies of interpretation.

[5] Chapple, "Fazil Iskander's *Rabbits and Boa Constrictors*, 34–36.

The ideologies of each likewise mimic aspects of Stalinist ideology. The Great Python justifies his hold on power with a materialistic mentality that might is right and one is what one eats. Indeed, the boa constrictors, who spend all their time hunting and eating rabbits, are characterized as being all appetite and stomach and no brain. This condition becomes the rather comic basis for a Stalin-like paranoid ideology. The Great Python's constant reminder to his cohorts that "The enemy is within us" parodies Stalin's famous dictum "The enemy is in our midst" (RB, 89). The boas see themselves as biologically superior to the rabbits. Echoing the oft-repeated Soviet idea that communism is a higher stage of socialism, the Great Python pronounces, "Boas are just rabbits at a higher stage of their development" (RB, 94). The Rabbit King originally legitimizes his power with the utopian icon of the Cauliflower, an image of ideal happiness and welfare. Like the sign with the ten rules of the ideally just society in Orwell's *Animal Farm*, a banner depicting the Cauliflower hangs over the King's throne. The banner changes colors from time to time, an event that the rabbit citizens interpret as a good omen, the "mysterious but ceaseless work of history in favor of the rabbits" (RB, 98). With time and growing restiveness among the citizenry, the King invokes kinship ties, specifically fatherhood, to legitimize his hold on power. Much like Stalin, who called himself the "father of all peoples," the King calls himself the "father of all rabbits" (RB, 144).[6]

Two other sources of ideological strength that would seem to challenge the Rabbit King, on the one hand, and the Great Python, on the other, have no real correlative in Soviet society, thus further undermining an Aesopian allegorical reading. These are the rabbit-philosopher, Thoughtful (Zadumavshiisia), and the young boa who becomes known as The Hermit (Pustynnik). Thoughtful is a protester who actively challenges the power of the boas over the rabbits. Having once been swallowed, he has won his way back to freedom. A Christlike figure, he preaches inner strength, claiming that the boas' alleged power to hypnotize and catch rabbits is really the rabbits' own fear of the boas. If they could conquer their fear, they would be free of the threat of the boas. His protest has further ramifications in that it reveals and directly challenges the real psychological basis for the Rabbit King's power: paranoiac fear of the enemy. He makes a bid for

---

[6] For more on kinship relations in Stalinist literary culture, see Clark, *The Soviet Novel*, 114–35.

power and is defeated, in part because the Rabbit King fixes the election and in part because of his own political miscalculations. He is too morally principled for ordinary rabbits. In addition to his primary message of liberation, he exhorts rabbits to cease poaching in the gardens of the "aborigines" or "natives," that is, human beings. Rabbits are not willing to be that responsible. The King meanwhile plots Thoughtful's demise. He has an opportunistic young rabbit, Resourceful (Nakhodchivyi), sing out a riddle that will tell the boas where to find Thoughtful. The young, ambitious boa who will eventually become The Hermit stalks Thoughtful on his favorite hillock. The wise rabbit uses this opportunity to test his theory that rabbits will not be paralyzed into submission if they overcome their fear of the boas. Thoughtful confronts the young boa with the thought that his powers of hypnosis are spurious. He indeed outwits the snake and would easily have escaped if he did not learn that he had been betrayed by his own kind. Falling into despair, he then decides to sacrifice himself, lying still while the boa eats him.

The young boa who consumes Thoughtful knows that he has eaten the most intelligent and best of the rabbits. Being a typical boa with a typically simpleminded, materialist boa philosophy, he believes that he is what he eats and, thus, that Thoughtful's brain will make him smarter, too! Exiled by the Great Python, who, like the Rabbit King, is embarrassed by the whole incident and anxious to have it forgotten, the young boa, now known as The Hermit (Pustynnik), works on new ways of hunting rabbits and perfects the method of smothering that older boas at the start of the story had rejected as "uncivilized." He realizes that this "technological innovation" will give him a basis to challenge the authority of the Great Python and make a bid for power. And, indeed, when he arrives back in court, the Great Python is impressed with The Hermit's power and appoints him as his successor. As the new leader, The Hermit turns his kingdom into a technocracy and works on perfecting the new hunting technique, turning it into a vehicle for mass murder of rabbits.

These two types, the moral leader, with his great powers of suasion, and the technician or "scientist," who commands concrete knowledge, do not really correspond to any specific person or situation in the Soviet experience and in a way expand the horizon of a possible Aesopian reading to universal limits. Thus, what is necessary for an Aesopian reading, that is, a clear context for interpretation, is lacking in this story, in which the contextual ground is continually shifting.

The Aesopian way of writing and reading is specifically parodied in the figure of the rabbit called The Poet, a Maksim Gorky figure who, as we saw earlier, thinks of himself as a strong moral voice and loves to write allegorical poetry about "storms" of political dissent and moral indignation. His poetic style mimics Gorky's famous revolutionary fable "The Song of the Stormy Petrel" ("Pesnia o burevestnike," 1901) in its forceful, even overbearing trochaic rhythms. Iskander parodies their inexorable, forward-pushing beat as The Poet repeats ad nauseum the root trochee in the word *bùria* (storm), for example, "Bùria! skòro grìanet bùria! [The storm! Soon the storm will burst!]" and "Pust' sil'nèe grìanet bùria! [Let the storm burst more violently!]" The Poet promises himself that he will write a long poem, "The Storm of Disappointment" ("Bùria razocharovàniia"), about the ultimate storm of discontent over the Rabbit King's abuse of power, his nightly orgies, and, still worse, his secret liquidation of his closest "friends" and supporters. The result is just a pile of notes made on dry magnolia leaves and a series of rhythms that the King will later sequester and use for self-aggrandizement and for jingles satirizing citizens who pay their taxes late. Worst of all, he takes and alters The Poet's composition "Variation on the Storm Theme" to make the verse-riddle with which Resourceful betrays The Poet's good friend, Thoughtful, to the boas.

The Poet cannot bring himself to write his real poem of protest as long as he is still enjoying the benefits of palace life, which include the promise of a ceremonial burial with lots of pomp and circumstance. With such promises and privileges the King controls his court jester and silences a potential voice of social conscience even into the grave. The Poet does read bits of poetry to close circles of friends, who recognize the Poet's "mad bravery"—a reference to Gorky's hymn to "the madness of the brave" in "The Song of the Falcon" ("Pesnia o Sokole," 1895)—and appreciate the social protest couched in Aesopian language. In the lines "Break over the world, storm, / Strike down the carrot oak tree! [Razrazìs' nad mìrom, bùria, / Porazì morkòvnyi dùb!]" The Poet's friends guess at his "bold" protest expressed in this "encoded part of the poem" (RB, 124). Aesopian language is thus shown concretely to be a weak and ultimately ineffectual form of social or political protest.

The other interpretive habit that Iskander confronts in *Rabbits and Boa Constrictors* is the didactic response, the habit of seeking an easy moral lesson, a "message." Instead, Iskander urges in his readers a complex response, evoking and then pointing out conflicting responses of feeling and intellect. He desensitizes the reader to both boas and rabbits, in part by describing how the rabbits are eaten, a process that, it seems, would cause the rabbits pain, but in fact does not, since they are whole and breathing and able to talk when they are inside the boas. The whole hunt, thus, is made somewhat absurd, at least until the end when rabbits are being smothered left and right and are in grave danger of being exterminated.

At the end the narrator describes the kind of reader he likes best, the "sensitive" kind who is able to feel for someone else:

> I have noticed that some people grow gloomy on hearing this story about rabbits and boa constrictors. Others start to get excited and prove that the situation of the rabbits isn't so bad, that they have several interesting ways to improve their life.
>
> With all my inherent optimism I must say that in the given situation I like the gloomy reader more than the excitable one, who is maybe trying to use the narrator to influence the rabbits. (RB, 190)

Having made this general appeal to feelings of sympathy in his implied reader, the narrator undercuts its pathos with an absurd example describing the reactions one encounters when one tries to cadge money from an acquaintance. The acquaintance who "gets excited and points to the multitude of ways to make money relatively easily" is much less sympathetic than the gloomy one who looks gloomy because he "has mentally parted with his money, or, having decided not to give any, is preparing for a severe rebuff" (RB, 190). With the second type, he concludes, one still has a chance.

Iskander similarly plays with the ideological judgments of his reader. Traditional Stalinist literature points the reader to one possible evaluation, to the "right" ideological viewpoint. Iskander circumvents two ideological positions in particular: on one hand, what is traditionally known as a "utopian" vision, that is, an idealized vision not linked to concrete power, and, on the other, an endorsement of any one ideology that legitimizes existing power. The main point is that, whatever one's ideological premises, power corrupts and, when one has power, preserving it automatically becomes one's first priority.

Of the four ideological figures in *Rabbits and Boa Constrictors*, the Great Python is by far the most primitive. He rules largely through a policy of physical coercion, a kind of struggle among the boas for survival. Any boa who shows mercy toward rabbits or a nonconformist boa, for example, a vegetarian who eats vegetables and fruit instead of rabbits, is "a boa whom we don't need." As we know, he also preaches a crude materialist ideology of biological superiority of boas over rabbits: "Boas are rabbits at a higher level of their development." Iskander gives no credence to this ideology, every utterance of which mimics Stalinist thinking.

Through the Rabbit King Iskander makes a travesty of a "liberal," utopian vision of universal education, rule by democratic vote—in short, of a kind of civil society. The Rabbit King manipulates the symbols and rituals of civil rule, using them to hide his paranoiac abuse of power. He alters the colors in the banner symbolizing the utopian dream of the Cauliflower that hangs over his throne. Thus, he mystifies citizens, playing on their ignorance and linking himself in their minds with the benevolent forces of history. When his power is challenged by Thoughtful, he insists on a vote of confidence. He fakes the voting process by organizing a session of mass aerobics as a supposed prelude to the vote. All the rabbits start to stretch, paws raised and lowered in rhythmic succession. The King puts the vote for himself when all paws are raised in a stretching motion.

On assuming power the King promises universal education and for that purpose has stored up vats of fermented elderberry ink. But he delays enactment of his educational policy for the foreseeable future. The ink becomes a symbol of social decline and degeneracy as palace functionaries, among them The Poet, discover its intoxicating effect and use it not to write and to enlighten but to get drunk. The vision of the good society gives way completely as the King builds security force upon security force to quell dissent. In this context, all his rhetoric rings false.

The Hermit's claim to the beneficial influence of technology is likewise undermined. Once this boa ascends to power, he shows himself to be much the same as his predecessor. Based on a crude materialism, his way of thinking is in no substantial way different from that of the Great Python. His belief that his "new" technique of smothering rabbits comes from having eaten the smartest rabbit, Thoughtful, is an offshoot of the Great Python's notion that one is what one eats and that "boas are rabbits at a higher stage of their development."

Finally, the notion that this change in hunting technique represents "progress" is suspect. The "discovery" of smothering is the very thing that an older boa known as Cross-Eyed (Kosoi) had rejected as uncivilized at the very beginning of the story. All in all, he shows himself to be rather ruthless, refusing to save a boa who has twisted himself into knots while practicing the new technique of suffocation. This case he dismisses as "not worth the trouble [ne rentabel'no]."

Most dramatic and full of pathos is the claim of the philosopher-rabbit, Thoughtful, to moral sway. His drama has elements of a serious parody of Demian Bednyi's 1912 satire of Russian liberalism, "Rebelling Rabbits" ("Buntuiushchie zaitsy").[7] Bednyi's poem starts with thirty or forty rabbits taking council on a hillock. They agree that life has become hopelessly oppressive and urge each other on to give up their lives for freedom. But when there is a faint rustling in the grass (possibly, although not definitively, from a snake), all the rabbits take to their heels and scatter. The poet ends the poem with the sarcastic comment that after this incident all the animals, and especially the wolves, will certainly be so scared of the rabbits that they will run away with their tails between their legs.

In both works rabbits gather on a hillock to discuss strategies for overthrowing tyranny and gaining civil rights. The difference is that, when there is a rustling in the grass in Iskander's story, Thoughtful does not flinch but acts on his theory that the boas have no real power of hypnosis. What the rabbits call "hypnosis" is really their own horror of the boas, which causes them to freeze in immobility. Thoughtful does not allow himself to become petrified with fear and, thus, proves himself to be superior to the young boa who wants to eat him. But he falls into such deep despair when he learns that he has been deceived by his fellow rabbits that he essentially decides to commit suicide and allows the predator to eat him. In this act we find Iskander's answer to Bednyi's scoffing at liberals' "cowardice."

When Thoughtful makes his discovery that the boas' power of hypnosis is really the rabbits' fear of confrontation with the boas, he wins a following and, for a brief time, has a broad impact, threatening even to unseat the King. His ideology of inner discipline and power seems

---

[7] Dem'ian Bednyi, *Stikhotvoreniia i poemy* (Moscow-Leningrad: Sovetskii pisatel', 1965), 76–77, 531. This poem allegedly satirizes the liberal political leader A. I. Guchkov and the supposedly faint efforts of his "Octobrist" party to bring about a parliamentary form of government in Russia after the revolution of 1905.

a genuine alternative to the utopian fakery of the King. And yet the narrator undermines his would-be hero: he points to the ultimate absurdity of Thoughtful's lonely, caring moral consciousness. As Thoughtful contemplates his political fate from his favorite green hill, the "dog-eat-dog" realities of natural life in the jungle play themselves out before him:

> Thoughtful sat on his green hill near the river. To the left stretched the pampas, and to the right the broad Frog Ford. Thoughtful watched surrounding life with sad yet penetrating eyes. More exactly, with penetrating and therefore sad eyes Thoughtful watched surrounding life.
>
> Over there a mosquito got lazy [zazevalsia] and flew too low over Frog Ford and was snapped up by a frog. The frog got lazy, and a heron stabbed it with her spearlike beak. And over here a heron, looking enviously at the first heron swallowing the frog, got lazy, and a crocodile snapped her up in his terrible jaws. And there the natives had managed to catch a crocodile who had let down his guard, after which they chopped him into what seemed to them to be tasty morsels and loaded him onto the boat and crossed to the far shore. They had not quite reached the village when one of them who had bent too low over the water was grabbed by another crocodile. (RB, 132–33)

This picture has so much death in it that one becomes desensitized to it, and is inclined to laugh at the absurd repetition of the natural cycle. It is Thoughtful's response, "And that's what they call life," that brings one to one's moral senses for a moment.

After Thoughtful sacrifices himself to the young snake who will become The Hermit, the narrator actually abandons his lightly humorous narrative tone to pontificate angrily about the faults and failings of Thoughtful's thinking and behavior. This emotional outburst certainly suggests that the narrator is most moved by Thoughtful, over all the other political figures who arouse in him only a strong sense of irony and the absurd. Here parody will not work. Thoughtful's thinking and language are indeed too fresh and powerful; only polemic can answer it.

Finally, the question arises: What sort of attitude does Iskander encourage in his implied reader, cynicism or a sense of searching? Although his treatment of all his characters is absurdist, his polemic with Thoughtful suggests an underlying indignation and a sense of urgency about understanding how moral ideals and feelings anticipate the practice of real power and how actual power distorts the ideal. Only through seeking out and defining the tension between the two can people possibly go beyond the twin dead ends of despotism and failed utopia.

Voinovich's implied reader is a consumer of popular potboilers, particularly science fiction. In his play with this implied reader, Voinovich goes a good deal further than other meta-utopian writers, even Iskander. He makes the ingenious distinction between the mass reader who seeks entertainment in literary "fantasy" and what I will call here the intrusive reader who seeks in literary "realism" a lever of ideological control.[8] This intrusive reader can be a form of censorship or a political or religious leader who tampers with the spontaneous relationship between a writer and his audience, who treats art as a tool for creating an ideologically desirable version of reality.

The tension between these two kinds of reader is established concretely in the novel's first chapter when Kartsev is drinking beer with his German friend Rudi in Munich's English Gardens. Kartsev has given copies of his books to Rudi, an avid reader of science-fiction novels and mechanics journals. He knows that Rudi has not read any of them, although he loves to boast to his acquaintances about his Russian friend who is a writer. It is Rudi as the model of the popular reader who throws down the challenge to Kartsev that realism is passé, that no one reads it anymore and that Kartsev should start writing science fiction since it sells much better. He invites Kartsev to compare the size and number of printings of his books with those of any current science-fiction novel (M, 11). A Russian emigré writer, Kartsev has never encountered this attitude of irreverence toward realism or the possibility of a spontaneous mass readership. Affronted, he responds stiffly that popular narrative forms, such as detective novels or science fiction, are on a level with computer games: all they do is contribute to mass idiocy. He insists that art is not about technological predictions (Rudi points to Jules Verne). Nor, in his view, is it capable of real political prediction: Orwell's novels, he says, are

---

[8] See Carol Avins, "Reaching a Reader: The Master's Audience in *The Master and Margarita*," *Slavic Review* 45, no. 2 (Summer 1986), 272–85. Avins speaks of the "intrusive presence" of the state in the communicative process between reader and writer. This presence may also be viewed as a type of reader per se, one inimical to the creative and often subversive workings of imagination.

satires of a political situation existing in Orwell's own time. (Kartsev does not mention Zamiatin.) He claims that people would much rather read about themselves than about some Martian civilization. Despite this rather curt dismissal of popular fiction, Kartsev's curiosity is piqued. Clearly interested in exploring the gap between fantasy and reality, he inquires about the realizability of various elements of science fiction, such as time travel. Rudi claims that time travel has indeed become possible, although not necessarily desirable. (He has already traveled to ancient Rome, where he barely escaped with his life from a gladiator fight in the Coliseum.) Thus, one of the fantastic elements in classical science fiction becomes realizable for Kartsev, who as a faithful "realist" refuses to write about people and events he has not actually witnessed. He answers Rudi's challenge by participating in a story that inadvertently (for Kartsev) mimics science fiction as well as another popular narrative form, the international spy thriller.

Voinovich makes fun of the rather simpleminded mass consumer of science fiction by ironizing over such generic conventions as time travel (which is no different from any other airplane flight), space travel (the only strange phenomenon Kartsev encounters is his old KGB friend Leshka Bukashev, who has been put into orbit around the earth for being too outspoken and controversial in his role as Genialissimus), and the full-fledged communist utopia of the future (which repeats and reinforces all the bad aspects of the Soviet experience). However, Voinovich also challenges and extends the mental skills of this reader by presenting him with paradoxes related both to the nature of time and space and to the interaction of memory and imagination of the sort already discussed in Chapter 3. Moreover, Kartsev, who has presented himself as a thoroughgoing realist, soon subverts this posture. As a true realist, he has claimed in his foreword to rely on memory in writing about his exotic adventures and assures the reader of the reliability of his memory. He also insists on the realist's basic claim to have "seen" everything that he has recounted here. It soon becomes clear, however, that he is a wholly, if inadvertently, unreliable narrator who unwittingly treads the boundaries between fantasy and reality. His muddled assurances about the verisimilitude of his project invite the reader also to explore these boundaries:

> I am telling only about what I saw myself with my own eyes. Or heard with my own ears. Or that someone whom I really trust told me. Or

don't really trust. Or don't trust at all. In any case, what I am writing here is always founded on something. Sometimes it's not even founded on anything at all. But every person who knows the slightest thing about the theory of relativity knows that nothing [nichto] is a variation of something [nechto], and something is also something definite (but I'm not sure exactly what) [chto-to], from which one can derive a certain something (but I won't tell you what) [koe-chto]. (M, 6)

As he plans his trip to Moscow, Kartsev runs into trouble with the intrusive reader. He is not permitted simply to appeal to and play epistemological games with a mass audience. All of the figures of the intrusive reader type in *Moscow 2042* are Russian writers and political leaders of the type familiar to anyone who knows the long history of Russian literary politics.[9] Unlike Iskander, who characterizes the implied reader as naturally having didactic expectations of the literary text, Voinovich suggests that it is the intrusive reader, in the form of the self-righteous, moralistic writer and the political censorship, that has created these expectations. Karnavalov, for example, goes beyond his historical prototype Solzhenitsyn in that he not only views himself as a "second government," an independent moral voice, but has ambitions to become a "primary government," that is, to rule Russia. He uses his "art," as it turns out, very successfully to harangue his reader into rebellion. And he treats Kartsev as little more than a servant of the "cause," at first demanding that he distribute copies of his sixty-tome opus, *The Big Zone*, around Moscow. On Kartsev's return, he insists in a tone more in keeping with that of a despot that Kartsev modify his account of his trip in order to manipulate the opinion of the leaders [zaglotchiki] in power sixty years hence.

Karnavalov hardly differs in intelligence and literary discrimination from his opponents in the Kremlin of 2042. In the twenty-first century literature has all but died out. Indeed, only "works" of The Genialissimus are printed on paper. Everything else is punched into a "computer" without a screen that, as it turns out, is not even plugged in. Despite this nonsensical situation, certain precommunist (*predvaritel'nyi*) classics, among which are works of Kartsev (and Siniavsky-Terts!), do appear. True to Soviet tradition, what Tynianov called "literary personality," that literary legend assimilating the

[9] A good recent study on writers and political leaders is George Gutsche, *Moral Apostasy in Russian Literature* (DeKalb: Northern Illinois University Press, 1986).

writer's biography with the lives of his or her characters, is most carefully cultivated while the actual literary works are all but impossible to find. Thus, Kartsev's only readers turn out to be the five leaders of the ruling Pentagon and a few others. With them, as with Karnavalov, the usual writer-reader relationship is reversed: rather than the author "teaching" the reader, it is the reader as censor who controls and forms the author. Like Karnavalov, they treat Kartsev very much as a tool of their particular political aims (M, 154). Their attitude toward fiction is highly self-contradictory and all the more worrisome for all its contradictions. On the one hand, they view art as a kind of magic, a modern-day surrogate for the Bible, potentially more powerful than their own political power, with the ultimate capability of determining the outcome of historical events. On the other, they wish to manipulate the artistic text in such a way as to render it a harmless fantasy! Ironically, although they view fiction as the ultimate reality, they are wary of too much of what Vzroslyi calls "naturalism" (M, 223).

Voinovich is clearly playing with the notion of the reader's "horizon of expectation" when he names the chief censor and deputy to the ineffable Genialissimus Gorizont Timofeich Razin. It is indeed Gorizont, or "Horizon" in English, who artificially fixes the expectations of the contemporary readership. Like the members of the ruling Pentagon, Gorizont is very pleased with Kartsev's initial bright dream from his first night in Moscow of a communist utopia filled with light, beautiful people, and lots of consumer goods. He encourages Kartsev to include more such material and to delete the "naturalist" part. As Vzroslyi cynically puts it, "we all live by our illusions. Dreams are primary, and life is secondary" (M, 224). Clearly the ruling elite-as-censor hope to neutralize the historical "reality" of Kartsev's work by reducing it to a series of absurd dreams. Their worst fears are confirmed when Kartsev gives into the unbearable pressure to alter his text. They believe their hold on power to be saved when in a public forum before the citizens of Moscow he agrees to delete Sim Simych Karnavalov from his work. This announcement comes in the nick of time, just as they have received a telegram from Sim Simych warning of his imminent invasion of Moscow and urging Muscovites to surrender peacefully. They are horrified to learn that Kartsev has decided to take out the name but to keep the character type, renaming him "Serafim." A look at the same telegram after Kartsev's announcement reaffirms their notion of literary text as historical truth: the telegram is now signed "Serafim"! (M, 307)

Kartsev has the last laugh over this kind of reader as well as the mass consumer, showing the intrusive reader to be still more benighted than the reader of pulp fiction. It is in the epilogue that he has his final say about both readers, one intended and the other an imposter. He suggests that a truly mass readership has not been allowed to develop in the Soviet Union because of tampering, on the one hand, by despotic, preachy would-be rulers like Karnavalov and, on the other, by actual leaders fearful of uncontrolled ideological opposition. He looks forward to the time when political leaders will stop meddling with the fictive worlds created in works of art and will apply themselves to what is really their domain, improvement of the social environment. Thus, they would assure that the so-called prophecies in fiction did not come true. Forced to acknowledge political leaders as his chief readers, Kartsev challenges them indirectly to make a liar of him and ruin his reputation as a "realist." By such reverse psychology Kartsev conveys a hope for an opportunity eventually to write books for a popular readership of the sort represented by Rudi, who will enjoy his work as the "fruit of an empty and harmless fantasy" (M, 339).

The two works considered in this chapter challenge the reader's interpretive skills considerably more than Zinoviev's, the Strugatsky brothers', Tendriakov's, or Aksënov's popular experiments do. While those tackle interpretive problems especially of Aesopian language, doublespeak, the subjugation of memory and imagination to very restrictive, exclusive ideological systems, and the coercive, censorious relationship between rulers and writers, they do it in a more or less close relationship with traditions of "realism." Iskander and Voinovich take their implied reader beyond these bounds. Iskander engages the reader in an interpretive game that calls into question both typical emotional responses and interpretive approaches to the text. He particularly foils any effort of the reader to take sides emotionally, to find a simple one-to-one allegorical correspondence between animals and possible political prototypes, or finally to seek out a "good" single ideology. Through the use of a narrator who is in exile, living physically beyond Soviet borders, Voinovich goes beyond the bounds of canonical Russian reader-writer relationships, implicitly contrasting a Western notion of the mass reader, such as Rudi, with the Soviet intrusive reader, and their two uses of popular art. This vantage point beyond the borders of the Soviet cultural sphere allows him to question the very notion of a true mass consumer of popular literature in the context of a politically controlled reading culture. Thus, Voinovich and Iskander both use their parodies of popular form to penetrate to the heart of problems raised more superficially in other popular meta-utopias: simplistic reading habits and the noncritical approach to ideological constructs implied in them and the coercive power relationship between reader and writer that inheres in the Russian literary tradition.

* CHAPTER TEN *

Play with Closure in Petrushevskaia's "The New Robinsons" and Kabakov's "The Deserter"

META-UTOPIAN FICTION written since 1987 is, as might be expected, more radically reductive than its forebears, finding naked coercion behind all but the most locally defined ideologies. It exposes a similar matrix of responses as the critical discussion about utopia. On the one hand, it harbors the same fear of the abyss as the only real alternative to stable, if oppressive, order, while, on the other, it is strongly concerned with reopening language to untried possibility, with reexamining deep social scripts, and with probing automatized readerly expectations. Two "best-selling" pieces, Liudmila Petrushevskaia's short story "The New Robinsons" ("Novye Robinzony: Khronika kontsa XX veka," *Novyi mir*, 1989) and a screenplay by the writer Aleksandr Kabakov, "The Deserter" ("Nevozvrashchenets," *Iskusstvo kino*, 1989), are at the forefront of current discussion.[1] Although close to simple dystopia and strongly reductionist in their conceptualizations of all forms of ideology, including utopia, both exhibit a meta-utopian tendency to engage rather than wholly reject utopian thinking and to juxtapose utopian thinking of all kinds. Both appear to be about their protagonists' attempts to "escape" coercion to some private sphere. Both seem on the surface to deny the possibility of a productive social imagination and to foresee a dead end. And yet although close to the pathologies of dystopia, each work admits of a multiplicity of ways to imagine society, of utopias (in the plural) instead of one absolute Utopia, of the sort that Mikhail Epstein envisions.[2] In the face of terrible odds, in a world all but overwhelmed by brute political violence, each story asserts some notion of social vitality.

[1] See, for example, Andrei Vasil'evskii, "Opyty zanimatel'noi futuro(eskhato)logii, II," *Novyi mir*, no. 5 (1990): 258–62.

[2] "'Kruglyi stol,'" 25.

Petrushevskaia's story deals with a family that moves to a run-down country cottage located in rural Russia sometime in the late twentieth century to escape adversaries in the city. The story moves in large cycles: the father continues to build and stock other hideaways so that when their current dwelling is discovered, they will have someplace to run to. Much as in Kafka's story "The Burrow," the characters' anticipation of a foe is much stronger a force than the actual fact of its existence. Although we never actually encounter the enemy, it is such a concrete presence in the minds of the characters that we are led to believe that their precautionary measures are based on danger more real than imaginary.

Kabakov's screenplay deals with a researcher in an institute of amorphous description in 1992 or 1993 (the story itself is unclear on the date) when perestroika has failed and a Kornilov-like military dictatorship has the most fragile grasp on power. A Committee for National Security conducts raids on the houses of the former *nomenklatura*, hanging signs on their doors proclaiming that they are "free of bureaucrats" once the sweep has been completed. Order is continually disrupted by warring bands, among whom are the "Levelers" and various fundamentalist religious groups, each fighting for its own political vision and its own bit of turf. The narrator, Iury Ilich, is approached by two intelligence operatives, reminiscent of the two buffoonish but deadly spies from Kafka's *The Trial*, and asked to write a report of his experiences in the street, to reveal the identities of all enemies of the government.

Both stories depart from traditional utopias and dystopias in that they envision not one but a variety of possible social scenarios. Both importantly divide utopian imagination into at least two types: a "realized ideology" masking some coercive power structure, and what might be called "imaginative" utopia, or social fantasy that resists political violence. While certainly against such realized utopias, they are not against all utopias. Petrushevskaia's story is narrated by an eighteen-year-old girl, the daughter of the family that has left the city. At least to start with, her consciousness is as close as possible to being nonideological. Her perceptions and judgments are based firmly on the five senses, focusing on the concrete aspects of life and death, pain and pleasure, giving precise details of what the family builds with, what they plant, what they eat, how people look and act. Petrushevskaia refuses to disclose the ideological leanings of the family's persecutors, implying that, when physical coercion is at stake, the ideological justifications given on its behalf really are of no consequence. On the other hand, the narrator shows a great deal of sympathy for that utopian scenario often denied in twentieth-century Russia, based on the enterprising spirit of Robinson Crusoe.[3] The young girl compares her beloved father, an image of vitality, to Crusoe. He is a new kind of hero, a self-made man. And toward the end a simple account of a struggle to survive persecution goes far to become an endorsement of socioeconomic values of hard work and personal prosperity. Here is a form of social imagination renewed and regenerated for the late twentieth century.[4]

The only remotely abstract issues to which the narrator alludes are those of life and death. In her treatment of them, they do not stand out as ideological bases, even in the broadest sense, but rather as concrete facts of daily life, related to feelings and physical conditions. If anything, life is a palpable, tactile quantity, while death is treated as the absence of life, a kind of nonsensical, empty, even stupid non-event that the living character automatically distances from herself. As the story in all its six pages develops, the concrete details of life do take on a noticeable cyclical pattern, as events, seasons, even generations are perceived to renew themselves. This pattern of regeneration becomes the basis for some sort of existential continuity and by the end acquires the vague contours of myth (NR, 172). Nonetheless, it is essential to the texture of the narrative and, as will become clear, to Petrushevskaia's use of language to understand that this patterning is fundamentally counterideological: the strange, Platonovian combination of visceral detail, awkward abstraction, and the dispassionate tone of the teenaged narrator all work against all serious effort to construct abstract valuative frameworks.

Kabakov's story also distinguishes between coercive "realized" utopia and other imaginative alternatives. Iury finds himself persecuted by a large number of organizations, each with its own claim to

---

[3] Petrushevskaia's story makes concrete allusion to Defoe's novel in its details, for example, the use of goats as the basis for the family's subsistence and the motif of periodic construction of new hideaways ever farther from human contact.

[4] For a very entertaining Stalin-era parody on the Robinson Crusoe theme, see the story "Kak sdelalsia Robinzon" by Il'ia I'lf and Evgenii Petrov (1933; Letchworth: Bradda, 1968). It is interesting that Zverev, in his excellent article "'Kogda prob'et poslednii chas prirody,'" also refers to the Robinson Crusoe story as a utopia that has not led to totalitarianism and the strict confinement of the creative imagination or the rights of the individual, in general.

power and its own view of the good life. Besides the two spies who appear to represent some more or less "Stalinist" security organs and the militarist regime of General Panaev that is still nominally in power, Iury encounters various groups on the street. These include the Revolutionary Committee of North Persia, the fanatical Holy Militia, the rightist, anti-Semitic Knights (Vitiazi), and the Commission on National Security, with its plan for the "radical leveling" of Moscow society—that is, the forcible "liberation" of Moscow neighborhoods of the privileged *nomenklatura* (D, 163).

All these forms of force used in the name of exclusivist religious and social ideals do nothing but copy in fragmented form the same reliance on brute force familiar in the Stalinist system. They can only lead to civil war and the destruction of any notion of civilization and civil society. Clearly they are to be avoided. However, in "The Deserter," as in "The New Robinsons," other utopian possibilities and alternatives are raised, thus making it essentially different from a dystopian narrative. Iury hears over his radio of a new novel by Aksënov entitled *The Continent of Siberia*, which, like its historical referent, *The Island of Crimea*, offers a pluralist social alternative to Stalinist authoritarianism. This single allusion to the title of a popular meta-utopian fantasy is followed by Iury's encounter in the subway with a shadowy figure with an easy "aristocratic" demeanor whom the two functionaries dub Lazhechnikov. The two spies think he is an *ekstrapoliator*, a kind of foreign intelligence operative, and want to get rid of him, viewing him as a threat to whatever state control has survived. And yet it is he who formulates a real alternative to ideological monologism. He sarcastically congratulates Iury and the Russian intelligentsia to which Iury belongs for seeing through the destruction of Marxism-Leninism, the "anomaly that has been mortifying [umertvliavshaia] this country for nearly a century" (D, 170). He argues that the cure had to be severe and, in fact, was not severe enough since the cancerous sore "metastasized" in the form of General Panaev, who promises yet another bloodbath "for the sake of the future radiant kingdom of love and, most importantly, justice" (D, 170). In other words, "Utopia" (in the singular), understood as a unitary, maximalist ideological system, rages on as Russia's sickness. Lazhechnikov criticizes the Russian intelligentsia for lacking the wit to go beyond this maximalism. As a contrastive model, he offers pluralist European social practice: instead of murdering each other, citizens with differing opinions and beliefs create a neutral zone of symbolic action, a theatrical acting-out of grievances, as it were, in the form of political demonstrations. This "street theater" allows people to convey their malaise to a national audience, to be seen and heard, without irreversible consequences. Russians, Lazhechnikov implies, must learn to let each person or group have a say without immediately wanting to punish or destroy them for their dissenting opinion. Here would be a new departure in the Russian tradition of ideological frameworking.

Both "The Deserter" and "The New Robinsons" go beyond the utopian–anti-utopian stalemate in yet other ways. Although the chronotopes in which these stories are embedded show a meta-utopian taste for "civilization," both stories confront the failure of present urban civilization. Like the dystopian novel, they have a strong sense of spatial and temporal borders, focusing on escape from a disintegrating civilization and, in Kabakov's story, even on apocalypse, that is, a crisis point of total fragmentation and collapse. Still, neither story endorses the dystopian primitivism, for example, that Zamiatin admires in his Scythians or Huxley in his Savage. Each story supports some notion of civilization. Petrushevskaia stresses the notion of building one's own independent universe, one's own notion of order and prosperity, not in the city but on the land. And Kabakov's shadowy aristocrat ruminates about the advantages of European cultivation over a Russian tendency to seek solutions in direct, physical coercion.

The innovative treatment of utopia in these works is buttressed importantly by experiment with style, narrative, and implied reader, all of which are conducive to fresh ideological conceptualization. In other words, both of these works evince strongly "constitutive" traits in their formal structures, representing a strong move beyond the constraints of literary dogma, of Socialist Realism, and the like. For example, Petrushevskaia's refusal to use ideologically "tainted" language leads to a use of language that possesses a remarkably vital, sensuous force. Here is, indeed, a return from utopian madness to one's "senses." As the narrator recounts the details of her family's life, we are made to feel as if anew the "weight" and quality of life at its minimum. The second paragraph of the story gives a feeling of this existence through detailed description of the physical work needed to survive and lists of the things that the family collects and uses for their new life:

And father started feverish activities [deistviia], he dug up a garden, taking over the neighboring plot as well, for which he dug across to the other side of the fence posts and took out the fence of the absent neighbors. We finished digging the garden plot, planted about three bags of potatoes, dug around the apple trees, father went and cut peat in the woods. A wheelbarrow with two wheels appeared—as a rule father actively [aktivno] poked around the neighbors' boarded-up houses, stockpiling whatever came to hand: nails, old boards, roofing paper, tin, pails, benches, door handles, windowpanes, various good old things like tubs, spinning wheels, grandfather clocks, and various unnecessary old things like cast-iron pots, cast-iron doors from wood stoves, stove doors, crowns for samovars, and the like. (NR, 166)

Another way in which Petrushevskaia brings to bear on her story the concrete value of life is to draw attention to the cost of separate items. A scythe, for example, costs the mother ten backpacks of grass; three days' worth of goat milk is obtained for one tin of preserves; one baby goat is bought for one kilo of salt and soap.

In contrast, Petrushevskaia's narrator treats death as an absurd event, strangely disjointed from the matter of life and survival. In this desensitization of death Petrushevskaia's style is reminiscent of Platonov. The narrator assumes a dispassionate distance from human suffering by using paralogisms such as non sequiturs and incongruous combinations of awkward abstractions and concrete images. For example, at the very start the narrator observes as a matter of fact that the "crazy" (*odichavshaia*) old peasant woman, Marfutka, does not count as a person. She sits "like a mummy wrapped in a *multitude* [*mnozhestvo*] *of greasy scarves, rags and blankets*," in an unheated house, eating rotten potatoes, just, as the narrator puts it, waiting to die (NR, 167; emphasis added). The collective noun *mnozhestvo*, with its suffix *-stvo*, which denotes some abstract group of things or people, belongs to an academic or journalistic style and jars with the picturesque detail of the rest of the sentence. The girl shows no compassion for the old woman's plight, perhaps partly because Marfutka herself responds neither to kindness nor to cruelty. She is the same whether they bring her fresh potatoes or ravage her garden. Toward the end the narrator decides that only when one has become like Marfutka and has nothing do the powers-that-be leave one alone. But then, she implies, one has really ceased to be alive.

Other images of death are equally absurd. When they first come to the country the local doctor, Tania, brings them as a gift a piglet, crushed accidentally by its mother and wrapped in a clean cloth, that reminds the narrator incongruously of a child: "little eyes with eyelashes, etcetera" (NR, 168). The narrator draws attention to the inappropriateness and incongruity of her emotional distance by putting so much emphasis on the phrase *etcetera*, spelling out the Russian letters *i te. de.* (for *i tak dalee*). The split between emotion and rationality is further stressed when the narrator comments that the very same evening her father cut up and salted the (childlike) piglet.

A young woman's suicide is also treated in just such an offhand manner as another fact, which the narrator treats matter-of-factly and without emotion. After the narrator has been describing how in the course of one short year she and her mother have turned into peasant women with dirt ingrained in their skin and fingernails, she suddenly adds a non sequitur: "By the way, Tania's constant visitor, the shepherd Verka, hung herself in the woods" (NR, 169).

It is important to point out that these images of death serve to highlight the narrator's and her family's commitment to survival. Death is consistently held at arm's length and not allowed to penetrate the family's determination to live. For example, the family adopts Verka's little daughter, Lenka, who is then claimed by her grandmother. When the narrator's mother refuses to give Lenka up, the grandmother "started to cry and left without Lena and the baby carriage; apparently, she left to die" (NR, 169–70). Elsewhere, as the narrator thinks about her former city life, she wonders about her own grandmother and grandfather. She remembers the fight with them over a large, comfortable apartment and the family's failure to secure the apartment; then, in another non sequitur, she supposes that her grandparents are "already corpses [Nam v nei ne privelos' zhit', a teper', navernoe, moi babushka i dedushka byli uzhe trupami]" (NR, 170). This absurd, abstracted treatment of death as something illogical and incongruous with life is as close as Petrushevskaia comes even to implying a "philosophical" or "ideological" point of view. If she has one, it is to reiterate the value of life, especially at its most concrete level.

Unlike Petrushevskaia, who avoids all abstract discussion, Kabakov openly raises the issue of literary style. The narrator, Iury, is afraid that he lacks a style that can win over his readers' trust and create the necessary sense of plausibility. He regrets his lack of literary talent. As he puts it, the "colorless and expressionless or, at times, too pretentious style with which I at times have noted down the results of my experiments is totally inappropriate in the present circumstances" (D, 150). However he may feel about his own literary abilities, he is equally critical of what normally passes for "great style," which, he says, masks ideological chicanery. The greatest proselytizers, among them evildoers, often have a riveting style that can be compared in its effect on the human psyche to narcotics:

> The great preachers who knew how to divert [uvlech'] the masses undoubtedly possessed great literary talent. The Evangelists would have done but little to spread the truth revealed to Christ if they had not been writers of genius. Unfortunately, just as often, if not more often, the gift of the word has been bestowed on evildoers, charlatans, and shortsighted, limited do-gooders. The last were if anything more dangerous than the run-of-the-mill good-for-nothings [negodiai]—narcotics are all the more terrible the more naturally they are included in the [body's] exchange of materials.... (D, 151)

Thus Iury's ambiguous attitude to what would traditionally be judged to be good style is, in a way, a reassertion of literary disinterestedness, a warning about language as it is used to bewitch, to captivate and unnerve, and a call for critical perspective.

Kabakov's primary focus, however, is on narrative technique, on reestablishing the borders between the ideological abuse of narrative, as denunciation or as political document, and fiction as a form of "purposiveness without a purpose," a form of disengaged play. The narrator makes this distinction as he is compelled by the two spies to use his writing as a political tool to catch enemies. While he serves up one narrative to his enforcers, secretly he tells another story of his own potential liberation. His refusal to disclose certain information and to finish either of the two narratives is another assertion of independence. In its lack of closure it reminds us again of one of its chief literary subtexts, *The Trial*, in which K. is confronted by his two persecutors, given a knife, and expected to kill himself. Kabakov's narrator is also threatened with destruction just as he is about to meet his aristocrat and escape. But this narrator leaves the scene open to a variety of outcomes, thus refusing to give into the scenario forced on him by the intelligence operatives.

The endings of both "The New Robinsons" and "The Deserter" differ in essential ways from the traditional dystopian dead end in which the rebellious protagonist is returned to a state of complacency. Both lack a conclusive finale. "The New Robinsons" operates on a cyclical structure of seasonal and generational renewal of life. The family's flight from its persecutors is marked by a periodic gathering of their possessions, a move still farther from urban and village civilization, a construction of a new shelter, and establishment of a new garden. This cyclical remaking of life is punctuated by the refrain of the father's joyful exclamations at having escaped his enemies once again. Kabakov's narrator, Iury, likewise refuses to end his narrative in capitulation or death—the ending expected by his "intrusive readers," the spies, who by asking Iury to write a report on his nocturnal wanderings try to force a certain story line, or by the more subtle implied reader-intellectual who expects failure.[5] Indeed, he refuses to complete his story at all, abandoning it at a climax in which Iury and his wife are caught between confrontation with the spies and a rendezvous with Lazhechnikov. This last narrative act suggests that perhaps we, the informed reader, are just as suspect in our treatment of the text as the spies are: we, too, expect and even impose a certain kind of outcome, either capitulation or escape. In its open-endedness, Kabakov's narration negotiates between these two options, opening space for still others, one of which might be ongoing struggle. He forces all his readers to imagine their own endings and thus to examine their own social expectations and the deeper social values that inform them. Thus, here, as with Petrushevskaia's circular tale, a traditional plot and its outcome are denied, being implicitly viewed as a form of ideological coercion, and the horizon of social imagination is expanded.

These two works echo the ambiguity of their time. Glasnost is a time of "pluralist" debate: it is deeply meta-utopian in that many ideologies—utopian, anti-utopian, and counterutopian—are being subjected to needed critique, but on the relatively neutral ground of journal pages, literary fiction, and unprecedented peaceful street demonstrations. And yet it is a time of deep skepticism and distrust of all rhetoric, all grand schemes. The greatest danger lies in cynicism and despair, the inability to distinguish between productive and pathological alternatives, those that open up a way to survive and those that lead merely to a dead end. What is finally at risk is the will to keep searching and to resist the urge to capitulate to familiar but failed social and political scenarios.

[5] Avins, "Reaching a Reader."

Was meta-utopian writing during glasnost merely a dark anti-utopian mirror of Stalinism, rebelling against all authority? Certainly at times it does seem to imply that there is no alternative other than total ruin. Nonetheless, we do find strong efforts to recast language use and narrative patterns in such a way as to free the reading and writing public from the prison house of Marxist-Leninist thinking and to suggest other options for interpreting and living one's social existence.

* CONCLUSION *

The Utopian Impulse after 1968

RUSSIAN META-UTOPIAN FICTION IN A EUROPEAN CONTEXT

WHERE does meta-utopian narrative stand in the general crisis of social imagination and the parallel crisis of representational aesthetics? Born in isolation, Russian meta-utopian fiction is certainly not an isolated phenomenon. It parallels the renewed attention to language, semiotic play, and narrative structure that has figured so importantly in the West in opening up new insight into ideological structures. Its challenge to maximalist, bipolar thinking and its argument for the middle ground makes meta-utopian fiction very much of a piece with current social, literary, and philosophical discourse. Indeed, if anything, it forces us to raise the question of social imagination, of ideal, collective self-projection—of "utopia"—in criticism and fiction that appears long since to have abandoned utopian thinking as yet another monologism.

There is an obvious historical parallel between the Soviet and the Western collapse of utopian "faith." Despite the general horror at social practice in the two Stalinist and fascist utopian experiments of the first half of the twentieth century, there was a suprising resurgence of a positive utopianism in the 1950s and 1960s, in both the East and the West. This is true of Soviet culture, in which, as the critic Natalia Ivanova notes, Khrushchev and even the most "liberal" Soviet journal of the 1960s, *Novyi mir*, made every effort to resurrect hope for the imminent success of socialism.[1] In the West the renegade Marxist Ernst Bloch spoke of utopian hope and anticipatory imagination, and Martin Buber saw fresh utopian possibilities in the newborn state of Israel.[2] Skinner, Marcuse, MacLuhan, and others were

---

[1] Ivanova, "Proshchanie s utopiei," 7.

[2] See, for example, Ernst Bloch, *The Utopian Function of Art and Literature: Selected Essays* (Cambridge, Mass.: MIT Press, 1988); Martin Buber, *Paths in Utopia* (New York: Macmillan, 1988).

dreaming of yet other variants of utopia, both personal and communal.³ The politics of the Great Society, with its emphasis on social equality and justice for American blacks, were strongly utopian. With the removal of Khrushchev, the arrest of Siniavsky and Daniel in early 1966, and the invasion of Czechoslovakia in August 1968, the credibility of the new Soviet utopianism was destroyed among progressive Soviet and Western intellectuals. And in the West the Vietnam War, the failure of the French student movement, and, five years later, the toppling of Allende's liberal Marxist government in Chile helped to disabuse intellectuals of their utopian visions.

During the 1980s we saw the dismantling of realized utopia in the twentieth century—the toppling of the Soviet state, the disemboweling of the structure of American civil rights, and the crumbling of the economic base for the American Dream. We have witnessed the reemergence of various counterutopias, some based on old nationalist rivalries, others on religious fundamentalism—all of which challenge the (Enlightenment utopian) concept of a secular, tolerant civil society. In its very ambivalence the emerging postmodern culture, however one defines it, would seem to avoid the question of utopian imagination. But utopia lurks everywhere as a word unspoken. As Jameson puts the question in his rather unpostmodernist book *Postmodernism, or the Cultural Logic of Late Capitalism*, "If postmodernism is the substitute for the sixties and the compensation for their political failure, the question of utopia would seem to be a crucial test of what is left of our capacity to imagine change at all."⁴

While Russian meta-utopian experiments offer an explicit critique of traditional utopian thinking, in recent "postmodernist" social thought and fiction, with one or two important exceptions, the critique is usually implicit, present in significant silence or in a series of euphemisms. Everywhere we find an impulse to confront ideological fixation, whatever direction it may take. Here one can find separate examples of meta-utopian sensibility that admires some qualified idea of social perfectibility, but rejects what is perceived as the monologism or ideological "totality" traditional for utopian thinking.⁵

---

³ Krishan Kumar, *Utopia and Anti-Utopia in Modern Times* (Oxford: Basil Blackwell, 1987), 393–400.

⁴ Fredric Jameson, *Postmodernism, or the Cultural Logic of Late Capitalism* (Durham, N.C.: Duke University Press, 1991), xvi.

⁵ See, for example, P. Dews, ed., *Habermas: Autonomy and Solidarity. Interviews with Jürgen Habermas* (London: Verso, 1986), 146.

CONCLUSION

This thinking stresses the power of dialogue and negotiation to open up imaginative possibilities.

Whether one reads Voinovich or Zinoviev or the essays of Jameson, Foucault, or Habermas, or, indeed, such novels of the last two decades as Ursula LeGuin's *The Dispossessed* (1973), *Foe* (1987) by the South African writer J. M. Coetzee, and *Paradise* (1991) by the Chilean writer Elena Castedo, it is patently clear that the emancipatory utopian impulse that Jean-François Lyotard sees at the heart of the Enlightenment "project" is still very much alive, if most ambiguously treated. As Paul Ricoeur puts it in his *Lectures on Ideology and Utopia*, "At a time when everything is blocked by systems which have failed but cannot be beaten, . . . utopia is our resource."[6] The point is that since 1968, few have been willing to grapple directly with a kind of fantasy that one "can't live with and can't live without." There is no doubt, however, that in these texts the utopian impulse is emerging in quite a different, less self-righteous and less single-minded mode. Socially concerned intellectuals, in both East and West, are much more self-aware and skeptical about what Lyotard calls "totalities"— systems of value, including utopias, that make exclusive claims to verity.[7] Such intellectuals reject the "faith" demanded in the utopias realized in fascist and Stalinist societies, and particularly in technologically advanced "democracies." Unlike the writers of the dystopias of the early twentieth century, who were typically disillusioned radicals, these intellectuals come from a variety of philosophical backgrounds. Still, none is willing to abandon the cultural and technological achievements of their age, and all see through the dystopians' attraction to a primitive existence and to "natural" man.

Admitting the liberating force of a utopian impulse, Russian meta-utopians and Western thinkers alike find themselves in search of a series of checks and balances to curb the excesses of utopian monologism, to limit utopia to the realm of intellectual play, and yet to retain its potential energy and imaginative force. To achieve this goal most of them insist on some notion of dialogue, dialectic, or balance between utopian thinking and other ideological constructs. Such is the thrust of Michael Holquist's 1968 essay "How to Play Utopia" and Paul Ricoeur's extended juxtaposition of ideology and utopia.[8] We find a point of view shared by Ricoeur, who urges on us the idea of

---

[6] Ricoeur, *Lectures on Ideology and Utopia*, 300.

[7] Lyotard, *The Postmodern Condition*, 13.

[8] Holquist, "How to Play Utopia."

utopia as a "preservation of opposition," and Zinoviev, who in *The Yawning Heights* stresses a social consciousness resting on the "constant experience of resistance" (YH, 253).[9]

It is interesting that one of the most influential of recent thinkers, Michel Foucault, makes broad use of utopian discourse and assumes a kind of meta-utopian perspective. In *Discipline and Punish* (1975), he tests the borders of the utopian-ideological space of liberal democracy, not to discard the notion of liberal democracy but to see more soberly how it has actually functioned in its utopian effort to improve human nature. He examines those who have not fit the utopian space, the criminals, and questions how utopian thinking has since the eighteenth century changed the notion of punishment to mean rehabilitation and perfection of aberrant people in such a way as to bring them into (utopian) civil society. More importantly, he uses this institution on the periphery of the utopian locus to show the weakness of the whole utopian idea in its realization. In a situation in which some humans control others totally, the notions of rehabilitation and perfectibility are refigured as externally imposed discipline and normalization. He goes on to speculate that this same pattern obtains in the institutions central to liberal democracy—factories, hospitals, and, most importantly, schools.[10] It bears repeating that

---

[9] Ricoeur, *Lectures on Ideology and Utopia*, 180.

[10] Michel Foucault, *Discipline and Punish: The Birth of the Prison*, trans. A. Sheridan (New York: Vintage, 1979), 138, 228. See especially pp. 200–249. It should, however, be noted that Foucault does use a dystopian image in his critique of liberal democracy, the image of the panopticon designed by Jeremy Bentham. The panopticon is an edifice with a tower at the center from which cells on the periphery are observed and controlled. Foucault asserts with some justification that the panopticon is fundamentally dystopian: "[T]he Panopticon must not be understood as a dream building, it is the diagram of a mechanism of power reduced to its ideal form" (205). It is important here to emphasize the parallels of perfect transparency and visibility that obtain between this architectural design and Zamiatin's dystopian glass city that centers on the Cube on which The Benefactor stands. For both transparent glass is an image of subjugation to total political and physical control. The panopticon, in Foucault's view, epitomizes corporal discipline, the "other, dark side" of civil society's explicit law codes, egalitarian judicial framework, representative government, and the like. Taken to the extreme, which is only implicit in Foucault's book, the panopticon, used primarily in prison design, can be extended to other institutions, such as education, health care, and production of wealth, and their architectural expressions, that are central to civil society. If indeed this were so, Foucault's vision would be fully dystopian, for the liberal democratic utopia would be exposed as a prison in which physical discipline replaces the civil liberties.

Foucault's aim is not "anti-utopian": he does not appear to seek the dismantling of this system. He is concerned rather to show how actual social authority distorts the original utopian idea and to warn about the possible ruinous reaction that this practice might bring.

In his essay "The Crisis of the Welfare State and the Exhaustion of Utopian Energies" (1989) the German social thinker Jürgen Habermas supports the contention that a utopian impulse is still alive and well but that it has moved out of that "particular utopia that in the past crystallized around the potential of a society based on social labor," that is, the Marxist utopia of *The German Ideology*.[11] He notes particularly the historical failure of Soviet communism, the "authoritarian corporatism" of fascist societies, and the social democratic idea of the welfare state.[12] A utopian impulse based on an "undamaged intersubjectivity," a communication in which both collective needs and individual autonomy are addressed, in his opinion, is necessary and a possible way for the utopian impulse to function productively in the contemporary world.[13] Habermas particularly stresses the need for "space for individuals to shape their own lives."[14] Other alternatives, Habermas suggests, are more or less authoritarian and hostile to intellectual speculation and aesthetic and social experiment. He mentions, for example, a reversion to the forced cohesion of religious communities or the neoconservative programs of leaders such as Reagan, Thatcher, and Kohl.[15] In his article "Discourse Ethics" (1983) Habermas imagines an "ideal" scenario of ongoing dialogue, of continual negotiation among citizens, each with a personal notion of the good life, talking themselves toward what he calls "consensus." Here he develops a notion of ethics as "communicative interaction," a condition achieved "when the participants coordinate their plans of action consensually, with the agreement reached at any point being evaluated in terms of the intersubjective recognition of validity claims."[16] In other words, commu-

---

[11] Jürgen Habermas, "The Crisis of the Welfare State and the Exhaustion of Utopian Energies" (1989), in *Jürgen Habermas on Society and Politics: A Reader* (Boston: Beacon Press, 1989), 287.

[12] Ibid., 288.

[13] Ibid., 299.

[14] Dews, *Habermas: Autonomy and Solidarity*, 147.

[15] Habermas, "The Crisis of the Welfare State," 287.

[16] Jürgen Habermas, "Discourse Ethics: Notes on a Program of Philosophical Justification" (1983), in *The Communicative Ethics Controversy*, ed. S. Benhabib and F. Dallmayr (Cambridge: MIT Press, 1990), 63.

nicative interaction succeeds only when the players agree on the rules of the game and thus create a common ground for legitimating and periodically evaluating their contract.

Lyotard in *The Postmodern Condition* treats the problem of utopian imagination without actually mentioning the word *utopia*. He arrives at his own much looser notion of consensus by way of confrontation with Habermas's thinking. He defines consensus as a local and provisional agreement based on autonomy of disparate groups and modes of discourse within society. The fault of Habermas's idea, Lyotard argues, lies in its unarticulated assumption that dialogue ought to end in agreement. Lyotard views this notion of consensus as a new "totality" and a new "terror" aimed against all experimentation and innovation, and urges thinking people to "wage a war on totality."[17] He finds an antidote to ideological totality in what he calls "paralogical" thinking, by which he means forms of thought that emphasize incommensurabilities and ruptures in logic. A utopian impulse is nonetheless clear in Lyotard's search for liberating forces in society, for example, in social and cultural difference and in the practice of discursive autonomy. Most importantly, we find a utopian impulse behind Lyotard's recuperation of "justice" as the recognition of the "heteromorphous nature of language games" and the recognition that all contracts are limited and temporary, subject to change as the players of the game change.[18]

In the course of our discussion it has become obvious that Russian meta-utopian fiction is saturated with a similar kind of skepticism about ideological totalities. Such skepticism can have a beneficial, indeed, liberating, effect on both literary and social forms of imagination. One move is to expose the either/ormentality, the valuative vicious circle of binary oppositions, that obtains between Marxist-Leninist utopianism and Russian Orthodox, nationalist counterutopianism—each of which claims for itself total truth and legitimacy and denies both of these to its polar opposite. Meta-utopian fiction flattens and puts into perspective the seeming differences between these two, showing how they do *not* provide real alternatives to each other, and, indeed, how they function as secret allies against the middle—against political dissent and social moderacy. Exposing the looking-glass war that obtains between the two and collapsing them onto one

---

[17] Lyotard, *The Postmodern Condition*, 82.
[18] Ibid., 66.

psychological template opens to the imagination other possible social spaces and social behaviors. But in keeping with its nonmonological character, meta-utopian fiction does not defend any one social or political program.

The Soviet theorists Iury Lotman and Boris Uspensky see maximalist thinking as a pathology specific to pre-nineteenth-century Russian culture. It is interesting that French poststructuralists have given their greatest attention to the binary oppositions that obtain in Western thought. The British Marxist critic Terry Eagleton calls binary thinking one of the deep issues in all kinds of ideological construction:

> Deconstruction ... has grasped the point that the binary oppositions with which classical structuralism tends to work represent a way of seeing typical of ideologies. Ideologies like to draw rigid boundaries between what is acceptable and what is not, between self and nonself, truth and falsity, sense and nonsense, reason and madness, central and marginal, surface and depth. Such metaphysical thinking ... cannot be simply eluded: we cannot catapult ourselves beyond this binary habit of thought into an ultra-metaphysical realm. But by a certain way of operating upon texts—whether "literary" or "philosophical"—we may begin to unravel these options a little, demonstrate how one term of an antithesis secretly inheres within the other.[19]

It is not my purpose to suggest any deeper parallel between deconstructionist theory, Russian semiotics, and Russian meta-utopian writing except to suggest that all are products of a recent resistance to what may be called valuative vicious circles. And both show a willingness to explore middle grounds between ideological extremes as a way at least to modify the vicious circle.

Positions on a variety of more specific issues bring Western thinkers and Russian meta-utopians into similar discursive spheres. Among these are a concern for the epistemological strategies we use to arrive at a consensus as to what constitutes "truth." Paramount here is a reconsideration of scientific and historical thinking in their relationship to realized-utopian ideology. Another important issue is the function of popular literary forms in the legitimization and fixation of utopian ideas as ideological orthodoxy. Finally, all these par-

---

[19] Eagleton, *Literary Theory*, 133.

ties are concerned with the problem of so-called realist representation in art, the limitations it places on memory and imagination, and the claims it makes to truth.

The relationship of scientific thinking to the construction and legitimation of ideologies is centrally important to both Zinoviev and Lyotard. Although each side approaches the problem from quite a different position, both are suspicious of institutionalized science and the harnessing of science to ideology, whether in Nazism, Stalinism, or the postwar welfare state, in order to fortify the claims to truth and beneficence made by these ideologies. Zinoviev adheres to a long-standing Russian scientific-intellectual consciousness when he abhors the abuse of scientific inquiry by bureaucracies and by political interests. He sees rigorous thinking in a traditional way, mainly as a challenge to ideology (YH, 153, 168). He gives priority to scientific analysis as a liberating discourse, which Lyotard decidedly does not. It should also be repeated that Zinoviev does see the importance of received narrative discourse in which ideological constructs are embedded for the creation of his preferred social personality, the citizen operating in a social context of multiple interests and pluralist dialogue (YH, 253). Nonetheless, an important trait of his favorite kind of citizen is, indeed, an ability to think critically and rigorously, a habit created by giving pride of place to scientific logic.

Lyotard, by contrast, is much more suspicious of science as an epistemological strategy that places itself above other ways of knowing, particularly narrative or received knowledge. Scientific discourse is blind to its own ideological interestedness and, thus, doubly at fault. Lyotard remarks on a variety of ways in which scientists make unacknowledged use of narrative discourse, for example, in the legitimation of scientific methods and results, in the process of popularization before a variety of political, industrial, and civic audiences, and, most importantly, in education, that is, the process of reduplication of the social type of the scientific researcher in the next generation. At the end of his essay *On the Postmodern Condition* he pays lip service to the British zoologist and Nobel Prize winner Peter Medawar, saying that science is also a narrative system, but one whose practitioners feel duty-bound to verify their claims.[20] As a final qualifier to Lyotard's argument, it would seem that Lyotard gives short shrift to the last part of that statement, namely, the compunction to

---

[20] Lyotard, *The Postmodern Condition*, 60.

verify. By contrast, Zinoviev's oppositionist social scientists and philosophers are forced to practice Medawar's definition of science, to verify and justify their claims.

Another issue paramount in the last quarter-century has been the reanimation of historical memory. Traditional utopian thinking dismisses history as a "dustbin," while paradoxically reappropriating historiography to create a prefiguration of itself. We have discussed at length Voinovich's, Aksënov's, and Zinoviev's concerns with the defixation of memory and imagination. Certainly similar concerns are at hand in Western debates about society. Perhaps the most eloquent defender of a historical consciousness is Habermas, who sees the "clash of historical and utopian thought," of memory and imagination, as the very lifeblood of modernity. Since the French Revolution, the polarity-in-dialogue of these two ways of thinking has released the energy necessary for the continued functioning of civil society. Now Habermas sees Western societies in crisis: as the Russian meta-utopian writers repeatedly make clear, in the twentieth century the utopian imagination has fused with historical experience, leading to a fear of the past and the future alike and forcing what Habermas calls a "contraction" of the "horizon of the future."[21]

In this crisis period people are at greatest risk of losing social and political identity. Habermas worries about the "traceless disappearance of the historical path," that is, that citizens of the welfare state will forget about the pain and suffering with which their forebears achieved material well-being.[22] One knows who one is, he argues, only by knowing and remembering one's origins and the path that one has followed into the present. In this limbo of historical consciousness, Habermas cautions, neoconservative utopian "totalities" can find fertile ground: "Whenever one portrays totalities, whole forms of life, whole life-histories, whole areas of life in their concretion, and suggests that these can be directly politically realized, the result can easily be the kind of consequences which our neo-conservative friends have indicated."[23] He has in mind the historical miasma and the return to simplistic and, in the long run, inadequate social and religious ideologies typical of the conservative side of the political spectrum.

---

[21] Habermas, "The Crisis of the Welfare State," 286.

[22] Jürgen Habermas, "Conservative Politics, Work, Socialism and Utopia Today" (Interview with H.-U. Reck [1983]), in Dews, *Habermas: Autonomy and Solidarity*, 139–40.

[23] Ibid., 146.

In recent social and literary discourse the revitalization of historical memory is closely connected to issues of representation and verbal play. Russian meta-utopian fiction, French poststructuralist theory, and American New Historicist thinking reject the single most widely accepted historical "reality" of the last century, the Hegelian notion of History as a force generating a single grand narrative.[24] Historical sensibility is reframed through attention to the problematic relationship between writing as historical document and writing as imaginative construct. Both meta-utopian fiction and "New Historicist" criticism stress the process of the "textualization" of history. They focus on the way in which event is transfigured as document and, thus, is subtly fictionalized and made subjective by acquiring a point of view and an ideological motivation. A major concern here is how the act of describing an event is secretly an act of assigning that event a value and a role in an assumed metanarrative.[25] A goal shared by New Historicism, such recent historical novels as Coetzee's *Foe*, with its play with the author and plot of *Robinson Crusoe* and (eighteenth-century) colonialism, racism, and sexism, and Russian meta-utopian fiction is to explore this shifting border between document and fiction, to tease out hidden behavioral codes, "other," dissenting views hinted at but not fully articulated, hidden under the armor of a firmly embedded ideological interest.[26]

The notion of reengaging historical experience through parody put forward by Linda Hutcheon in *The Poetics of Postmodernism* implies that historical narratives are continually in the process of being automatized and thus invite parodic challenge. It is our responsibility actively to bring them into confrontation with present experience and thereby gain what history has to offer, a perspective that allows us to locate and define ourselves. In Hutcheon's view, current fiction works toward this revitalization through constant attention to the border between memory and imagination, between fact and fiction, by "framing" the historical document in a fictional context.

---

[24] Michel Foucault, "The Discourse on Language" (1971), in *The Archaeology of Knowledge and the Discourse on Language*, trans. A. M. Sheridan Smith (New York: Pantheon, 1972), 215–38.

[25] See, for example, the helpful discussion of New Historicism by Hayden White, "New Historicism: A Comment," in *The New Historicism*, ed. H. Aram Veeser (New York: Routledge, 1989), 293–302.

[26] I am grateful to Richard Reitsma for discussions about Coetzee and African postcolonial literature.

Hutcheon's remarks on how, for example, John Fowles's *The French Lieutenant's Woman* and Umberto Eco's *The Name of the Rose* expose the ideological fixation of academic historiography, but also add to a sense of the revitalization of historical memory. A critic who until recently stood out as an opponent of the concept of "postmodernism," Fredric Jameson, concurs here with his critical opposition. In a move that sounds surprisingly like Ortega y Gasset in *History as System* and, more recently, Hutcheon, he usefully proposes a "dialectical view that seeks to grasp the present as history."[27] Thus, although none of these Western post-1968 developments is committed to perceiving history as a vital, legitimate "other," at least we are witnessing the reintroduction of an important impulse that counterbalances the utopian tendency to dismiss past experience as irrelevant to one's sense of self.

Western critics and Russian meta-utopians both worry about the resurgence of a simple, nostalgic, unreflected utopianism in various forms of neoconservatism. For example, during the 1980s Americans witnessed, and many welcomed, the "counterutopian" vision in Ronald Reagan's science-fictional star-wars reveries and the image of a gleaming city on a hill as the future of American society.[28] In Western and Russian thinking this social sentimentalism is linked to a resurgence of faith in simple representational art, in "realism," and to an anti-intellectual discreditation of both aesthetic and social experiment.[29] Voinovich, Zinoviev (YH, 441), and Terts, in particular, call into question the ideological claims of Solzhenitsyn, whose art couples conventional realism with conservative Russian nationalism. Lyotard worries about the attempt to muzzle creative imagination and aesthetic experimentation that he finds in the new surge of "realism," which, he claims, perhaps somewhat unfairly, has always stood "somewhere between academism and kitsch."[30] Habermas puts the problem in more moderate terms, criticizing the tendency of Reaganism and other neoconservatisms to discredit intellectual debate and aesthetic experimentation.[31]

[27] Frederic Jameson, "The Politics of Theory: Ideological Positions in the Postmodernist Debate," in *The Syntax of History*, vol. 2 of *The Ideologies of Theory: Essays, 1971–1986* (Minneapolis: University of Minnesota Press, 1988), 113.

[28] This image was borrowed from John Winthrop. I am grateful to Nicole Schonemann for her work on utopian imagery in the speeches of Ronald Reagan.

[29] Habermas, "The Crisis of the Welfare State," 293.

[30] Lyotard, *The Postmodern Condition*, 75.

[31] Habermas, "The Crisis of the Welfare State," 294.

Despite meta-utopian criticism of ideologically conservative uses of realist art, it is essential to note the ambiguity that obtains between theory and practice: both Western postmodernists and Russian meta-utopians practice a representational form of art. While upholding aesthetic experiment and fantasy as essential means for exposing embedded ideological interest, neither kind of fiction locates itself as "avant-garde" or esoteric. On the contrary, both stake out a claim to the middlebrow reader, whom they are not willing to relinquish to the ideological monologisms either of the right or of the left. While maintaining a dissenting consciousness, both trends make an appeal to more than just socially or politically marginalized or culturally highly competent readers. In practice they meld realist technique with meta-aesthetic contemplations on realism and its epistemological implications and with forays into the fantastic.

Thus, Russian meta-utopian writing and discrete trends in recent Western fiction and social thought share a number of features. All play with realized utopian orthodoxies fixed in conventional, popular literary forms. They call for a reconsideration of the ways in which we limit our collective memory and imagination. And, finally, there is a strong suspicion of binary modes of thinking that deny an imaginative middle ground. Taken together, these shared concerns are the hallmark of a "meta-utopian" mentality.

As we have defined what we believe to be a significant dominant in the social imagination of the post-Stalinist era, we have suggested throughout that this kind of social imagination participates in its own way in a more widespread, if not to say global, shift in imagination. In closing it will be well to stress the profound differences between Russian meta-utopian experiments and Western postmodernist thinking. First, young Russian writers have all had to live with a kind of "total," police-state totality that their Western counterparts have only theorized and played with. In contrast to intellectuals to the west, Russians have little in the way of a usable tradition of political pluralism or civil society that did not end in complete unraveling of the social and political fabric.[32] Second, Russians would appear to have a recent cultural heritage quite different from the one posited for postmodernism. As Hutcheon defines it, postmodernism is cast as a parodic response to modernism and modernist cultural texts. It bears

[32] See E. Clowes, S. Kassow, and J. West, eds., *Between Tsar and People: Educated Society and the Quest for Public Identity in Late Imperial Russia* (Princeton: Princeton University Press, 1991).

repeating that, because of the repression of modernist aesthetic experiment in Russia in the early 1930s, post-Stalinist experimental writers had no recent models to respond to. Because of this rupture Russian readers and writers tend to feel a nostalgic reverence for the lost modernist past, while their Western counterparts look on this heritage irreverently. However, this situation shifts in the recent postmodernist revision, *The Total Art of Stalinism*, by the young Russian intellectual historian Boris Groys, who argues that, while he repressed *merely* aesthetic experiment, Stalin himself created in the Soviet state the ultimate, *grand* aesthetic experiment, the *Gesamtkunstwerk*, which, Groys contends, many modernists yearned for.[33] And, indeed, it is to Stalinism as an aestheticized, fabricated text, and to its merely aesthetic texts—its rhetoric, its songs, its novels—that meta-utopias address themselves.

Nonetheless, there is a very real and disastrous historical reality behind the aesthetic play—a reality of inner exile, forced silence, incarceration, terror, and mass murder—that makes the meta-utopian deconstruction of real totalitarian practice both more risky and more serious than the Western war on totalities. The Russian fiction is emotionally charged by comparison to Western counterparts partly because there is such a deeply felt lack of usable, credible value and a desire to invent a basis for truth beyond the traditionally available historical scripts.

A possible positive impulse implied in this most serious Russian game of parody might be a Russian reinvention of the notion of *Gesellschaft*, understood as a secular, multipolar, civil society. It should be said that this defense is pessimistic, born of the desperate determination not to let any single utopian vision become paramount and thus gain full and dangerous access to physical force. It is quite different from, say, Francis Fukuyama's quite unfounded assumption that pluralism and liberal democracy are now granted throughout the world, that the hegemony of ideological monologisms has been broken once and for all, and that, indeed, history has come to an end.

What, then, is the place of utopian imagination in an era that has quite rejected this kind of fantasy and its incursions into historical and social scenarios? It might be useful to frame the meta-utopian imagination in terms of narrative strategy. It has been claimed that

---

[33] Boris Groys, *The Total Art of Stalinism: Avant-Garde, Aesthetic Dictatorship, and Beyond* (Princeton: Princeton University Press, 1992).

the "grand" narratives of modern social-political history have been preceded by "little" narratives, read by or told to an audience, that make a major shift in social behavior thinkable and desirable. If Solzhenitsyn was producing such "petits récits," then Russian meta-utopian writers in the post-Stalinist underground wanted rather to expose the ideological commitments of all kinds of little narratives and their claims on a perceived grand narrative and, as well, to pose the question of the legitimacy of the grand narrative itself.

It is appropriate to end with a concept of place, the heart of utopia and of meta-utopian thinking. In her book *Strangers to Ourselves* (1991) a most unlikely, un-utopian thinker, Julia Kristeva, addresses the problem of utopia: "How can one be free without some sort of utopia, some sort of strangeness? Let us therefore be of nowhere, but without forgetting that we are somewhere."[34] Perhaps it is here, in this middle-ground meditation on polar opposites, this multipolar balancing act, that the utopian impulse can have a place in our time—between the "nowhere" of multipolarity and consensus and the ravaged, fragmented "somewhere" of the ideological either/or.

[34] Julia Kristeva, *Strangers to Ourselves* (New York: Columbia University Press, 1991), 117. I am grateful to Ivelise Faundez for this source.

Bibliography

Aksenov, Vasilii. *The Island of Crimea*. Trans. M. H. Heim. New York: Vintage, 1984.

———. *Ostrov Krym*. Ann Arbor: Ardis, 1981.

Al'tshuller, Mark. "'Moskva-Petushki' Venedikta Erofeeva i traditsii klassicheskoi poemy." *Novyi zhurnal*, no. 146 (1982): 75–85.

Amurskii, Vitalii. "Ia—odinochka vo vsem," *Novoe russkoe slovo* (July 12, 1991), 14.

Amusin, M. "Daleko li do budushchego?" *Neva*, no. 2 (1988): 153–60.

———. "Illiuzii i doroga." *Oktiabr'*, no. 6 (1989): 203–6.

Apel, Karl-Otto. "Is the Ethics of the Ideal Communication Community a Utopia? On the Relationship between Ethics, Utopia, and the Critique of Utopia." In *The Communication Ethics Controversy*, ed. S. Benhabib and F. Dallmayr, 23–59. Cambridge, Mass.: MIT Press, 1990.

Arapov, M. "Iazyk utopii." *Znanie-sila*, no. 2 (1990): 66–72.

Arzhak, Nikolai (Iulii Daniel'). *Govorit Moskva*. New York: Inter-Language Literary Associates, 1966.

———. *This Is Moscow Speaking, and Other Stories*. Trans. S. Hood, H. Shukman, and J. Richardson. London: Collins, 1968.

Aucouturier, Michel. "Writer and Text in the Works of Abram Terc." In *Fiction and Drama in Eastern and Southeastern Europe: Evolution and Experiment in the Postwar Period*, ed. H. Birnbaum and Th. Eekman, 1–10. Columbus: Slavica, 1980.

Avins, Carol. "Reaching a Reader: The Master's Audience in *The Master and Margarita*." *Slavic Review* 45, no. 2 (Summer 1986), 272–85.

Azhgikhina, N. "Razrushiteli v poiskakh very (Novye cherty sovremennoi molodoi prozy." *Znamia*, no. 9 (1990): 223–27.

———. "Vozvrashchenie Siniavskogo i Danielia." *Oktiabr'*, no. 8 (1990): 203–5.

Bakhtin, M. M. *The Dialogic Imagination*. Ed. M. Holquist. Trans. M. Holquist and C. Emerson. Austin: University of Texas Press, 1988.

———. *Rabelais and His World*. Trans. H. Iswolsky. Cambridge, Mass.: MIT Press, 1968.

Baudrillard, Jean. *America*. Trans. C. Turner. London: Verso, 1989.

Bednyi, Dem'ian. *Stikhotvoreniia i poemy*. Moscow-Leningrad: Sovetskii pisatel', 1965.

Belaia, Galina."'Da budet vedomo vsem. . . .'" In *Tsena metafory ili prestuplenie i nakazanie Siniavskogo i Danielia*, 4–14. Moscow: Kniga, 1989.

———. *Zatonuvshaia Atlantida*. Biblioteka "Ogonek," vol. 14. Moscow: Ogonek, 1991.

Beliaeva, Svetlana. "Ne podpol'em edinym." *Literaturnaia gazeta*, no. 33 (August 15, 1990): 6.

Beraha, Laura. "Iskander's Anti-Idyll." Paper presented at the national meeting of the American Association for the Advancement of Slavic Studies, Phoenix, Arizona, November 22, 1992.

Berdyaev, Nicolas. *The Russian Revolution*. Ann Arbor: University of Michigan Press, 1966.

Berlin, Isaiah. *The Crooked Timber of Humanity: Chapters in the History of Ideas*. Ed. H. Hardy. New York: Knopf, 1991.

Bethea, David M. *The Shape of Apocalypse in Modern Russian Fiction*. Princeton: Princeton University Press, 1989.

Bitov, Andrei. "Zapiski iz-za ugla." *Novyi mir*, no. 2 (1990): 142–65.

Bloch, Ernst. *The Utopian Function of Art and Literature: Selected Essays*. Cambridge, Mass.: MIT Press, 1988.

Bozhenko, L. A. "Chitaia Andreia Platonova." *Don*, no. 12 (1988): 163–65.

Brodsky, Joseph. Preface to Andrei Platonov, *The Foundation Pit*, ix–xii. Ann Arbor: Ardis, 1973.

Brown, Edward J. "Zinoviev, Aleshkovsky, Rabelais, Sorrentino, Possibly Pynchon, Maybe James Joyce, and Certainly Tristram Shandy: A Comparative Study of a Satirical Mode." *Stanford Slavic Studies*, no. 1 (1987): 307–25.

Buber, Martin. *Paths in Utopia*. New York: Macmillan, 1988.

Chalmaev, V. "Utonuvshii kolokol (Chitaia A. Platonova)." *Voprosy literatury*, no. 7 (1988): 58–92.

Chapple, Richard. "Fazil Iskander's *Rabbits and Boa Constrictors*: A Soviet Version of Orwell's *Animal Farm*." *Germano-Slavica*, nos. 1–2 (1985): 33–47.

Chuprinin, Sergei. "Literatura prinosit zhertvy." *Novoe vremia*, no. 18 (1990): 46–47.

Clark, Katerina. "Political History and Literary Chronotope: Some Soviet Case Studies." In *Literature and History: Theoretical Problems and Russian Case Studies*, ed. G. S. Morson, 230–46. Stanford: Stanford University Press, 1986.

———. *The Soviet Novel: History as Ritual*. Chicago: University of Chicago Press, 1985.

Clowes, Edith W. "Beyond the Abyss: Nietzschean Myth in Zamiatin's *We* and Pasternak's *Doctor Zhivago*." In *Nietzsche and Soviet Culture*, ed. B. G. Rosenthal. Cambridge: Cambridge University Press, forthcoming.

———. "Kafka and the Modernism-Realism Debate in Literary Criticism of the Thaw." In *The European Foundations of Russian Modernism*, ed. P. Barta in collaboration with U. Goebel, 295–325. Lewiston, Maine: The Edwin Mellen Press, 1991.

———. *The Revolution of Moral Consciousness: Nietzsche in Russian Literature, 1890–1914*. DeKalb: Northern Illinois University Press, 1988.

Clowes, E., S. Kassow, and J. West, eds. *Between Tsar and People: Educated Society and the Quest for Public Identity in Late Imperial Russia*. Princeton: Princeton University Press, 1991.

Dews, P., ed. *Habermas: Autonomy and Solidarity. Interviews with Jürgen Habermas*. London: Verso, 1986.

Diuzhev, Iurii. "Antiutopiia Vasil'ia Belova." *Sever* (Petrozavodsk), no. 6 (1989): 109–16.

Eagleton, Terry. *Literary Theory: An Introduction*. Minneapolis: University of Minnesota Press, 1983.

Elliott, Robert C. *The Shape of Utopia: Studies in a Literary Genre*. Chicago: University of Chicago Press, 1970.

Erofeev, Venedikt. *Moscow to the End of the Line*. Trans. H. W. Tjalsma. New York: Taplinger, 1980.

———. *Moskva-Petushki*. Paris: YMCA-Press, 1977.

Erofeev, Viktor. "Pominki po sovetskoi literature." *Literaturnaia gazeta*, no. 27 (July 4, 1990): 8.

Evtushenko, Evgenii. "Sud'ba Platonova." *Sovetskaia kul'tura* (August 20, 1988), 5–6.

Fanger, Donald. "Conflicting Imperatives in the Model of the Russian Writer." In *Literature and History: Theoretical Problems and Russian Case Studies*, ed. G. S. Morson, 111–24. Stanford: Stanford University Press, 1986.

Fantasticheskii mir Abrama Tertsa. New York: Inter-Language Literary Associates, 1967.

Filosofskaia entsiklopediia. Moscow: Sovetskaia entsiklopediia, 1960–1970.

Foucault, Michel. *The Archaeology of Knowledge and the Discourse on Language*. Trans. A. M. Sheridan Smith. New York: Pantheon, 1972.

———. *Discipline and Punish: The Birth of the Prison*. Trans. A. Sheridan. New York: Vintage, 1979.

Frye, Northrop. "Varieties of Literary Utopias." In *Utopias and Utopian Thought*, ed. F. E. Manuel, 25–49. Boston: Houghton Mifflin, 1966.

Gaiser-Shnitman, Svetlana. *Venedikt Erofeev: Moskva-Petushki ili "The Rest is Silence."* Bern: Peter Lang, 1989.

Gal'tseva, R., and I. Rodnianskaia. "Pomekha—chelovek: Opyt veka v zerkale antiutopii." *Novyi mir*, no. 12 (1988): 217–30.

Geertz, Clifford. *The Interpretation of Cultures: Selected Essays*. New York: Basic Books, 1973.

Greenblatt, Stephen. "Towards a Poetics of Culture." In *The New Historicism*, ed. H. A. Veeser, 1–14. New York: Routledge, 1989.

Greenfeld, Liah. "Kitchen Debate: Russia's Nationalist Intelligentsia." *The New Republic* (Sept. 21, 1992), 22–25.

Griakalov, A. A., and Iu. Iu. Dorokhov. "Ot strukturalizma k dekonstruktsii (zapadnye esteticheskie teorii 70-80-kh godov XX veka)." *Russkaia literatura*, no. 1 (1990): 236–49.

Groys, Boris. *The Total Art of Stalinism: Avant-Garde, Aesthetic Dictatorship, and Beyond*. Princeton: Princeton University Press, 1992.

Günther, Hans. "Aspekte und Probleme der neueren Utopiediskussion in der Slawistik." In *Utopieforschung: Interdisziplinäre Studien zur neuzeitlichen Utopie*, 1:221–31. Stuttgart: Universität Bielefeld, 1982.

Gutsche, George. *Moral Apostasy in Russian Literature*. DeKalb: Northern Illinois University Press, 1986.

Habermas, Jürgen. "Conservative Politics, Work, Socialism and Utopia Today" (Interview with H.-U. Reck [1983]). In *Habermas: Autonomy and Solidarity*, ed. P. Dews. London: Verso, 1986.

———. "The Crisis of the Welfare State and the Exhaustion of Utopian Energies." In *Jürgen Habermas on Society and Politics: A Reader*. Boston: Beacon Press, 1989.

———. "Discourse Ethics: Notes on a Program of Philosophical Justification." In *The Communicative Ethics Controversy*, ed. S. Benhabib and F. Dallmayr, 60–110. Cambridge, Mass.: MIT Press, 1990.

Hassan, Ihab. *The Dismemberment of Orpheus: Toward a Postmodern Literature*. 2d ed. Madison: University of Wisconsin Press, 1982.

Ho, Koon-ki, Tommy. "Why Utopias Fail." Ph.D. diss., University of Illinois, 1986.

Holquist, Michael. "How to Play Utopia: Some Brief Notes on the Distinctiveness of Utopian Fiction." *Yale French Studies*, no. 41 (1968): 106–23.

Hosking, Geoffrey. *The Awakening of the Soviet Union*. Cambridge, Mass.: Harvard University Press, 1991.

Howe, Irving. *The Decline of the New*. New York: Harcourt, Brace and World, 1970.

Hutcheon, Linda. *A Poetics of Postmodernism: History, Theory, Fiction*. New York: Routledge, 1988.

Il'f, Il'ia, and Evgenii Petrov. *Kak sdelalsia Robinzon*. Letchworth: Bradda, 1968.

Iskander, Fazil'. *Kroliki i udavy*. Moscow: Knizhnaia palata, 1988.

———. *Rabbits and Boa Constrictors*. Trans. R. E. Peterson. Ann Arbor: Ardis, 1989.

Ivanova, Natal'ia. "Proiti cherez otchaianie." *Iunost'*, no. 2 (1990): 89–94.

———. "Proshchanie s utopiei, ili Siuzhet dlia nenapisannogo romana." *Literaturnaia gazeta*, no. 29 (July 18, 1990): 4, 7.

———. "Tret'e rozhdenie." *Druzhba narodov*, no. 4 (1988): 157–60.

Jakobson, Roman. "On Realism in Art." In *Readings in Russian Poetics: Formalist and Structuralist Views*, ed. L. Matejka and K. Pomorska, 38–46. Ann Arbor: University of Michigan Press, 1978.

Jameson, Fredric. *The Ideologies of Theory: Essays, 1971–1986*. Vol. 2: *The Syntax of History*. Minneapolis: University of Minnesota Press, 1988.

———. *The Political Unconscious: Narrative as a Socially Symbolic Act*. Ithaca, N.Y.: Cornell University Press, 1981.

———. *Postmodernism, or, the Cultural Logic of Late Capitalism*. Durham, N.C.: Duke University Press, 1991.
Jauss, Hans Robert. *Literaturgeschichte als Provokation*. Frankfurt: Suhrkamp, 1970.
Kabakov, Aleksandr. "Nevozvrashchenets." *Iskusstvo kino*, no. 6 (1989): 150–75.
———. *No Return*. Ed. D. Stumpf. Trans. T. Whitney. New York: Morrow, 1990.
Kanchukov, E. "Mezhdu proshlym i budushchim." *Literaturnoe obozrenie*, no. 9 (1988): 25–29.
Kantor, Karl. "Siiaiushchaia vysota slovesnosti." *Oktiabr'*, no. 1 (1991): 30–35.
Kasack, Wolfgang. *Dictionary of Russian Literature since 1917*. Trans. M. Carlson and J. T. Hedges, with revisions by R. Atack. New York: Columbia University Press, 1988.
Khodasevich, V. F. "Gor'kii." *Sovremennye zapiski* (Paris), no. 70 (1940): 131–56.
Kratkaia literaturnaia entsiklopediia. Moscow: Sovetskaia entsiklopediia, 1962–1978.
Kratkii filosofskii slovar'. Moscow: Gosudarstvennoe izdatel'stvo politicheskoi literatury, 1952.
Kristeva, Julia. *Strangers to Ourselves*. New York: Columbia University Press, 1991.
"'Kruglyi stol': Nereshennye problemy teorii literatury." *Voprosy literatury*, no. 12 (1987): 3–74.
Ksepma, V. O. "'Po tu storonu lobnoi stenki': Konspekt neproiznesennogo dialoga po povodu nekotorykh sochinenii pisatelia A. G. Bitova." *Literaturnoe obozrenie*, no. 3 (1989): 24–27.
Kumar, Krishan. *Utopia and Anti-Utopia in Modern Times*. Oxford: Basil Blackwell, 1987.
Lahusen, Thomas. "Inversiia utopicheskogo diskursa. O 'Zapiskakh iz podpol'ia' F. M. Dostoevskogo." *Wiener Slawistischer Almanach*, no. 20 (1987): 5–40.
Lakshin, V. "'Antiutopiia' Evgeniia Zamiatina." *Znamia*, no. 4 (1988): 126–30.
Latynina, Iuliia. "V ozhidanii Zolotogo Veka: Ot skazki k antiutopii." *Oktiabr'*, no. 6 (1989): 177–87.
Literaturnaia entsiklopediia. Moscow: Izdatel'stvo kommunisticheskoi akademii, 1929–1939.
Loktev, Nikolai. "Allegorii Dzhordzha Oruella." *Literaturnyi Kirgizstan*, no. 1 (1989): 151–53.
———. "O tsene utopii. Literaturnyi dnevnik." *Literaturnyi Kirgizstan*, no. 2 (1989): 125–30.
Loseff, Lev. *On the Beneficence of Censorship: Aesopian Language in Modern Russian Literature*. Munich: Sagner, 1984.

Lotman, Iurii. *Struktura khudozhestvennogo teksta*. Providence, R.I.: Brown University Press, 1971.

Lotman, Jurij, and Boris Uspenskij. "The Role of Dual Models in the Dynamics of Russian Culture (Up to the End of the Eighteenth Century)." In *The Semiotics of Russian Culture*, ed. A. Shukman, 3–35. Ann Arbor: Ardis, 1984.

Lyotard, Jean-François. *The Postmodern Condition: A Report on Knowledge*. Trans. G. Bennington and B. Massumi. Minneapolis: University of Minnesota Press, 1984.

McHale, Brian. *Postmodernist Fiction*. London: Methuen, 1987.

McMillin, Arnold. "Zinoviev's Fiction in the Context of Unofficial Russian Prose of the 1970s." In *Alexander Zinoviev as Writer and Thinker: An Assessment*, ed. P. Hanson and M. Kirkwood, 61–70. New York: St. Martin's Press, 1988.

Manuel, Frank E., and Fritzie Manuel. *Utopian Thought in the Western World*. Cambridge, Mass.: Harvard University Press, 1979.

Marin, Louis. *Utopics: The Semiological Play of Textual Spaces*. Trans. R. A. Vollrath. Atlantic Highlands, N.J.: Humanities Press International, 1990.

Morson, Gary Saul. *The Boundaries of Genre: Dostoevsky's "Diary of a Writer" and the Traditions of Literary Utopia*. 1981. Evanston, Ill.: Northwestern University Press, n.d.

Mumford, Lewis. "Utopia, the City and the Machine." In *Utopias and Utopian Thought*, ed. F. E. Manuel, 3–24. Boston: Houghton Mifflin, 1966.

Murikov, Gennadii. "Oni i 'my.'" *Zvezda*, no. 1 (1989): 187–91.

Nietzsche, Friedrich. *The Gay Science*. Trans. W. Kaufmann. New York: Vintage, 1974.

Novikov, Vladimir. "Vozvrashchenie k zdravomu smyslu: Sub'ektivnye zametki chitatelia antiutopii." *Znamia*, no. 7 (1989): 214–20.

O'Brien, Conor Cruise. "Paradise Lost." *New York Review of Books* (April 25, 1991), 52–60.

Ortega y Gasset, José. *History as System*. New York: W. W. Norton, 1961.

Orwell, George. *1984*. Harmonsworth, Engl.: Penguin, 1979.

"Otkazyvat'sia li nam ot sotsialisticheskogo realizma?" *Literaturnaia gazeta*, no. 21 (May 25, 1988): 3.

Paperno, I. A., and B. M. Gasparov. "'Vstan' i idi.'" *Slavica Hierosolymitana*, nos. 5–6 (1981): 387–400.

Pavlova-Sil'vanskaia, M. "Eto sladkoe 'My,' eto kovarnoe 'My.'" *Druzhba narodov*, no. 11 (1988): 259–62.

Pertsovskii, Vladimir. "V novoi situatsii: Polemicheskie zametki." *Ural*, no. 4 (1989): 171–78.

Peterson, Nadezhda L. "Fantasy and Utopia in the Contemporary Soviet Novel, 1976–1981." Ph.D. diss., Indiana University, 1986.

Petro, Peter. "Aleksandr Zinov'ev's *Yawning Heights* as an Anatomy." *Canadian Slavonic Papers*, no. 23 (1981): 70–76.

Petrushevskaia, Liudmila. "Novye Robinzony." *Novyi mir*, no. 8 (1989): 166–72.

Platonov, Andrei. *Kotlovan*. Ann Arbor: Ardis, 1973.

Putrenko, T. "Pushkin—nash smeiushchiisia genii." Interview with A. Siniavskii. *Literaturnaia gazeta*, no. 32 (August 8, 1990): 7.

Radischev, Aleksandr. *Puteschestvie iz Peterburga v Moskvu*. Leningrad: Khudohestvennaia literatura, 1969.

Radzikhovskii, L. A. "Pochemu my ne doshli do '1984' goda?" *Filosofskie nauki*, no. 12 (1990): 71–81.

Reiss, Timothy J. *The Discourse of Modernism*. Ithaca, N.Y.: Cornell University Press, 1984.

Revich, Vsevolod. "Preduprezhdenie vsem." *Literaturnoe obozrenie*, no. 7 (1988): 44–46.

Ricoeur, Paul. *Lectures on Ideology and Utopia*. Ed. G. H. Taylor. New York: Columbia University Press, 1986.

Rishina, Irina. "Ia vernulsia by." Interview with Vladimir Voinovich. *Literaturnaia gazeta*, no. 25 (June 20, 1990): 8.

Ross, D. A., ed. *Between Spring and Summer: Soviet Conceptual Art in the Era of Late Communism*. Cambridge, Mass.: MIT Press, 1990.

Rostovtseva, Inna. "U chelovecheskogo serdtsa." *Oktiabr'*, no. 11 (1988): 158–62.

Sabinina, O. B. "Zhanr antiutopii v angliiskoi i amerikanskoi literature 30-50-kh godov XX v." *Vestnik moskovskogo universiteta: Filologiia*, no. 2 (1990): 51–57.

Saraskina, L. "Strana dlia eksperimenta." *Oktiabr'*, no. 3 (1990): 159–70.

Scherrer, Jutta. *Die Petersburger Religiös-Philosophischen Vereinigungen*. Berlin-Wiesbaden: O. Harrassowitz, 1973.

Schutte, Ophelia. *Beyond Nihilism: Nietzsche without Masks*. Chicago: University of Chicago Press, 1984.

Seidman, S., ed. *Jürgen Habermas on Society and Politics: A Reader*. Boston: Beacon Press, 1989.

Semenova, Svetlana. "Mytarstvo ideala: K vykhodu v svet 'Chevengura' Andreia Platonova." *Novyi mir*, no. 5 (1988): 218–31.

Serbinenko, V. "Tri veka skitanii v mire utopii: Chitaia brat'ev Strugatskikh." *Novyi mir*, no. 5 (1989): 242–55.

Servier, Jean. *L'utopie*. Paris: Presses universitaires de France, 1979.

Sesterhenn, Raimund. *Das Bogostroitel'stvo bei Gor'kij und Lunačarskij bis 1909*. Munich: Sagner, 1982.

Shestakov, V. P. "Evoliutsiia russkoi literaturnoi utopii." In *Russkaia literaturnaia utopiia*, ed. V. P. Shestakov, 5–32. Moscow: Izd. moskovskogo universiteta, 1986.

Shikhalev, L. G. "Utopiia na ruinakh utopii." *Literaturnaia gazeta*, no. 6 (February 13, 1991): 14.

Shklovskii, Evgenii. "Neugasaiushchee plamia: zhurnal'naia proza—88." *Literaturnoe obozrenie*, no. 2 (1989): 20–37.
Shklovskii, Viktor. *O teorii prozy*. 1929. Ann Arbor: Ardis, 1985.
Spindler-Troubetzkoy, Laure. "Le Discours sur le Fantastique dans les revues soviétiques du début des années 80." *Cahiers du Monde russe et soviétique*, no. 2 (1987): 201–8.
Spivak, M. "'Lazurnoe blazhenstvo zabyt'ia': detstvo v antiutopiakh XX veka." *Detskaia literatura*, no. 9 (1989): 18–24.
Stel'makh, V. "Novye starye knigi." *Izvestiia*, no. 32 (January 31, 1989): 3.
Stepanian, Karen. "Nuzhna li nam literatura? (Zametki o proze ukhodiashchego goda)." *Znamia*, no. 12 (1990): 222–30.
Stites, Richard. *Revolutionary Dreams: Utopian Vision and Experimental Life in the Russian Revolution*. New York: Oxford University Press, 1989.
Strugatskii, Arkadii, and Boris Strugatskii. *Gadkie lebedi*. Frankfurt: Posev, 1972.
———. "Grad obrechennyi." *Neva*, no. 9 (1988): 64–117; no. 10 (1988): 86–128.
———. *The Ugly Swans*. Trans. A. Nakhimovsky and A. S. Nakhimovsky. New York: Macmillan, 1979.
Sussman, Elisabeth. "The Third Zone: Soviet 'Postmodern.'" In *Between Spring and Summer*, ed. D. A. Ross, 61–72. Cambridge, Mass.: MIT Press, 1990.
Tendriakov, Vladimir. "Pokushenie na mirazhi." *Novyi mir*, no. 4 (1987): 59–116; no. 5 (1987): 89–164.
Terras, Victor. *Handbook of Russian Literature*. New Haven: Yale University Press, 1985.
Terts, Abram (Andrei Siniavskii). "Anekdot v anekdote." *Sintaksis*, no. 1 (1978): 77–95.
———. "Chtenie v serdtsakh." *Sintaksis*, no. 17 (1987): 191–205.
———. "The Literary Process in Russia." Trans. M. Glenny. In *Kontinent*, 77–118. Garden City, N.Y.: Anchor/Doubleday,1976.
———. *The Makepeace Experiment*. Trans. M. Harari. Evanston, Ill.: Northwestern University Press, 1989.
———. "Solzhenitsyn kak ustroitel' novogo edinomysliia." *Sintaksis*, no. 14 (1985): 16–32.
———. *Spokoinoi nochi*. Paris: Sintaksis, 1984.
———. *"The Trial Begins" and "On Socialist Realism."* Trans. G. Dennis. New York: Vintage, 1960.
Toporov, Viktor. "V poiskakh utrachennogo smysla: zarubezhnaia literatura v otechestvennoi periodike." *Literaturnoe obozrenie*, no. 1 (1989): 37–42.
Trotter, David. *The Making of the Reader: Language and Subjectivity in Modern American, English, and Irish Poetry*. London: Macmillan, 1984.
Tsena metafory ili prestuplenie i nakazanie Siniavskogo i Danielia. Ed. L. S. Eremina. Moscow: Kniga, 1989.

Tupitsyn, Margarita. *Margins of Soviet Art: Socialist Realism to the Present.* Milan: Giancarlo Politi Editore, 1989.

———. "U-turn of the U-topian." In *Between Spring and Summer*, ed. D. A. Ross, 35–51. Cambridge, Mass.: MIT Press, 1990.

Vail, Petr, and Aleksandr Genis. *Sovremennaia russkaia proza.* Ann Arbor: Hermitage, 1982.

Vasil'ev, Vladimir. "Natsional'naia tragediia: utopiia i real'nost'." *Nash sovremennik*, no. 3 (1989): 172–82.

Vasil'evskii, Andrei. "Opyty zanimatel'noi futuro(eskhato)logii, II." *Novyi mir*, no. 5 (1990): 258–62.

Veeser, H. Aram, ed. *The New Historicism.* New York: Routledge, 1989.

Voinovich, Vladimir. *Moscow 2042.* Trans. R. Lourie. New York: Harcourt Brace, 1990.

———. *Moskva 2042.* Ann Arbor: Ardis, 1987.

White, Hayden. "New Historicism: A Comment." In *The New Historicism*, ed. H. Aram Veeser, 293–302. New York: Routledge, 1989.

Wittgenstein, Ludwig. *Philosophical Investigations.* Trans. G.E.M. Anscombe. New York: Macmillan, 1962.

———. *Tractatus Logico-Philosophicus.* Trans. D. F. Pears and B. F. McGuinness. London: Routledge and Kegan Paul, 1974.

Wollen, Peter. "Scenes from the Future: Komar & Melamid." In *Between Spring and Summer*, ed. D. A. Ross, 107–20. Cambridge, Mass.: MIT Press, 1990.

Zalygin, S. P. "1984." *Literaturnaia gazeta*, no. 19 (May 11, 1988): 15.

Zamiatin, Evgenii. *Litsa.* New York: Inter-Language Literary Associates, 1967.

Zinov'ev, Aleksandr. *The Radiant Future.* Trans. G. Clough. London: The Bodley Head, 1981.

———. *Svetloe budushchee.* Lausanne: L'age d'homme, 1978.

———. *The Yawning Heights.* Trans. G. Clough. New York: Random House, 1979.

———. *Ziiaiushchie vysoty.* Lausanne: L'age d'homme, 1976.

Zolotusskii, Igor'. "Krushenie abstraktsii." *Novyi mir*, no. 1 (1989): 235–46.

Zverev, Aleksei. "Bez starshego brata . . . O slozhnom cheloveke i neprostom avtore—Dzhordzhe Oruelle." *Novoe vremia*, no. 37 (1989): 38–40.

———. "'Kogda prob'et poslednii chas prirody . . .': Antiutopiia. XX vek." *Voprosy literatury*, no. 1 (1989): 26–69.

* Index *

Aesopian language, 29, 147, 153–154, 184, 196
Aitmatov, C., 173
Aksenov, V., 17, 35, 201, 216; *The Island of Crimea*, 12, 67, 146, 163, 164, 177–81; *Metropol*, 35
Allende, S., 209
Altshuller, M., 50
Andreev, L., 19
anti-utopia, 5, 9, 10, 32–33
Arapov, M., 29
Armah, A. K., 74n.11
Arzhak, N. *See* Daniel, Iu.
Azhgikhina, N., 17, 37

Bacon, F., 72
Bakhtin, M., 41, 93, 118, 122
Bednyi, D., 125, 183, 190
Belaia, G., 9
Belinsky, V., 172
Bellamy, E., 72; *Looking Backward*, 75
Belyi, A., 13, 17
Bentham, J., 211
Berdiaev, N., 128, 129
Bible, 34, 170, 195
Bitov, A., 14, 15, 95, 117
Bloch, E., 208
Blok, A., 13
Bogdanov, A., 13, 19, 30, 42, 72; *Engineer Menni*, 30; *Red Star*, 30, 80
Bosch, H., 21
Brezhnev, L., 35, 152, 158–59
Brodsky, J., 14, 96
Buber, M., 208
Bulgakov, M., 19; *Heart of a Dog*, 26; *The Master and Margarita*, 171, 173

Campanella, T., 172, 174; *City of the Sun*, 18, 64
Castedo, E., *Paradise*, 210
Chapple, R., 184
Charlemagne, 16
Chekhov, A., 51, 74, 126

Chernyshevsky, N., 7, 42, 72; *What Is to Be Done?* 42
Christianity. *See* ideology
chronotope, 41–69
Civil War, Russian, 4
Coetzee, J., 171, 210, 217
communism. *See* ideology
conceptualism, 35–36, 79–80n.12
counterutopia, 5, 59, 212, 218
critical realism. *See* realism

Dal, V., 134
Daniel, Iu., 10, 35, 37, 209; *Moscow Speaking*, 12, 19, 67, 122, 129–32
Dante, 21
Davydov, Iu., 33
deconstruction, 3, 214
Defoe, D., 200; *Robinson Crusoe*, 18, 75, 81, 90, 217
democracy. *See* ideology
Doctorow, E. L., 171, 182; *Ragtime*, 20
Dombrovsky, Iu., 32
Domostroi, 135
Dostoevsky, F., 7, 128, 129, 139, 157; *The Brothers Karamazov*, 49, 55, 66, 157; "Dream of a Ridiculous Man," 59; *Notes from the Underground*, 11, 18, 43, 73, 125
dystopia, 5, 9, 10, 17, 19, 96, 150, 211n.10; chronotope in, 43, 46; compared to meta-utopian writing, 12, 97, 124, 127, 129, 136–39; linguistic innovation in, 93, 96–97; Soviet reception of, 25–38

Eagleton, T., 109, 214
Eco, U., 171, 218
Efremov, I., 183
Engels, F., 92
Epstein, M., 31, 162, 198
Erofeev, V., 17, 30; *Moscow-Petushki*, 12, 106–7, 122; concepts of space in, 46–49, 50; concepts of time in, 67–68; critique of science in, 92; narrative structures

Erofeev, V. (*cont.*)
  in, 91–92; meta-utopian consciousness in, 139–40
Escher, M., 66
Evtushenko, E., 32

Fanger, D., 9
fascism. *See* ideology
Fedorov, N., 18, 42
Foucault, M., 210, 211
Fourier, Ch., 7
Fowles, J., *The French Lieutenant's Woman*, 218; *Magus*, 145
Frye, N., 124
Fukuyama, F., 220

Galtseva, R., 27, 32
glasnost, 4, 206
Godbuilding, 7, 13, 16, 18, 29, 128
Godseeking, 13
Gogol, N., 9, 51, 68; *Dead Souls*, 110
Goncharov, I., 90; *Oblomov*, 73
Gorbachev, M., 3, 34, 68
Gorky, M., 14, 125, 135, 140, 183; and Godbuilding, 7, 29, 128; *Confession*, 42, 59; *The Lower Depths*, 103, 104; myth in, 42; parody of, 101–8, 133, 187; "The Song of the Falcon," 103, 187; "The Song of the Stormy Petrel," 187
Grossman, V., *Life and Fate*, 32
Groys, B., 220

Habermas, J., 210, 212, 216, 218
Hegel, G., 16
Hitler, A., 7
Holquist, M., 210
Howe, I., 20, 145
Hutcheon, L., 20, 145, 217, 219
Huxley, A., 129

ideology, 6–8, 86; Christianity as, 34, 151, 205; communism as, 108; democracy as, 134, 134n.10; fascism as, 208; liberalism as, 181, 189, 190; Marxism as, 152, 160, 212; Marxism-Leninism as, 4, 11, 23, 33, 59, 78, 140, 151, 172, 173, 180, 207, 213; nationalism as, 33, 218; Nazism as, 8, 82, 166–67; pluralism as, 9, 29–30, 134–35, 135n.11, 206; Roman Catholicism as, 23; Russian Orthodoxy as, 23, 33–34, 213; and science, 8, 70–93, 215–16; Slavophilism as, 180; Stalinism as, 8, 23, 27, 163, 184, 185, 207, 208; totalitarianism as, 8, 9; and utopia, 6–8
"The Igor Tale," 89
Ilf, I., and Petrov, E., 81
Iskander, F., 35, 37; *Rabbits and Boa Constrictors*, 12, 19, 30, 123, 147, 183–92; Aesopian language in, 147, 184–87; parody in, 101–2, 111
Ivan the Terrible, 135
Ivanov, V., 13
Ivanova, N., 31, 208

Jakobson, R., 109
Jameson, F., 41, 42, 209, 218
Joyce, J., 17

Kabakov, A., 5; "The Deserter," 198, 199, 200–202, 204–6
Kabakov, I., 35, 36, 79–80n.12
Kafka, F., 17, 169; *The Castle*, 3, 25; *The Trial*, 199, 205
Kantor, K., 5
Kasack, W., 83
Khrushchev, N., 19, 129, 208, 209
Kim, A., 20
Kingston, M. H., 20, 171
Kireev, R., 34
Koestler, A., 25
Kohl, H., 212
Komar, V. and Melamid, A., 35, 36
Kristeva, J., 221
Ksepma, V., 21, 145, 146
Kublanovsky, I., 34

Latynina, J., 31
Le Carre, J., 117
Leguin, U., 210
Lenin, V., 140, 157
liberalism. *See* ideology
Lomonosov, M., 47
Loseff, L., 153
Lotman, Iu., 22, 23, 33, 58, 73, 214

Lunacharsky, A., 13, 128; *Religion and Socialism*, 42
Lyotard, J.-F., 22, 70–71, 210, 213, 215, 218

MacLuhan, M., 208
Maiakovsky, V., 126
Mannheim, K., 6
Marcuse, H., 208
Marin, L., 41, 43
Marx, K., 92; *Das Kapital*, 34; *The Communist Manifesto*, 34, 82; *The German Ideology*, 212
Marxism. *See* ideology
Marxism-Leninism. *See* ideology
McHale, B., 74
Medawar, P., 215
Melamid, A. *See* Komar, V.
meta-utopia: compared to dystopian fiction, 12, 97, 124–25, 127, 129, 136–39; concepts of space in, 41–59; concepts of time in, 59–69; as consciousness, 9, 26, 33–34, 122–41; ideological critique in, 22–24, 70–93; implied reader in, 146–207; and language, 13–16, 95–121; and history, 16–19, 162–82; as novelness, 92–93; and popular narrative forms, 183–97; and postmodernism, 20–22, 70–71, 208–21
modernism, 18
More, T., 16, 72; *Utopia*, 18, 41, 70, 75, 162
Morson, G. S., 42

Nabokov, V., 3, 17
Narbikova, V., 3, 17
nationalism. *See* ideology
Nazism. *See* ideology
Nietzsche, F., 94, 95, 107, 113, 158, 167; *The Gay Science*, 70; *Thus Spoke Zarathustra*, 43; *The Use and Abuse of History*, 59, 62, 64
nouveau roman, 171
Novikov, V., 12, 33

Ortega y Gasset, J., 177, 218
Orwell, G., 4, 129, 147, 150, 192; Russian reception of, 19; *Animal Farm*, 25, 183, 184, 185; *1984*, 11, 25, 28, 32, 67, 97, 124, 135
Ostrovsky, N., 140

Pasternak, B., *Doctor Zhivago*, 26
Pavlova-Silvanskaia, M., 27, 28, 69
Peter the Great, 23
Petrushevskaia, L., 95; "The New Robinsons," 5, 19, 117, 123, 198, 199–200, 202–6
Plato, 16, 43; *The Republic*, 18, 42, 57, 74, 162
Platonov, A., 4, 14, 17, 19, 96; *Chevengur*, 25, 29; *Foundation Pit*, 25, 26, 43; "Juvenalian Sea," 25
pluralism. *See* ideology
Popov, E., 3
postmodernism, 20–22, 70–71, 208–21
Proletcult, 19
Pushkin, A., 9, 176; "The Bronze Horseman," 49; "The Memorial," 89

Rabelais, F., 50; *Gargantua and Pantagruel*, 18
Radishchev, A., 46
Rasputin, V., 59
Reagan, R., 212, 218
realism, 14, 61, 66, 123, 181, 219; and implied reader, 149; parody of, 110–17; and romanticism, 112; truth value of 102–3, 108–12, 196; critical, 117, 123, 133, 166; Socialist, 72, 126, 131, 165, 167, 172, 202; critique of, 29, 33, 34; Gorky and, 103, 117, 133; heritage of, 36
Reiss, T., 70–71
Revich, V., 27
Ricoeur, P., 6–8, 9, 210
Rodnianskaia, I., 32
Roman Catholicism. *See* ideology
Russian Orthodoxy. *See* ideology

Sabinina, O., 32
Saint-Simon, H., 7, 16
Schiller, F., 51
science. *See* ideology
Shklovsky, V., 13
Siniavsky, A. *See* Terts, A.

235

Skinner, B.F., 208
Slavophilism *See* ideology
Socialist Realism. *See* realism
Socrates, 16
Solovyov, Vl., 7
Solzhenitsyn, A., 5, 133, 135, 151, 152, 194, 218, 221
Stalin, J., 4, 7
Stalinism. *See* ideology
Sterne, L., 91
Strugatsky, A., and B. Strugatsky, 35, 37, 118, 124, 183; *The Condemned City*, 19; concepts of space in, 45, 49, 56–57; narrative structures in, 67, 68, 79, 82–83; *The Snail on the Slope*, 20, 30; *The Ugly Swans*, 12, 30, 122, 146, 165–71; concepts of space in, 45–46; concepts of time in, 67; parody in, 104; implied reader in, 164
Suslov, M., 5

Tendriakov, Vl., 37; *A Potshot at Mirages*, 10, 13, 30, 140, 146; concepts of time in, 64; critique of history in , 163, 172–77; implied reader in, 164
Terras, V., 83
Terts, A., 17, 35, 95, 145, 194, 209; as literary persona, 125; critique of Gorky, 102–03, 105; critique of Solzhenitsyn, 108, 135n.11, 218; publication of, 37; *Liubimov*, 4, 10, 12, 136–39, 146; concepts of space in, 43, 46, 49, 55–56; concepts of time in, 64, 67; critique of science in, 87–90; narrative structures in, 76–79; critique of realism in, 110–17; "What Is Socialist Realism?" 64–65, 97–98, 125–29, 132
Thatcher, M., 212
Tiutchev, F., 15
Tolstaia, T., 3
Tolstoi, L., 135, 174; as archetypal realist, 90, 115, 133, 152, 167
Tönnies, F., 27
totalitarianism. *See* ideology
Turgenev, I., 90

Tynianov, Iu., 11, 194
Tupitsyn, M., 35

Uspensky, B., 22, 23, 33, 214
utopia, 5; Great Society as, 209; and ideology, 6–8; and language, 14. *See also* anti-utopia, counterutopia, dystopia, meta-utopia

Verne, J., 192
Vidal, G., *Burr*, 176; *Julian*, 176
Voinovich, V., 10, 17, 35, 95, 210, 216, 218; *Moscow 2042*, 4, 11, 12, 36, 163; concepts of space in, 44, 50, 52–55; concepts of time in, 61–64, 67; critique of realism in, 123, 132–36; implied reader in, 192–97; language play in, 99–100; narrative structures in, 79–82
Voronsky, A., 29

Wells, H., 72; *Modern Utopia*, 75
Wittgenstein, L., 94, 96
Wolf, C., 145

Zamiatin, E., 4, 13, 17, 19, 128 129, 150, 193; *We*, 3, 11, 14, 43, 67, 69, 124; dystopian architecture in, 211n.10; dystopian protagonist in, 127; reception of, 25, 28–30, 32
Zinoviev, A., 5, 132, 210, 216, 218, reception of, 17, 35, 37; *The Radiant Future*, 13, 19, 21, 44, 67, 73, 120, 146, 147, 149–61; *The Yawning Heights*, 4, 11, 16, 146, 153, 160, 211; concepts of space in, 44, 49–50, 53–54, 57–58; concepts of time in, 60–63, 65–68; critique of science in, 215; implied reader in, 21, 147–49; language play in, 95, 98–101, 118–21; meta-utopian consciousness in, 122, 123, 124, 140–141; narrative structures in, 12, 73, 75–76, 78, 83–87; and Orwell, 19
Zverev, A., 28, 32, 33, 69, 200
Zvezdochetova, L., 35

GPSR Authorized Representative: Easy Access System Europe - Mustamäe tee 50, 10621 Tallinn, Estonia, gpsr.requests@easproject.com

www.ingramcontent.com/pod-product-compliance
Lightning Source LLC
Chambersburg PA
CBHW070601300426
44113CB00010B/1344